HOODOO FOR LIFE

THE COMPLETE GUIDE TO ROOTWORK AND CONJURE WITH 125 AUTHENTIC HOODOO MAGIC SPELLS

3 BOOKS IN 1

ANGELIE BELARD

HENTOPAN
PUBLISHING

CONTENTS

HOODOO FOR BEGINNERS

WORKING MAGIC SPELLS IN ROOTWORK AND CONJURE WITH ROOTS, HERBS, CANDLES, AND OILS

ANGELIE BELARD

INTRODUCTION

I had just turned 23 when Mama Estelle was buried. She was my favorite person in this world. Mama Estelle was my grandmother, but everyone loved her. I know that we all say this about our grandmothers, but this is the honest truth about Mama Estelle. She was exceptional. She raised me, for the most part, even though I did spend some time with my parents. Most of who I am as a woman today can be attributed to Mama Estelle. This book begins on the day she was buried because that was the day the rest of my life began. Throughout my life, right up to the moment she died, Mama Estelle would sit me down and tell me stories about her childhood and share secrets with me about our way of life.

Hoodoo for her was not some folklore or black magic, although certain aspects of it could take on a really dark tone. Still, it wasn't this dark and mysterious thing that has been portrayed in the movies. It was about being attuned to your environment and knowing your roots, understanding the power of your ancestors and manipulating the elements in your favor. Unfortunately, I never really appreciated any of this until the day I saw Mama Estelle being put into the earth. And so, there I sat, listening to the slow, monotonous sound of the priest reciting the final rites. Mama Estelle was a devout member of the small local church and many people knew and loved her. I was physically present to witness the somber event taking place around me, but I felt as though I was somewhere else.

What registered the most in my mind was the thick air of silence that seemed to envelope the whole graveyard. When it was time to pick up dirt and pour it on the coffin, I thought I wouldn't be able to do it. I thought it would break me for sure. But the moment my hands connected with earth, I experienced what felt like a transference of energy. I felt peace and quiet so intense that it felt as though I was betraying the grief I was feeling inside. You could say the day Mama Estelle was buried was the day I was reborn. Because right there by her grave site was where I became consciously aware of the powers that surround us. Of the divinity that dwells on the inside of us. It was that day all of her teachings came alive for me.

It has been over 40 years since that moment when I made the decision to become a Hoodoo practitioner, and I have never looked back. Now, I want to honor Mama Estelle's legacy by sharing some of her wealth of knowledge, in addition to some of my own experiences in the practice of Hoodoo.

I don't know what brought you to this book. Most of my clients come to see me when something in their life has gone very wrong, and they've already tried all the "normal" ways to fix it. Some come out of plain old curiosity. Maybe you're just looking for a simple spell to make your life a little easier to bear. Whatever it is that brought you here, you should know that there are no coincidences in this life. I hope my book can help you find what you're looking for, and maybe find something even more important than that.

This book is foundational knowledge of the practice of Hoodoo. If you are looking for academic research, you won't find much here, because everything I know, and everything I have done, has been passed down from mother to daughter for generations. Some of the information is unique to my family. But it will serve you well just as it has served my family and clients and all those we have helped. In this book you will find:

- A brief history on Hoodoo and some common misconceptions
- A foundational knowledge of key elements of Hoodoo practices
- A breakdown of the symbolism of purification rites and their application in day-to-day life

- How to create an enabling environment for spells to manifest
- Simple and powerful spells for love, luck, money and life in general

Before you delve into Chapter 1, I urge you to proceed with an open mind. At the end of the day, your mind is the birthplace of whatever spell or enchantment you will cast. If you are filled with doubt, unresolved emotions and negative thoughts in general, especially about the practice itself, you may find that most of what you learn will be rendered impotent.

So be open-minded, be generous with your positive emotions and most importantly, embrace the power that is within you.

1

MY HOODOO ROOTS

The first Hoodoo working I performed without help from Mama Estelle was for a young man who was just setting up a convenience store. This was his third attempt at starting a business, and after previous failures, he was worried that he was cursed. For a novice, this was a lot of pressure on me. I could barely put a protection spell together and here I was being called on to reverse the misfortunes of this man and invite wealth into his life.

I started with a floor wash of his store, using roots and herbs that cleanse and protect, and a few more to draw luck and money. After cleansing the floor, I cleansed the door and the path leading to the store. When we finished with the cleanse, I buried nine pennies at the entrance, underneath earth that had been dug up from a bank, along with a lodestone, and then sealed this by pouring quality whiskey over it. Two weeks later, the store opened. Six months after that, he opened another branch in another part of town and then just kept growing. In the decades following my first attempt, I have performed this cleanse and money attraction spell several times, and each time it has been effective.

I imagine that you are currently just starting out your journey as a Hoodoo practitioner and you want to find effective ways to achieve results. You have probably taken note of this money invitation spell and perhaps even put down the book long enough to put the ingredients together. The spell I mentioned above is one of the basic beginner spells. At the end of this book, I am certain that you will be able to create your own money spell, change your fortune in the process and do a whole lot more. But I am also sure that there is a logical side of you that is seeking an explanation as to how the elements I listed above; the coins, the lodestone and the earth from the bank, were able to manifest wealth.

To see the connection between all these things and the world that lies beyond our physical realm, you need to peer behind the curtain and expand the borders of your mind. Now, because it was easy for me to accept my transition into Hoodoo practice, I know that I will not completely understand what you are struggling with. That said, I should point out that I firmly believe my first ritual was effective for one primary reason - I believed it would work. If this is completely new to you, this is going to be a journey that will require you to change your perspective about certain things.

So, why was it easy for me to believe? I was the love child of a young Haitian immigrant and a Creole girl. They were too young to raise a child, so I ended up with my grandmother. My mother later married another man. I spent some time at both my mother's house and my father's, but most of my childhood was spent with Mama Estelle. I suppose my childhood was a bit odd, but it helped me see things differently from the way others saw them.

In the Beginning...

Growing up with Mama Estelle, Hoodoo was always a part of my life. I never had to go through training or any kind of ceremony to be introduced to it. I saw it around the house just the way you probably saw things in your childhood. Like the herbs in your mother's kitchen or the newspaper that was always lying on the coffee table, or the toys in your playroom. It was natural to me in my day-to-day life.

For example, when my grandmother had a headache, she would never take aspirin. Instead she would make a tincture from specific herbs and spices. She would take this mixture and go to sleep, and when she woke up she would be right as rain. And she always had a white cloth with a candle on it beside her bed. I didn't think anything of what I suspect would seem bizarre to you. It wasn't until Mama Estelle explained it that I realized it was part of a protection spell.

Growing Up With a Hoodoo Background

Mama Estelle descended from a long line of Hoodoo practitioners who go back generations, and for her this was a way of life. She never shied away from her identity and was very proud to be recognized as a "two-headed" doctor. It wasn't just a title for her. People came to her for solutions. I remember a woman who traveled across the country to come and see Mama Estelle. She was desperate to get pregnant and had been trying for several years. Medicine hadn't made the advancements that it has today, and even the little that was available in the way of fertility treatment was too expensive. So, in her desperation, she sought out my grandmother.

That night, my grandmother performed the fertility ritual. She asked me to witness it because I was a young woman and she explained that my energy would help make the ritual more effective. It was a beautiful ceremony and in my young eyes it was both magical and mysterious. The woman and her husband had moved into town so that they could be closer to my grandmother in order to be able to receive her regular herbal treatment. I didn't think anything of this until six months later we ran into her at the store. She was pregnant and glowing. I cannot count the number of times I witnessed miracles such as these. It was just a part of growing up and I think this is one of the reasons I took it for granted, that is, until I lost my grandmother.

Sharing My Rich but Mysterious Heritage

People have many misconceptions about Hoodoo, and in this book I want to try as much as possible to address most, if not all of them. I want to start by letting you know that Hoodoo is not some mysterious dark force that taints your life. In truth, it can enhance your experiences and help you navigate very difficult moments.

Hoodoo is as spiritual as it is physical. There are aspects of Hoodoo practice that simply focus on the use of herbs. The idea generally is to connect with nature. Mother Earth is the most powerful element in the world. She is home to the soil that is a direct link to our ancestors. She is the conduit for light and life, and if you channel her essence, you can bring about productivity and multiplication in your life. Practicing Hoodoo gives you a very pragmatic perspective about life. For instance, your views about certain objects or places are no longer tainted by negative emotions like fear, anger or pain. Instead, you are able to see these places as connections to a world beyond our physical world. I know that sounds mysterious so I will give you an example. The cemetery is generally regarded as sacred ground where our loved ones are put to rest. But there have been a lot of dark notions perpetuated about the cemetery as a place or gathering of evil. This is far from the truth. A graveyard is a source of immense power. This power can be channeled for good or for evil. It is as simple as that.

In the next chapter, I will talk about the history of Hoodoo, and hopefully bring you to a place of understanding. With better understanding, you open yourself up to the benefits of Hoodoo practice.

2

THE HISTORY OF HOODOO

Hoodoo, Conjure, or Rootwork, as it is sometimes called, can be traced back to the arrival of enslaved Africans here in America. When our ancestors arrived here, the African practices that they came with merged with European and Native American influences. African beliefs and customs met with European folklore and the botanical knowledge of American Indians came together under one umbrella - Hoodoo.

People consulted with Hoodoo doctors when they needed spiritual help. Whether it had to do with physical health or changing their fortunes for the better, Hoodoo was always used to make the lives of people easier and better. Slave owners, however, tried to vilify African spiritual practices, calling it demonic or devil worship or witchcraft. If you've ever heard negative things about Hoodoo, that's where it all started.

A Spiritual Journey

In my personal opinion (and I believe this is a sentiment shared by many who practice Hoodoo), Hoodoo is more of a personalized spiritual journey than it is anything else. In a religion, you worship a deity, something considered supernatural and supreme. This deity, or in some cases, multiple deities, dictates what is right or wrong, good or evil. In Hoodoo, however, you are free to practice any religion, or none at all, and still practice Hoodoo.

In Hoodoo, you create your own personal magic using the knowledge you have of the various roots, herbs and other elements. It is about establishing a connection with the spirits around us. It is a way of life. There is no devotion that you have to perform, other than the physical rituals required for the results that you demand.

In the practice of Hoodoo, magic comes from roots, stones, bones and even discharge from the human body, such as blood, sweat and so on. By combining their power, you are able to tap into the force it produces and channel it to deliver the results you want. Your desired results could range from healing to jinxing, love potions to money spells and much more. You have the ability to manifest whatever it is you desire. All you need is knowledge of the right combination of these elements and acceptance of the power that you possess. But most importantly, you need to acknowledge and have a reverence for the spirits of our ancestors. In Hoodoo, we understand that there are spirits constantly around us, and those spirits can either serve or harm, depending on how you treat them. I will get into more of that later but for now, just understand that Hoodoo has less to do with faith and more to do with changing fate.

Voodoo vs. Hoodoo

A lot of people use Voodoo and Hoodoo interchangeably, thinking that they mean the same thing, but you need to understand that while they have roots in central African religions, they are very different practices. Think of them as distant cousins, at best.

Voodoo is a religion primarily practiced in Haiti. There is a similar, but distinct practice also called Voodoo in Louisiana. Practitioners of both forms of Voodoo serve the Lwa, powerful spirits believed to control the physical world. Haitian Voodoo is more a religion than Louisiana Voodoo, with regular congregations and initiated priests. Louisiana Voodoo is less of what you might think of as a religion, but beyond that, there's not much of a distinction between the two. You'll meet people who practice Voodoo in all kinds of ways.

Hoodoo is not a religion at all, and worship and service to the Lwa is not part of it. That's probably the best way to draw a line between Hoodoo and Voodoo - if the Lwa are involved, it's definitely Voodoo.

Hoodoo and Christianity

When African slaves were brought to North America, they were not allowed to practice their old religions. Slaves were forcibly baptized into Christianity, either Catholicism or Protestantism, depending on their owners. They had to hide their old religious practices under a veil of Christianity.

Many aspects of Christianity weren't so very different from traditional African religions. The African slaves already believed in one creator, God. Many believed in powerful spirits that helped run the world, and recognized Catholic Saints as just another aspect of those spirits. The Bible was seen as a powerful spell book, and even today many traditional Hoodoo workings include reading various psalms while casting a spell.

Mama Estelle was a devout Baptist and took me to church with her every Sunday. After the service was over, I would see people go up to her and talk quietly. Sometimes she would hand them small objects, and sometimes I saw them hand her money. For Mama Estelle, and the people she helped, there was no conflict between their Christianity and their belief in the power of Hoodoo.

Hopefully, I have been able to open your mind concerning some of the most difficult areas of understanding Hoodoo. The next step is to delve deeper into the practice and our first stop will be to look at those elements that I have been talking about. In the next chapter, I will focus on seven important elements of Hoodoo. As you continue your study and practice of Hoodoo outside of this book, you will learn a lot more on this subject. But for now, these seven elements are your starting point.

3

THE ELEMENTS OF HOODOO

In many magical practices, the elements focused on evolve around water, air, fire and earth. In Hoodoo practice, the force in these elements is recognized but the practice goes a lot deeper. We see the connection between the things in the world around us and the spiritual realm. There is also a lot of symbolism and representative magic used to create spells that are potent and life-altering. In this chapter, I will highlight some fundamental forces that power Hoodoo practice and explain how spirits interact with these elements. Your understanding of this concept will be very useful in helping you create and develop your very own personalized Mojo, spell or ritual. You should understand that the more unique a spell is to you, the greater the chances of it working for you.

The spells that I will share with you in this book are standard spells that are very effective. However, every situation is different, and if you can craft your own spell specific to your own needs, the results will be far more powerful.

Your understanding of individual roots and the power they hold is a crucial factor in determining the potency of a spell. Think of it like going to the grocery store to buy some vegetables because you want to get healthy. Vegetables are good for you in general, but if you know what each vegetable is best for with regard to your health goals, you can buy the right ones for you. Likewise, choosing the roots that are right for your particular magical needs will save you time, money, and will help you achieve better results.

I had a client who used to have a problem that perfectly illustrates the message I am trying to get across. She was in love with a man and they had been in a relationship for a long time, but suddenly he started drifting away from her. Now, she knew that he loved her, but he was having difficulty staying focused on that love and their relationship. So, she went online and found some love potions. For the first few days after administering the love potion, everything seemed to be going well. But within a few weeks, they would be back to struggling with the same problems again. This went on for several months until she came to see me. She assumed that she had not performed the ritual and the spell well enough or that perhaps it was completely wrong. But this was not the problem.

The problem was that she was using a general love drawing spell - but the man already loved her. She needed something unique to her situation. Oftentimes I'll prescribe a series of steps for a client to take to bring about the result they're looking for, and in this case we began with a love drawing bath that included coriander, because it brings about fidelity. We followed this with a candle spell using a red candle and cinnamon to add some heat to the relationship. It worked well for my client. They've been married for over a decade now.

Ancestral Spirits

We are often called to "know" ourselves. We translate this to mean knowing our likes, our dislikes, our socio-cultural identity and connecting with our innermost thoughts. All of this is fantastic because having a strong sense of self is necessary for making your way in this world today. How else will you be able to distinguish yourself from every other individual in a world with a current population of nearly 8 billion? Knowledge of self will help you stand out from the rest of the pack. That said, the practice of Hoodoo requires you to take things a step further. You need to know your roots. Your ancestors are your roots; those who came before you, those with whom you share a blood connection.

Of all of the forms of magic available, blood magic is considered to be the most powerful, the most potent and the most dangerous. Blood contains a direct link to the people who came before you. In a scientific sense, your history is written in your blood. This is how science is able to connect your DNA with your blood relatives, and this DNA can be traced back generations. Ancestral magic goes beyond blood. It refers to the essence left behind by those who came before you. You came from someone who came from someone who came from someone and so on. Acknowledging this lineage connects you to the power of this linkage.

The truth is that whether you acknowledge your ancestry or not, there is always a possibility that you are paying for something that your ancestors did. It could be good or it could be bad. Their actions, inactions, spoken words and emotions all flow through anyone who is a part of their lineage. Ever met a person with an uncontrollable temper? Look into the person's lineage and you may find that there is someone who actually exhibited those traits.

This is why some people tend to experience an unusual amount of luck. It is not because lady luck is standing over their shoulder. Instead, there is every chance that their ancestors did something that brought about a reward that is being passed from one generation to the next. Unfortunately, the opposite is also the case. If your ancestor is known to have committed an offence so grievous and grave that it attracted a curse, this curse might be transferred to their descendants. Even beyond the transference of curses and blessings, there is power linked to our lineage. Failure to acknowledge this power weakens its potency over time, until it feels almost non-existent.

That doesn't mean that the power is suddenly extinguished. It remains dormant until you awaken it by acknowledging your ancestry. Think of your bank account. When you continuously carry out transactions with that account, it remains active but when you leave it for a long period of time, it gradually becomes dormant. The account is not closed, but is simply inactive. Ancestral spirits guide us because they see things that we do not see. They have experienced things that have happened before and, as they say, history has a way of repeating itself. Who else is in a better position to prevent you from repeating the mistakes of your past, if not an ancestor? Also, when it comes to rituals that require their help, a spirit with a direct link to you is usually more willing to provide assistance than one that is merely drifting. Consider all of these factors and understand them before you proceed.

To show your respect for your ancestors, consider setting aside a portion of your home for them. An ancestral altar is an important place in Hoodoo, because it's a place to invite your ancestors into your life. You can use your altar to call on them for not just aid in your magic, but for advice about your life. A small table is a fine place for an altar. If you have pictures of your ancestors, you can place these on the table, along with a glass of water. You might even leave offerings of food or alcohol, like whiskey or rum, every week, if you wish.

The Spirits of Roots

The practice of Hoodoo was originally called Rootwork, because the bulk of Hoodoo practice centers around the use of roots and herbs for both physical and spiritual aid. For example, if you are having a chronic headache, there are plants that you can use to treat that headache. If you need to bring luck into your life, there are roots that can help with that as well.

Before humankind fell in love with science and technology, we had a deep connection to nature. Part of that fundamental connection to nature was our relationship with plants. By utilizing plants in specific ways for unique spells, you are able to tap into the spirit within that plant to create the results you desire.

We have always known that plants can help provide a connection between our minds, bodies and spirits. Some plants are blessed with the unique ability to break the veil between our world and the spirit world. They allow you access to the other world, where you can reach out to the spirits and receive direct answers to your problems.

There are roots that can draw love or luck, protect you from evil and keep unwanted people away. There are roots to help you get a job or a promotion, roots to cleanse your spirit and cleanse your home. Knowing which roots do what is crucial if you ever want to do more than buy commercial love spells.

Much like words, roots have nuances. There are many roots that can draw love, but it's important to know which one you should choose and for which occasion. Coriander draws fidelity in love, while ginger adds passion and heat. Grapevine ties people together, lemon balm removes bad luck in love, and myrtle keeps love passionate in long-term relationships or marriages. There are many more roots for love, and the same kind of nuance applies in every other kind of spell.

The Spirits of Earth

In the opening of the first chapter of this book, I talked about a spell for attracting wealth in which I used earth that had been dug up near a bank. I used it because the energy of a place leaks into the ground around it, much like a sponge absorbing water. A bank is a place that draws money to it, and that money-drawing energy is transferred into the soil.

In the same way, you can use earth from near a hospital for healing, or earth from a casino to draw luck. Or you can use earth from the grave of an evil person to draw evil to someone else. Hoodoo is not all love and luck spells, after all.

In Hoodoo, we also add earth to magic spells to ground them, the same way electrical lines are grounded in the earth. Magic from roots or ancestors is powerful, but the strength of that power needs to be focused and controlled or you can end up with some unexpected results. Earth in a spell can stabilize it, calm it, and direct it where you want it to go. If I have a client asking for a spell to draw love into her life, I'll often add dirt from a church, so that the man we draw will be a good one. It's easy to draw love from the wrong man.

We all know that the earth is full of riches. When you think of precious stones and plants, in fact, you could say that the kind of wealth that the earth possesses is the most sustainable type of wealth. So it makes sense that when you include it in your spell and call upon the spirits of the earth, you draw on that wealth energy and divert it to your will.

It is for these reasons that you should try to be selective about the places where you obtain earth for your spell. For instance, if you take earth from a desert, the general idea is to attract dryness and barrenness. This is why, when placing curses, most practitioners go to places that symbolize what they want to visit upon the intended victim of the spell.

When carrying out any kind of spell, regardless of the elements or tools you will use, you must be very selective about what goes into it. Even the slightest mistake can alter the balance of the spell you are trying to create. So, when you choose earth, choose wisely. Understand its meaning. Try as much as possible to know its history before you use it. For the standard spells that I talk about in this book which require the help of earth spirits, I recommend going to places where the soil is rich and fertile. Places where you can see actual vegetation growing and thriving. As you continue to grow in the practice and craft of Hoodoo, you can expand your search to soils from other places.

Graveyards

Working Hoodoo in a graveyard is, honestly, not for beginners. Working with the spirits there requires a high degree of intuition that beginners usually don't have. Also, spirits in the graveyard can be dangerous. Just like walking into a strange neighborhood, some of the folks there may not be happy to see you and may wish you harm. I strongly suggest you get a good deal of experience working with your ancestral spirits, at home at your ancestral altar, before you move to working in a graveyard. However, I would be remiss in not at least discussing graveyards, because graveyards, and the spirits that live there, as such an important part of Hoodoo.

Graveyard magic is like combining the power of ancestral spirits with earth spirits. You can imagine how powerful this combination is. Many people associate a graveyard with sorrow and grief, or perhaps are just terrified of them, thanks to Hollywood movies. In Hoodoo, we do not share this perspective. In fact, death is not always regarded as the worst thing that can happen. Neither is it seen as an entirely negative experience. Of course, we hope that the people we love will always be with us in physical form, so losing them causes us pain. But because we also understand that there is a world beyond ours, where death is a bridge, we simply view death as the end of one journey and the commencement of another.

Graveyard magic is powerful, but maybe not for the reasons you think. Graveyard earth is used because it is a place of transition; of endings and beginnings. So if you are looking to end a cycle in your life that has proven to be very disruptive and destructive, graveyard earth might be just what you need. Also, if you have a relationship that has taken its toll on your mental and physical health, you might want to consider graveyard earth.

But it can also be used to herald new beginnings. The end of one thing often means the beginning of something new. If you find yourself in a place where you are about to start something new and you need something to initiate and activate the blessings associated with this new phase, graveyard earth might be the best option for you.

I should point out here that, just as you should be selective about where you get your earth, you should also pay close attention to the particular cemetery or grave from where you got your earth. If you go to a grave where the deceased was a dangerously psychotic person, you risk introducing very unstable elements into the spell you are trying to create.

When going to graveyards to collect grave dirt, you must be respectful. It is important to appease the spirits whose earth you are taking for your spell. You should always pay for the dirt you take, either by burying a few pennies or spilling some whiskey on to the ground. And because of how strange it looks for others to see someone digging around a cemetery for earth, I have learned over the years to do it under the guise of planting new flowers by grave sites.

To find a spirit to work with, you can use a method of divination like cards or a pendulum, but I usually work by instinct and intuition since I've been doing this for a long time. Walk around the graveyard, taking your time to get a feel for the place and the spirits that live there. Eventually you may feel pulled to one grave in particular. Before you strike up a conversation, I suggest doing some research about the person who was buried there, if you can. Were they a good person in life? A mother, a father, a nurse, a gambler? I'll say it again – spirits can be dangerous. Do your research.

If you've found a spirit you want to try working with, start off with an offering. Use your intuition or divination technique to get a feel for what the spirit might want, be it alcohol or food or cigars. Strike up a conversation and learn to listen to what the spirits have to say. Do not go into this kind of relationship with transactional mindset. Try and make a friend. Later, days or weeks later, you can ask your friend for a favor, or if you can take some of the dirt from their grave.

Crossroads

Where two roads cross, possibilities open up. In Hoodoo, we visit crossroads for spells to open roads to new opportunities, and to rid ourselves of things we don't want in our lives, like bad luck or bad people. In Hoodoo, crossroads are associated with the beginning of a journey. Therefore, they are mostly used in protection spells. Like the graveyard, a crossroads symbolizes transition. The main difference is that it doesn't carry that grim connotation of endings.

There are places here in Louisiana where, when you arrive at a crossroads, you'll find by the corner of the road sacrifices or offerings. This practice is also common in parts of Africa, where the traditional form of Hoodoo is practiced. A crossroads is also considered the perfect place to dispose of the remnants of the spell that you created. This is because a crossroads is a neutral place in magic, generally speaking. So, if you have created something that was previously very potent and you would like to neutralize its power, you can take the leftovers from that spell and place it at a crossroads. With each day that passes, the power will diminish.

Spells involving crossroads are best performed late at night or early in the mornings. I suggest you have this at the back of your mind when you want to carry out such spells. For maximum effect, some people would advise that you go during the moments between midnight and the following day.

Finding Balance

When you are preparing a meal, one of the first things you try to achieve in the process is a balance of flavors. This is because you are bringing a lot of different ingredients together and each of these ingredients has their own unique flavor. If you fail to pay attention to how those flavors complement each other, some might overpower others. This will likely either ruin or at least negatively affect the taste of the food. The same principle can be applied when creating a spell. You have to be fastidious about ensuring that you are creating a balance of powers. You cannot allow one power to overwhelm another, because it would impact the results. It doesn't matter how seemingly simple the spell is. You must be conscious of the elements involved in the creation and development of that spell.

Some spells will require the use of items that may come with a lot of power, especially if they have not been blessed, cleansed or if the previous owner was mentally unstable and left a residue of their essence on the item. When you add this into you spell, you are already tipping the balance. You'll need to find other ingredients that will either even out or counteract the power that will be drawn from this artifact.

Earlier, I mentioned that earth is a stabilizing power, and so its use helps to ground spells and create balance. But this is not always enough, especially if you are unsure about the source of the earth you are using. Every Hoodoo practitioner, whether a beginner or an expert, must endeavor to master the tools of balance. Hoodoo channels things outside our realm and this means that we are often tiptoeing on the edges of things outside our consciousness.

This is why some Hoodoo experts will tell you that certain spells will leave you teetering on the edge. If you miss a single detail, no matter how little, it can tilt the balance and the outcome can be disastrous. I know that when you started this journey, you had the idea of creating simple spells to cause little changes that will impact your daily life. That is perfectly okay. But it does not exempt you from the responsibility of striving to maintain balance.

Another way to look at it is this; with each spell that you create, you are absorbing energy from one dimension and leaving an empty space in its place. Using tools at your disposal, you should try to ensure that the energy you have removed does not create chaos on the other side that could lead to problems in later life.

Purification and Cleansing

Cleansing and purification rituals are not unique to any religion or spiritual practice. They are done across the board. Whether you are a Christian, a Voodoo practitioner or a Buddhist, there are purification exercises that you must undergo that will open you up spiritually. This is also true with Hoodoo. Beginners often dive straight into a spell without carrying out this purification stage. If you were learning under a Hoodoo teacher, a cleanse and purification ritual would be one of the first things you would be taught, because it is vital to the process. It cleanses you mentally, emotionally and physically, and then opens you up spiritually for the next stage of your journey. Taking a spiritual cleanse does not mean you are physically dirty. It might just be an indication that you are tainted by something beyond your control and closed off to the desires that you want to manifest in your life.

With the right tools, ingredients and elements, you can create a spiritual opening that will allow you access to these blessings. Now, contrary to the image that a cleansing bath or purification ritual conjures, you will not be slipping into perfumed herbs and oils in a warm bathtub with scented oils and candles surrounding you. Instead, what usually happens is a methodical dumping of powerful herbs and potions onto your body to achieve the clinical objective of opening you up spiritually. But fortunately, the effect of a cleansing ritual is almost immediate. You can sense it the moment it happens. The way it happens depends on what your objectives for the rituals are. For example, if your objective is to make yourself more receptive to love because you are planning a love spell, the cleansing process will start from your feet upwards. If the goal is to ward off negativity, the cleansing process works in the opposite direction, from your head downwards.

It is also worth noting that you must pay attention to the timing of this ritual. It must be done before the sun rises. Do not do it as the last item on your to-do list before you go to bed. Also, make sure that you do not speak to anybody before you carry it out. Wake up before sunrise, begin the process and carry out the routines associated with it. It will be over sooner than you expect. At the end of a cleansing bath, the water should not be drained from the tub as it is when you take a regular bath. Instead, if you are trying to attract something into your life, take the water containing the remnants or residues of the spell and toss it towards the east, where the sun rises. But if you intend to ward off something, by creating a protection spell, for example, the remnants of this water must be tossed at a crossroads.

I will go into more details of the cleansing and purification rituals in a later chapter. For now, these are the basics with which you need to familiarize yourself. Read up as much as you can on the subjects that I have discussed in this chapter. Master what you need to learn and ensure that you are conscious of the mandate that you have been given; to ensure that a balance is maintained at all times. Now I think you are ready for the next stage, which is Rootwork.

4

ROOTWORK

As I noted earlier, an alternative name for Hoodoo is 'Rootwork', because so many of the spells and magic conjured have a connection to plants. I also explained the role that the plant spirits play in the casting of a spell. I talked about the belief that certain spirits inhabit plants, and so each plant has unique attributes that can influence the outcome of the magic you wish to create. Across every culture, plants have been known to possess healing properties, but in Hoodoo, or Rootwork, if you prefer, things are taken a step further. Here, the plants are utilized beyond their physiological markers. In this chapter, we'll explore this concept in its entirety at a beginner level, and you'll develop a basic understanding of the symbolism of specific herbs, as well as some of the best practices in Rootwork that will help you produce or even amplify the desired results.

Basic Instructions on Roots

When it comes to the instructions about using roots, the first place to start is with your intention. If you intend to simply dabble in a few spells to meet some of your short-term needs, it is okay to pop into the store, pick up the things you need and begin casting. However, if you want to be a proper Hoodoo practitioner, you must understand the role that Earth plays in the empowerment of the plants with which you will be working. You should get used to the idea of either having your very own herb garden or learning to be a gatherer. The reason is simple; the herbs you pick yourself are still very much connected to Earth, which we know is a powerful component when it comes to the creation of Hoodoo magic. That is not to suggest that the plants you purchase in the store will not give you acceptable results. For basic spells and, even in some cases, advanced spells, store-bought plants can be very effective. But if you want something that is spiritually enriched, sustainable and in alignment with our practices, you must learn to interact with nature. There is something deeply satisfying about reaching into the soil, nurturing a plant from its seed days to the point of harvest, and then taking that plant from the soil to your potion, or whatever it is you want to use it for.

Before you strap on your boots and head into the wild to forage for herbs, though, I urge you to do some research. This will help you to differentiate between the many types of herbs. My grandmother started by teaching me which ones were edible and which ones were not. As a beginner, there are common herbs you should have in your garden. Growing them does not require a large space or a great deal of maintenance. You can grow them in pots or recycled bottles and still enjoy the benefits that come with this process. The most common herbs used in Rootwork are sage, rosemary and mint. You can continue to expand this list as you become better at recognizing and growing them. One of the reasons I love having my own herb garden is the easy access it gives me to the plants I use in my potions and mojos. Because they are readily available to me, I am able to create mixes in my home that will enhance the atmosphere for creating magic at the drop of a hat. For instance, it is generally believed that sage is a cleansing plant that can be used to ward off evil. Imagine days when you feel that there is a lot of negative energy in your space. During the time it takes you to purchase what you need from the store, that energy is creeping into every corner of your home. When you have your own garden, you can simply dash out and pull up what you need, then put the right ingredients together and immediately begin the ritual.

If growing the herbs yourself does not sound appealing to you, the next best thing is to work with people who grow them for Hoodoo purposes. Most people who grow herbs for magical purposes are well-educated on the art and craft behind it. For example, they usually plant these herbs according to the moon cycle, which is believed to empower the plants with even greater magical properties. The timing of their harvest is also crucial, as certain plants are said to bloom and reach their magical peak at midnight during full moons. So, when you buy from a recognized magical herb dealer, you can be certain that you are getting the highest quality that will deliver the best outcome. Again, you can go to the store to get what you need for basic spells but I suggest you begin to see plants as more than just things that grow from the earth. If you are going to be a Hoodoo practitioner, you must understand the place of roots/plants in creating magic.

Root Capabilities

In this section, I will focus on just 10 of the more common herbs that we deal with. These herbs will be featured in many of spells throughout the book and I will also share quick tips on how you can use them even without an active spell or potion. Remember, if you want to get the most out of them, buy them from someone who grows them for magical purposes or else grow them yourself.

Alfafa: This is a plant commonly used to attract money. As a practitioner, if you have a few of these in your home, it will help to ensure that money is always in your house. You can also sprinkle a bit of it in your wallet or pocket to attract money into it.

Angelica root: This particular root will keep dark and negative forces at bay. If you are a woman, you can use this to amplify your femininity and can also utilize it to create protection spells for your children. I also have a few beginner spells that use the power in Angelica root to attract luck.

Black Mustard Seed: We also call this "the seed of strife," because its primary purpose is to create confusion in the mind of your enemies. If you have a dispute with someone who is constantly troubling you, sprinkling some black mustard seeds on the path where they are known to walk can stir up confusion that will destabilize them and throw them off your path.

Chamomile: In general herbal medicine, chamomile is believed to have a calming effect and is good for people who have sleeping problems. In Hoodoo magic, you can use this to neutralize spells that you think have been cast against you.

Dandelion root: If you ever have a spell where you need to draw on help from your ancestors, using a dandelion root can amplify your reach and connection, making it easier to access them. If you are having trouble sleeping and feel that you are the victim of spiritual attacks, using dandelion in some of the potions that I will share in this book can help provide additional protection and will help you sleep better.

Fennel: Ensure your home is a safe space, free of bad spirits and negative energy that might corrupt the magical atmosphere, by hanging fennel seeds on your windows. If you need a little dose of courage for something, putting fennel seeds in your pocket can help. When I first started casting spells myself, I used to have fennel seeds in my pocket or in my palm to give me extra confidence. I encourage you to do the same.

Ginger: Until you become an advanced Hoodoo practitioner, I advise you to chew a little bit of ginger before you cast a spell. It is one of those herbs with an "amplifying" ability. Another effective use of ginger root is in spells that are used to increase desire in a relationship. But in a general sense, it is used to attract success.

Hibiscus: Warding off dangerous spirits is very important in the practice of Hoodoo magic, but at the same time you need to connect with the right spirits. Using the hibiscus plants in specific spells can attract good spirits that will, in turn, be happy to help you achieve your goal. You also use this in spells that are related to love, marriages and relationships.

Lemongrass: If you feel that you are suffering from a curse or that you have been jinxed, some of the cleansing spells and baths that I will talk about in this book use lemongrass to wash away the negative effects of those curses or completely neutralize the jinx.

Mandrake root: This is a multipurpose plant that can be used for different spells and rituals. It can be bound to a doll and used for a love spell. It can be inserted into a mojo bag to either attract money or repel evil forces and is also commonly used in fertility potions.

Root Spells

The list of herbs provided above are just some of the most basic herbs you should keep in your home. I want to point out that herbs are not the only things used in creating spells. It is called Rootwork, of course, but other non-plant-related elements, such as bones and stones are essential for the preparation of certain spells.

You will find that many different roots and herbs are used in creating attraction spells to empower you or provide protection. You either want to attract wealth, luck or love or you are seeking to empower yourself emotionally by raising your confidence level, or want to protect yourself from negative energy, negative spirits and potential curses. Most of the spells that will be performed in this book, and that you will perform as you grow in the craft, will center around these needs. And that is why it is important that you learn about roots at this early stage.

There are a lot of online resources that can help teach you the different kinds of herbs that are used in Rootwork. We would need a whole second book if I were to go into all of them. But for now, I am covering what you need to know as a beginner. The next step, as I mentioned earlier, is to learn how to properly identify and differentiate between herbs. Some plants look alike, so you need to smell them in order to determine which is which. The final step is to learn what herbs to mix together and what not to mix. It is easy to assume that simply because they are plants, they can all go together without consequences. Creating a spell is very different from creating a salad. You are not relying on the flavor of the plant. Instead, you must assess the energy, and certain energies clash. When you have a clash of energy in a potion, it either nullifies the desired effect or amplifies a negative outcome.

My reason for adding this caution here is not to scare you but to help you understand that you are not dealing with ordinary elements and materials. You are dealing with a magical force and you have to practice your spell creations with respect for the craft. Take the time to learn and grow as a Hoodoo practitioner. Use the foundation that this book will provide as a stepping stone to your next stage in Hoodoo practice. Call on your ancestors for guidance because, yes, they are always willing to provide assistance. Some of the spells I know today were not handed down to me directly from Mama Estelle. I intuitively knew what to put together and I believe that that was as a result of my connection with my ancestors. They guided me through the process and yours are always willing to guide you if you open up to them. One way to open yourself up to your ancestors is by cleansing yourself. The spiritual cleanse is a vital part of a spell-casting process and we will get into that in the next chapter.

5

SPIRITUAL CLEANSING

"Purify me with hyssop and I shall be clean.
Wash me and I shall be whiter than snow"
Psalm 51:7

For a brief moment, let us remove magic from the equation and focus on the emotional, mental and psychological benefits of having a bath. When, after a long, hard day, you come home and immerse yourself in a bath with your favorite soaps and scents, regardless of your gender, it has an uplifting effect on the psyche. Now, if you turn this experience up a notch by including herbs imbued with specific powers, you can amplify the effect of a cleansing bath on your spirit and even on your physical well-being. If you have been paying attention, you have noticed that I use the word "amplify" a lot. This is not a coincidence or a grammatical addiction. It is because I believe that this word is exactly what Hoodoo practice is all about. You are taking what naturally exists and harnessing its power to increase your chances of achieving the outcome you desire. So, forgive me for using this word a lot. In time, you will understand why. For now, let us take a closer look at purification baths, cleanses and the rituals associated with them.

Purification Baths: Symbolism and Application

Purification baths are meant to purify you for the ritual you want to perform and open you up spiritually to create a channel that allows you access to the spirit world, where you can make your petition known. By doing so, purification baths increase the chances of your desires becoming reality. But beyond opening you up, a purification bath serves other purposes, and I want to talk about a few of these right now.

Severing Ties:

Some of us unwittingly get ourselves into sticky situations, either through love ties, ancestral curses or as a result of our own actions. One of the many ways to get rid of such a tie is to undergo a purification bath. It helps to separate you from that person, curse or consequence. When it comes to soul ties, it is possible you will come across an individual who is unnaturally addicted to you. Their obsession with you might have negative repercussions in your life. Even if they are not doing anything spiritual, the fact that you may have had some kind of physical interaction with them, whether through intercourse or some other shared intimate activity, may have created a tie with that person without you realizing it. These bonds can become dangerous, especially when the person becomes obsessed with you. As for the ancestral curse, there are times when the sins of the father are visited on the son, so just because you were born to this particular individual could mean that you carry some pain and hurt in your present life as a result of that lineage. There are special baths that you can prepare to break such a tie and make sure that it ends permanently. Finally, when you offend someone and that person holds a grudge against you, if they are the spiritual type, they could engage in declarations, sometimes through incantations and spells, that will negatively affect you. Putting yourself through a purification bath will separate you from those declarations and free you from the consequences.

For Protection:

As you ascend in your journey as a Hoodoo practitioner, one of the things you will come to realize is the fact that a lot of the things we deal with on a daily basis are more spiritual than they are physical. The energy that people project towards you can affect you without you even realizing it. The spaces that you inhabit are not entirely new, as they belonged to previous owners. These people may have left a very negative aura in that space, and if you do not perform a purification bath, you will find yourself absorbing some of that negativity in different areas of your life. A purification bath helps to give you additional protection against these unpredictable elements. We can never predict the intentions of another, but a purification bath will protect you from them. Think of it as boosting your immune system. You might not yet be sick but by feeding your body with the right vitamins and nutrients, you arm yourself against any disease that may want to invade your body. In the same way, there may not currently be any spiritual attack or negativity in your physical space, but to maintain that serenity and ensure that you are well-guarded against any future attacks, a purification bath will create a barrier that keeps such things out.

For Attraction:

Anything with the ability to repel the negative can also attract the positive, so if you are preparing yourself to attract certain events in your life, a purification bath is a good idea. With the right ingredients, you can use your body as a channel that attracts the kind of things you want to see in your life. There are stones and other elements that can be used for this very purpose in the preparation of a purification bath. If you are able to diligently follow through on some of the rituals I will share shortly, you can make yourself a magnet for wealth, love or even luck. The impact of attraction spells that call for purification baths is greater than simply manifesting what you desire. You can also attract positive energy so that you find yourself constantly associating with the people that you need in your life. The main thing to remember when performing a ritual of this sort is to ensure that your mind is clear and focused on what you want.

Internal Cleansing

In Hoodoo, the practice of carrying out an internal body cleanse has more to do with ensuring that you are in a better position to invoke or conjure the things you want. I use the word "cleanse" because it's something that a lot of us can relate to, but the appropriate term is purification. As you continue to learn more on this journey, you will find that the word "purification" will expand to accommodate concepts like anointing, blessing and consecration. An internal body cleanse requires the ingestion of certain mixtures and concoctions designed specifically for this process. The herbs used in these mixtures are meant to intensify your psychic connection and provide clarity of thought so that you are able to focus your mind and zero in on the specific thing about which you want to consult with your ancestors.

This is another part of Hoodoo practice that requires caution and consultation with those who know exactly what they are doing. Some of the herbs that I work with for jobs or preparations of rituals are not exactly meant for consumption, so you need someone who knows the ins and outs of the plants that you intend to use and how their interaction with one another could impact you physically. Failure to comply with instructions given by the Hoodoo doctor you work with might result in a failure of the spell or even health complications, especially if you ingest the materials. As a beginner, I would advise that you skip the internal cleansing ritual until you have reached a point where you have more knowledge on the subject. Instead, opt for ready-made herbal bath mixes. These mixes are often created with a specific purpose in mind. Go for the one that matches the expectation that you have and follow the instruction to the letter.

Finally, you should know that doing an internal cleanse is not solely reliant on ingesting herbs. There are crystals and other curios you might be able to use for such purposes. In some spells, you can light a candle and use the power of visualization to draw in the energy you need for an internal cleanse. I usually tell my beginner students that this is a better route to take unless you are working with an experienced Hoodoo doctor. The practice of Hoodoo is relatively safe, but it is important that you don't take this for granted by disregarding basic instructions. You might end up in a situation that is far worse than what brought you there initially or attract the wrong kind of energy into your life. I share these warnings because the practice of Hoodoo is not a hobby or to be engaged in on a whim. It requires dedication, devotion and due diligence.

Keeping Negative Energy Away

Many of us need to maintain a personal space filled with positive energy. This is why I feel like the perfect introduction to a purification bath is one that is meant to repel negative energy. In this segment, I am going to teach you how to create your own purification bath using some of the more common herbs, like the ones I listed earlier, and a few others you will need to obtain. I will also walk you through the step-by-step process to completing this ritual. As you continue to practice this, you will absorb more spiritual insight and guidance on some other necessary steps you can take to create results that are unique to different situations. But for now, let us fill your space with positive energy that will allow you to thrive spiritually and that will create a more enabling environment for your spells to work.

Duration:

This ritual takes place over a period of three days, so make sure you arrange your schedule to work without interruption. I would recommend that you do this once a month or once every quarter, depending on your experiences and personal needs. The first bath is meant to happen just after sunset. It is believed that this is the period that negative forces begin to assemble. So the first ritual is going to be made up of bitters herbs that repel the activities and intentions of negative spirits towards you. The second bath is meant to be performed just before dawn and it is meant to attract positive energy. The third bath is much like the second and its sole purpose is to reinforce your intentions from that second bath. It acts as a seal for the attraction magic you are trying to create.

Preparation:

For the first ritual and the first bath on the first day, you will need the following:

- Dandelion roots
- Yarrow
- Wormwood
- Nettle
- Red or purple colored petals
- Horehound
- Vinegar
- Ammonia

It doesn't matter if the herbs used are fresh, dried or powdered. Remember that this is not a sexy bath situation, so don't try to do the whole spa-like treatment. Start by setting the hot water in the bathtub at a temperature that is hot but not so hot that it scares you, then add the herbs and petals into the hot water. Add 1/2 cup of vinegar and a few drops of ammonia and you are set.

For the second and third day of the week will you will need the following:

- Angelica
- Chamomile
- Hyssop
- Allspice

- Comfrey leaves
- Powdered Nutmeg
- Powdered Cinnamon
- White petals
- Honey
- Milk
- Egg

Again, the herbs used here can be fresh, dried or powdered. In addition to the powdered nutmeg and cinnamon, you can throw in some whole nutmegs if you have them. The milk should be three cups, and one egg is enough. I should also point out that you have to prepare the herbal mixture from scratch on the second and third day. Do not use leftovers!

Process:

Day 1: When the time is right, begin by filling the tub with hot water. Then take two candles (preferably white) and place them on opposite ends to act as a doorway to the bath. You will walk through this doorway to enter into the bath when it is ready. Next, pour the herbal mixture into the water along with the ammonia and vinegar, remove your clothing and enter the doorway you made with the candles. If you are using fresh or dried herbs, you can place them in an organza bag to prevent your tub from clogging. If you are a woman on your period, do not take this bath. Blood interferes with the magic. Wait until it's over before you engage in this ritual. Once you are in the water, focus your mind on whatever negative circumstances you are going through and imagine the positive outcome that you desire. Completely immerse yourself in the bath water.

Dunk yourself in the water at least seven times. Do not ingest the contents of this water. Each time you emerge, spend a few minutes meditating on the positive outcome that you desire in your life. If you are in a situation where you are attached to something negative, like bad debts, a bad relationship or just bad experiences that happened to you, use these meditation moments to detach yourself emotionally from those feelings. By the seventh time you emerge, the water should begin to feel cooler. Step out of the tub through the doorway that you created with the candles. Take a cup and scoop the contents of this water. Set it aside and drain the rest. Do not dry yourself. Allow the water and herbs to seep into your skin so that the magic can work. When you feel dry enough, put on your robe, take that cup of water that you extracted and go outside. Turn your face towards the West, hold the cup over your head and say these words: *"Whatever hold the negative forces or spirits have over me has been broken. I am free from every negative bond. As I cast this water over my head, I am also casting out every negative spirit and energy in my life."* After reciting these words, toss the water out and go back inside. You are done for the night.

Day 2 and Day 3:

Cleanliness is a requirement for these next two rituals, so it is important that you take a personal bath before you commence. Also ensure that the bathtub you use is very clean. Once you have done this, you can start the process by running hot water in the tub and lighting the candles to create an entryway. Next, crack the egg and drop it in the water before adding the herbals and the white petals and spices. Pour in the milk and honey and then enter the tub through the gateway you have created. The mixture has a sweet-smelling aroma. Enjoy this and allow it to inspire positive images in your mind. Dunk yourself in this water five times. As you emerge from each dip, feel yourself opening up to the positive energy in the world around you, as a petal opens up to the rising of the sun.

When you are finished, step out of the tub. With an empty cup, once again scoop out the contents of the bath water. If you used whole nutmegs, try to have at least one in the cup. Drain the rest of the water. Allow yourself to air dry and then step outside. This time, you will be facing the East. Instead of holding the water above your head, hold it close to your chest and say these words: *"I welcome this day with joy and gladness. I open myself to the blessings that the world has to offer me. I attract light, love and positivity to every area of my life. I welcome all the good spirits into my heart and into my home."* Toss the water in the direction of the rising sun. You feel like immediately washing off all that egg gunk in your hair but resist the urge. Give yourself time to absorb all the positive energy that the ritual has provided by waiting until you are completely dry. Personally, I don't wash off until the end of the day, when I have to prepare myself for the ritual the next day. But if you feel that you must wash off, do it after you are dry. If you successfully completed this ritual, congratulations! You have just performed your first authentic Hoodoo spell. How does it feel? If the magic excites you, wait until you create your first oil.

6

CONJURE OILS

Oils are another curious part of religion that have been used throughout the ages. You will find the use of oils in virtually all religions. In Hoodoo, oils are used as an accelerant, as well as a sealant. In other words, when you put a specific oil on an object or place or person, you are accelerating the power of the spell that you want to invoke or conjure within that object, place or person. You can also use it to seal that power that has been placed in/on them. For example, if you consecrate a specific place and assign it as holy, you need an oil to seal this consecration process. So whatever kind of spell you want to create, there is an oil mixture that can aid that process and that is what we'll talk about in this chapter. I will share the core uses of oil in Hoodoo and then highlight a spell that utilizes oils in its incantation.

Understanding Magic Powder and Oils

Powders and oils are an integral part of Hoodoo tradition. They have been used for centuries; long before it became commonplace to use essential oils for aromatherapy. The only difference between the general use of oils and the way they are used in Hoodoo practices is that each oil is conditioned with a purpose. This tradition is perhaps what gave rise to the knowledge that certain scents are associated with certain emotions and can invoke certain feelings. For example, the scent of citrus is said to inspire creativity. There is a lot of science that backs up the effectiveness of these aromatherapy oils. But as you well know by now, Hoodoo is not exactly science that can be cooked up in a laboratory. It requires the merging of mind and spirit.

Oils and powders are extracted from plants, and so, with the understanding of plant spirits and what they represent, you can extract the essence of that plant, combine it with other herbs in specific portions and then bind that to a purpose with your mind. It really is as simple as that. However, the process is very delicate. Therefore, it is important to pay attention to how these herbs are extracted and combined in order to achieve the results you want. More often than not, oils and powders can be used on their own without any additional magical components. So, let's say, for example, you wanted to attract wealth, or you are more specific about attracting money. There are oils and powders that have been crafted for this particular purpose. All you have to do is ensure that you are getting them from the right source and use as directed by the Hoodoo practitioner from whom you bought them and you are as good as gold. But if you want to be a Hoodoo practitioner yourself, you will have to learn to create your own oils and powders.

While there are a lot of experts and people like myself who are deeply steeped in the practice of Hoodoo who can create the right oils for you, there is something beautiful about being able to create a mix that is unique to you. Eventually, as you advance and grow in the craft, you might be able to create these mixtures for other people as well. My goal and desire here is to pass on my knowledge to enable you to create your own herb mixes, oils and potions that are just as effective as mine, if not more so because they are specific to you. To create your own oil and powder mix, the first place to start is with the understanding of plants. Now you see why I said it is important to conduct research on all these herbs and plants. Don't just focus on their magical proper-ties. You have to identify them individually. There are different species of each plant, which are unique to their geographical location. Mastering their uses and extraction process requires constant practice and study.

Because we have touched on the role that plants and plant spirits play in this kind of magic, I am going to focus on how to extract these plants to make oils or powders. But first we'll look at how to use these powders and oils.

How to Use Conjure Oils

Oils and powders are primarily used in anointing and dressing purposes. For example, if you want to attract money and you have a channel that can act as a doorway for that money to enter, you can use powders to ensure that that money comes to you by dressing that medium with the powder. Here is what I mean. Let us say you have a business where you sell specific products or services. Before sending the physical invoice to them, you might sprinkle some powder on the back of the invoice or on the envelope and then invoke a clear image of what your expectations are. I would think you would expect your client to pay on time and to continue to retain your services. With this thought clearly in your mind, gently lace the invoice as I mentioned.

When you have someone specific in mind to whom you want to direct your spell, powders can be an effective way to get the results you want. Simply sprinkle the powder in the area where they are likely to step. The potency of a powder like this depends on how well it latches on to that person's imprint, which carries their essence. One thing you will quickly learn about Hoodoo magic is that the essence of a person is a very important ingredient in increasing the potency of the spell that you are casting. This is because the spell in question is no longer generic, but instead has a unique identity to work with. Let us say you live in a neighborhood that is relatively quiet, except for one annoying neighbor who is a nuisance to you. A quick way to get them out of your life without having to tip the balance of good and evil is to use Hoodoo powder. Sprinkle this powder on a well-known path where they walk. Mixing the powder with a little bit of dirt will help disguise it. Once you have sprinkled it, you have to seal the spell with your intention by vocally saying their name and what you want to happen. There are specific powder mixtures that can act as a repellent and when you attach your intention to such a mixture, you are guaranteed to get results almost immediately. This can also work if you are trying to get attention from that person.

Oils work a little differently from powders, which has a lot to do with their consistency. For instance, if you sprinkle oil on an invoice, it would look tacky and you would come off as unprofessional. This bad impression that the image creates will set the mind of the recipient against you. So it is better to use powder in certain situations and oils in others. One instance where both oil and powders can be used is when you are creating a spell or working with candle magic. There are candles that are created for spell purposes. Sprinkle a little bit of powder or oil on the uppermost part of the area where the candle is burning and then place your intentions on that candle so that as it burns, the spell will be activated and cause your desires to manifest in your life. You can also use oils and powders as a way to feed your mojo bags. In the next chapter, we are going to be talking in greater detail about mojo bags. But the thing you need to understand about them right now is that their power wanes over time. For this reason, you need powders and oils to continue feeding that energy if you want to keep the spell active and relevant.

There are many other ways to use Hoodoo oils and powders, but I am saving some of those tips for the chapters where we get into the creation of spells, so you can see this part of Hoodoo practice in action. For now, the only thing left to discuss is how to create or conjure up your own magic oils and powders.

Creating Personalized Oils

Creating you own oils will require having a neutral carrier oil as your base. Personally, I like to use homemade coconut oil. It is a very receptive oil and adapts its structure to whatever herbal elements you put in it, so if you add herbs that are very strong, it will adjust its physiological nature and adopt the potency of whatever you are using. It is also soft enough to be flexible when you want something very mild. For love potions, I prefer to use oils extracted from flowers, like roses. The nature of the rose plant is very open to love, and when used in a spell it can invoke very strong imagery in the mind of the recipients. As a beginner, I would recommend the oils I have listed below. When you become stronger in the craft, you can move on to oils like bergamot oil and so on. For your first lesson, the intention is to create a *"Get me a Job"* oil. These are hard times we live in and you might need a little spiritual boost to help you get ahead.

For this oil, you will need the following:

- Allspice - Used in prosperity spells
- Cinnamon - Attracts luck
- Coconut oil - An excellent base oil
- Dill - To make you irresistible
- Sage - For wisdom and to ward off evil eyes

Use a transparent glass bottle for this work. Pour your base into this bottle or jar and then add the cinnamon, allspice, dill and sage. If you are using fresh dill and sage, you will need to prep them ahead of time by bruising the leaves a little before immersing them in oil. Let them sit in the bottle overnight and then pour the oil and herb mixture into a strainer. Squeeze to extract and then use what is in the container. Ensure that no fresh leaves get into the mixture. Repeat this for three days with new dill and sage leaves.

On the third day, you should have enough to use for the mixture. Put the allspice and cinnamon into the oil/herb mixture. Shake it and set it down for an entire day. For the next week, continue shaking it several times every day. At the end of the seventh day, you have your first magic oil. Rub this on the sole of your shoe before you go for a job interview. You are bound to get positive outcomes. Another way to amplify the potency of this oil is to use it on a candle. Hoodoo incantations involving candles are a special kind of magic close to my heart and I will tell you all about them in the next chapter.

7

MAGIC CANDLES

M agic candles are commonly used in Hoodoo practice. You will find them used by themselves in spells, or with other elements such as powders, oils and roots. Outside of Hoodoo magic, candles create a kind of light that enables you focus and draw on your psychic energy. When your psychic energy levels are elevated, you are able to project your thoughts and direct them accurately towards your intentions. This is why a lot of exercises that involve meditation call for the use of candles. It provides light but with a glow that resonates with your spiritual aura. The elements that are used in the creation of a spell are only one part of the equation meant to give you the magic that brings about the manifestation of that spell. The second part of that equation is your mind. Having a candle in that process will help center and focus your mind. This is why I love candle magic. No matter how confused or disoriented you feel, when you put a candle in the mix, your mind is brought to the center of the problem and distractions are eliminated, thus giving you the ability to effectively carry out your incantations. In this chapter, I want to further explore this process and concept.

The Power and Intent of One

The mind is a very powerful tool but at the same time it requires utmost discipline and sometimes spiritual intervention to focus on a singular problem. There are people who are gifted with the singular focus that is required in the creation of a magical spell. However, this gift is extremely rare and even those who have require years of practice to harness it. When you have an immediate problem to solve and you want to use magic to fix it, time is a luxury you cannot afford. But having a candle in the mix can help cut that time significantly because it draws your focus to its light and helps you bring your intentions and willpower into one place.

Even with the right portions of mojo bags, purification baths and herbal mixtures, a spell can go wrong if an untrained mind is behind its activation. You need to be in agreement with the spirit behind all the elements required for the spell. You have the herbs that are meant to attract what you desire in your life and you have taken the bath that has opened you up spiritually. Your mind is the final gateway that will introduce the manifestation of the magic into your life and this is why it has to be unified in its intent. This is not always easy. As you well know, life pulls us in different directions. Even when you are very certain that the decision you are about to make is the right one, there will usually be that voice of doubt that makes you feel as if there is something else you should be doing.

A lot of people complain about how the spells they cast were not effective, or the portions they bought from the Hoodoo doctors were fake and so on. Sometimes these complaints are valid. But the real reason behind the failure of the spell is often the absence of unification of the mind. You need to be at one with the magic of the elements you are using in the spell. You need to align your thoughts and willpower with those of the spirits that you will conjure up for the spell. Many people who have come to study under me had to first learn to adjust their mentality about magic. You see, the spirits, herbs and all these wonderful things from which we are drawing magic are not just lying dormant waiting for someone to control them. They are active forces on their own and can only be moved by people who have mastered their own minds. This little bit of information is especially important if you are dealing with the kind of spell that is designed to influence the will of another. I am talking about love spells, commanding spells and others like them.

Therefore, because of the technicalities involved in the creation of magic, it is important to introduce candles and learn how to work with them. Some candles are imbued with magical powers and they help to amplify your thoughts. Some are simply representing your intentions and they draw on your energy to boost the spell. Then there are candles that you bind to your purpose with special oils and herbs. Whatever type of candle you use, the objective remains the same; to unify your thoughts, your willpower and your desires with the magical intent of your heart. This is the key to unlocking the power of the elements.

Colors and their Manifestations

Candles are shaped in different ways and this is deliberate. They have specific meanings that can help channel the magic you are trying to create in a certain way. This knowledge of the shapes of candles is something I think should be learned later on. As a beginner, your primary concern should be with the colors. Through technology, candles are being created in a greater variety of colors than we ever had in the early days. However, these different shades still fall into specific categories, so I am not going to focus on the range of colors in their different shades. Instead, I am going to start with the seven primary colors that are used in conjuring, Rootwork and magic. I will share the significance of the candles and explain what the color represents.

Black Candles: There is a general misconception that black candles are typically used for dark magic and deep-seated occult practices. While a part of this is true, black candles do not necessarily signify evil. In the world of Hoodoo magic, black is a protection color and so if you want to create a protection spell, a black candle would be most effective. If you also need a spell that involves dominance over the will of another person or entity, a black candle is a must. An example of such a spell would be a break-up spell or a banishing spell.

White Candles: Most purifying spells are done under the ethereal glow of a white candle. This is because white signifies purity, protection and, in many cases, peace. White is a deeply spiritual color that invokes harmony and a sense of calm. It is the traditional go-to color for most basic Hoodoo incantations. It provides clarity of thought and can help you center your focus if you are having trouble with it.

Red Candles: Red is a vibrant and passionate color and, as you can imagine, it a perfect color to use when the spell involves love. On the opposing end of this emotion is revenge, which can be dangerous. Red evokes powerful emotions and if you need a colored candle to stir up such emotions, you cannot go wrong with this one. Just be careful, though. As your feelings are being stirred up, you still need to maintain control and mastery over them. You don't want your feelings all over the place. This will only cause chaos with your spell.

Green Candles: Draw on the energy of money spirits with green candles. Green is also associated with vegetation, which means growth and prosperity. If the spell you are working on has to do with fertility, this is the right color of candle to use. Spells that have to do with luck, abundance and growth can draw energy from green candles.

Yellow Candles: Yellow is such a positive and upbeat color that even when it is used under the direst circumstances, it has a way of immediately brightening your mood. This candle is a personal favorite of mine. I usually light this when I am feeling down or depressed. Even without an active spell linked with it, the glow of the candle amplified by the color almost always cheers me up immediately. Unsurprisingly, it is used in spells that evolve around happiness, friendship and mental clarity.

Silver Candles: If the spell you are creating needs to draw on feminine energy, a silver candle is the surest way to get the results you want. Another interesting use of silver candles is to mirror moon magic. There are specific magic spells that need to be performed under the light of the moon. However, you would need to wait until that point in order to harness the moon energy. But in case of an emergency, lighting up a silver candle will cast a moonlit glow over the spell and improve its efficiency.

Blue Candles: Sharpen your communication skills under the light of a blue candle. Promote healing and sound mental health with spells cast in the glow of a blue candle. Using a blue candle is also excellent for meditation exercises. After carrying out a purification bath, I like to light a blue candle and meditate on the positive outcome I am expecting.

Candle Reactions

Candle reading is a Hoodoo practice that you will learn in time. When you light a candle and put it in a spiritual element, it draws on the energy in the environment and you can read the flames to interpret the energy in the space you are in. The art of candle reading is somewhat advanced because there is a lot of information to learn. At this stage, I will simply share what you need to know at this level. If you want more information, you will have to do a bit of online research on the topic. There are also books that will enlighten you about how to read candle flames. I am also considering writing a more advanced version of this book, so watch for that.

There are three basic things to look out for as a newbie Hoodoo practitioner. First, you look at the color of the flame, then the movement of the flame and finally the brightness of the flame.

Color Reaction

The power of the candle flame ranges from blue at one end of the spectrum to red at the other end, with yellow and orange in between. A blue flame is indicative of the presence of a friendly spirit, like an angel or a fairy or even a familiar ancestral spirit. A red flame, on the other hand, signifies the presence of a very powerful entity. Yellow and orange speaks of the presence of active energy that could be helpful in the spell.

Flame Movement

When candles flame, it is usually in the direction of the wind. But when you are in a closed space and the flame flickers, pay attention to what direction the flame is pointing towards. It will tell you the state of your spell. For example, an east-facing flame indicates mental soundness in the spell that you have created while a west-facing flame points to the strength of the emotion surrounding the spell. A north-facing flame is usually the result of a physical factor, while south-facing flames speak to the fact that your physical energy is powered by intent.

Flame Brightness

Candle flames burn at different levels. A low-burning flame might mean you need to up the energy levels required to push the spell forward. A flame that is burning bright and fast but unevenly means the spell is not grounded. You want a slow, steady burn that tells you your spell is going in the right direction.

8

MOJO BAGS

A mojo bag can be the most personalized form of magic. You use it to draw on powers that can be invoked in the spells that you create, in the daily activities that you carry out and also in your practice of Hoodoo. Everything you have learned up to this point was bringing you to this place where you learn how to create your own mojo bag. In this chapter, I will talk about what a mojo bag really is. I will also share some tips on how you can create your own personal mojo bag. Some of my tips will enlighten you on how to continuously activate the power of your mojo bag so that it remains potent for a very long time. This is one of the most exciting parts of this process, because you will see your magic begin to evolve and develop its own identity. The things that we learn from our ancestors provide a foundation for our growth but with practice, we are able to add our own individual ingredients to the mix to create a signature magical identity. When this happens, if you perform a spell, the energy that comes off of that spell will have your name written on it because it will be a marker unique to you. Doesn't that sound exciting? If this is something you look forward to, I promise you will enjoy this chapter immensely.

What are Mojo Bags?

In the general term, a mojo bag is your own personal talisman. It is regarded as an amulet. In other cultures and religions you will find references to it when it comes to protection. When I looked online to find out what people thought about a mojo bag, one definition I loved described a mojo bag as "a prayer in a bag." This is nice and somewhat fitting but in Hoodoo, it goes beyond that. A mojo bag in Hoodoo practice is a signature spell bound to you with immense power to drive a specific purpose over a long period of time. Unlike the standard spells, which basically go on errands for your desires, a mojo bag is tied to a core aspect of your destiny. For example, there are protection mojo bags designed to keep you away from anything that could possibly hinder your progress in life. This type of magic is not only about protecting you from evil spirits or those who want to harm you but is essentially about keeping you on track when it comes to your purpose in life.

There is a huge difference between the work of a protection spell and that of a mojo bag created for protection. One is like buying an alarm system for your home to notify you of imminent danger and enabling you to act to prevent that danger, while the other is like having a round-the-clock bodyguard who is knowledgeable about every form of defense so that if there is an attack, all you need to do is follow the instruction of this bodyguard. You see how distinctly different that is? You also have mojo bags that focus on specific emotions, like love. If you desire a partic-ular person and want to attract their attention and affection but feel that you are unable to do so the natural way, a mojo bag might be the only way for you to get those things in a sustainable way. This is because a regular love spell will do the initial work for you, but as soon as that work is done, it diminishes in power. A mojo bag, on the other hand, will continue to activate your desire for that person as long as you feed the power that backs it in order to keep it potent.

Mojo bags are powerful; from the way they are created to the way they are activated and the way they are fed. There are critical steps you must take and conditions that must be fulfilled in order to benefit from their power. Whether or not you are spiritually attuned, the second the power in your mojo bag begins to wane, you will feel its impact because that is how strong the energy is that it projects. Do not dabble lightly in the creation of a mojo bag. You want to ensure that there is a balance of energy in this process and that the spell you are working with is well-grounded. The potency of a mojo bag will amplify the intent you have for that spell and if you fail to get it right in the preparation stage, it will amplify the negative repercussions of that failure. So, always use caution when creating a mojo bag. But when you get it right, you will activate a supernatural energy so intense that it will almost be like having your own personal genie at your beck and call, particularly in the area for which the spell was meant. If, for instance, you created the mojo bag for protection, you will find yourself in ordinary situations where you are supernaturally guarded. In such situations, you will not be able to explain some of the unusual saves that you experience. Now that we have thoroughly explored what mojo bags are, let us look at how they can be used.

THE VARIOUS USES OF MOJO BAGS

Mojo bags have several uses but for this level of training and practice of Hoodoo, I will focus on only three of them. But before I cover the three main uses, I want you to think of mojo bags as your super-packed multivitamin supplements. They power up your life in many ways and can be personalized and adapted to suit your specific goals and objectives. Now let us look at the three uses of mojo bags.

1. To Activate the Power That Attracts Your Desires

If you have a burning desire to see something specific manifest in your life through a spell, a mojo bag is the perfect thing to give that desire and activated spell an extra boost. There are situations that call for more than just a one-time spell. And even if you go through a full ritual like a cleanse or purification bath, you might be required to do more. Now, instead of performing these spells or purification baths every other week, having a mojo bag dedicated to this spell will be enough to hold the power from the moment your spell is activated to the point where it manifests. It doesn't matter what that desire is for; whether you are attracting love, wealth, luck or simply trying to end a relationship with someone. A mojo bag will create an atmosphere that pulls the power required for the spell and then sustains it until that thing you desire has manifested.

2. To Power a Protection Spell

Even the most basic protection spell requires immense power, and as a beginner you might not be able to draw on those elements on your own. A mojo bag created specifically for protection will ensure that the protection spell you have cast over yourself remains active over a long period of time. Again, it doesn't really matter how powerful or how basic the spell is, if you are working with the right ingredients or Hoodoo doctor, you should be able to sustainably power up the spell. Long ago, mojo bags were mostly used as talismans. Essentially, this meant that they had the same duties as bulletproof vests on police officers. A mojo bag would absorb whatever negative energy was directed your way and threatened to cause you harm. In some cases, it can even redirect that negative force towards its origin. However, in very simple terms, it serves as a barrier between you and anything that intends to hurt you, whether physically or spiritually.

3. To Draw on Deeper Inner Strength

One of the things my grandmother taught me that has stayed with me all through my life is the knowledge that I am powerful. I am going to pass this gift on to you; you are incredibly powerful. The only difference between you and me is the wealth of information I have. This knowledge that has been passed down to me by my ancestors has equipped me with information that I have been able to use to my advantage. What is my point? You have a dormant power inside of you and a mojo bag can awaken it and tap into it to give you some of the results that you desire. For example, if you want to experience more confidence or more calmness in your life, you should not be looking to spirits for this. Instead, you should be able to awaken the god or goddess inside you and a mojo bag is the right tool to do exactly that. So, if you find yourself in a season that stresses you out, such as our current climate, having a mojo bag with you at all times can help you experience a calm and patience that may be unlike you but is perfectly natural at the same time.

Making Personalized Mojo Bags

One phrase I have used throughout this chapter in describing the mojo bag is how specific it is to a spell. But more than that, it is also unique and specific to you. This means that your mojo bag cannot be used by another person.

You also cannot allow someone else to see, touch or know about it. It is meant to be kept in a safe place on your person at all times. It can be made from a combination of herbs, stones and oils. But the most powerful ingredient is your intent. On that cheery note, let us create your first mojo bag. For this exercise, we are creating the inner peace mojo bag. You will need to gather the following items:

- A flannel bag in indigo blue
- A seashell
- A lapis lazuli stone
- Chamomile
- A peace symbol (optional)

Indigo blue is a color that calls on inner peace. This is why it is a perfect choice for this mojo bag. A seashell connotes the soothing and calming presence of the ocean during its gentle moments, and drawing on that presence is a great way to feed the energy you want to direct into this mojo bag. The lapis lazuli stone connotes harmony and tranquility and its potency in fulfilling the magic required for this makes it an excellent addition. Finally, throw in some chamomile seeds for that extra calming touch. Put these ingredients into the flannel bag and seal it with a peace symbol, if you like. I am particularly fond of the ohm sign, because it represents inner calmness. Find a symbol that you feel reflects what you want and then complete your mojo bag magic by placing your intent on it.

Hold the bag in your hands and speak what you desire. Your words could be something like this: "I experience calmness every time this bag touches me. I automatically relax and feel stress leaving my body every time I make contact with the bag. I never lose touch with this calmness that I have on the inside so that even in the most trying situations, I am able to keep my head above water. This is my intent and I speak it into action every single day of my life." Breathe on the bag so that it absorbs your essence and begins its cycle. Every other week, rub this mojo bag with an anointed oil to keep and sustain the power behind it and, just like that, your first mojo bag is activated.

With your first mojo bag creation, you have finished the basic training on your journey to becoming a Hoodoo practitioner. What you need now is a couple of spells for different situations to help you get started and to develop the knowledge you have right now. We will kick things off with some fundamental love spells.

9

SPELLS FOR LOVE

L ove is a beautiful and pure emotion. It is such a great feeling to love and be loved at the same time. However, when this mutual love does not occur, but it is something you desire, especially when you have someone particular in mind, you might need some kind of spiritual intervention to trigger the emotion in the other person. From a logical standpoint, it's easy to understand why many struggle with love potions. It seems like a potion is meant to compel someone to do something that they don't want to do. But in reality, magic, especially Hoodoo magic, simply creates an opportunity that might not have existed before.

A person's emotions and feelings are not exactly being compelled against their will, although it's true that there are dark forms of magic that will channel that sort of energy.

But in this case, an opportunity is presented for the seed of love to be sown. The person for whom the spell is intended is conscious of their willpower in the process. Imagine this scenario. You are pining for someone who doesn't even know you exist. You have nothing but good will and good intentions towards them, but you have no idea how to initiate a romance. Performing a love spell is not going to suddenly make them fall in love with you. On the contrary, it merely creates an opportunity for them to see you in a different light. What happens from then on is up to them. Now let's look into simple Hoodoo love spells and learn how to create them.

The Place of Love Spells in Hoodoo

The subject of love spells or magic associated with love has been a source of controversy in many circles because of the ethics involved. But as I explained earlier, traditional love magic does not compel a person against their will. The spell is not designed to make a person fall in love with you. It is meant to create the circumstances that will provide opportunity and enhance an atmosphere for love to blossom. In fact, I like to think of love spells as creating an ambience that attracts genuine love but also the attention of the person on whom you are fixated.

Think of a love spell like an advanced flirting technique, but in this case you are not using words, body language or other tactics to show this person that you are interested in them.

Instead, you are empowering the forces in your environment to provide the right signals that will welcome this love into your life. Of course, it would be unfair of me to not acknowledge the existence of dark magic that compels a person against their will. But the truth is that love spells are not the only spells in which a person's will is being subjected to that of another. There are spells designed to rob a person of their wealth or opportunity, and there are spells for vengeful reasons.

I am aware of these spells, but I do not use them because the idea repulses me, and also because there are negative reper-cussions. When you willfully subdue a person's willpower and impose your intentions on them, you create an atmosphere that attracts negative forces, which can build over time to the point where they become uncontrollable. Once that happens, you will find yourself regularly attracting negative circumstances into your life. I promise you it is not worth it.

In the next segment, I am going to talk about some things that you should never ignore, especially when it comes to love spells. It is better to err on the side of caution and walk on the path that is good.

Warnings You Must Never Ignore

When creating love spells, you must never ignore your own emotions that are attached to the spell you are creating. If your intentions are not out of love or genuine desire for good towards the person to whom the spell is directed, you will not have peace of mind. You will experience a sense of wrongness about the spell and once that sets in, you will receive a clear message from your subconscious that what you are doing is not appropriate. Whenever you sense this feeling, whether it is for a love spell or not, I urge you to stop. Look for other alternatives. The problem could be that the spell you want to cast is not the right one or that your intentions are not clear enough to activate the power you are seeking.

Another sign you must not ignore when creating a love spell is if you sense that the feeling this person has towards you is not genuine. It is possible that you have already had some kind of interaction with the person for whom the spell is intended but it did not move towards love. If that's the case, it might be an indication that this person does not feel the same way about you as you do about them. If you sense this, a spell will no longer be directed at creating opportunities but will instead work with the intention of forcing them to fall in love with you, which is not right. You should also watch for behavior that points towards an addictive personality. If the person has a history of drug or alcohol abuse, you should probably back away from the spell because if the right atmosphere is created, it could enhance their addictive tendencies and push that love emotion they have for you towards obsession, which of course is something you do not want.

Finally pay attention to their mental health. A person who has a history of mental health problems or who struggles with emotions like depression, anxiety and so on is not an ideal candidate for a love spell. Do not allow your own feelings to cloud your judgment. Watch for signs of these mental or emotional traits and have the decency to hold off creating a spell, because it will only complicate things for both of you.

POTENT LOVE SPELL RECIPES

There are five different types of love spells that I will share with you. Each of them is unique and serves a different purpose, as you will see. They can often be created using simple ingredients around the home but you may need to expand your search for some important ingredients:

Spell One: Come My Way Orange

Purpose: To create an atmosphere around you that acts as a magnet and attracts love

For this spell, you will need the following ingredients:

- Orange
- Rose
- Pins (Nine of them)
- Red thread
- A lock of your hair
- Follow Me Boy oil (I will share the recipe for this)

First, anoint the lock of your hair, the pin and the thread with the "look me over" oil. Then insert the lock of hair into the rose petal. Use a small carving knife to drill a hole into the orange. Insert the rose with the lock of your hair into this hole. Use the pins to close the hole and then weave the thread between the pins in order to "lock it." Bury this orange somewhere close to your phone and wait for love interests to begin to pour in. Always remember to keep your intent close at heart when you are creating a spell like this.

Spell Two: Call Me Hand

Purpose: To make someone specific contact you

Since you've probably attracted several love interests, it is possible that some have your phone number but have not reached out. This spell will help initiate the next phase. Like the previous spell, it is easy and can be done right in your kitchen. Here is what you will need:

- Licorice root
- A dime (mercury dime for something more potent)
- A paper with the name of the person on it
- A purple cloth

Wrap the dime and the licorice root in the paper that has the name of the person you want to call you. Wrap this paper in the purple cloth. Make your intentions known by calling out the person's name and saying, "I want you to call me." When you have done this, put it all on the floor and stomp on it. Do this nine times every day for nine days. Expect positive results.

Spell Three: Love Me Dearly Mojo Bag

Purpose: To increase the love that someone feels for you

This is the perfect spell if you have a love interest whose affection you want to boost to sustain the relationship. You will need the following items:

- A lodestone
- A pouch
- Hair from the head of your beloved
- Scraping from the sole of the shoe of your beloved
- A piece of paper

Write the name of your beloved on the piece of paper and put all of the items listed above into the pouch. Hold the pouch close to your heart and express your intentions clearly. This is not the time to evoke wishful thinking. Be clear about what you want them to feel and visualize your energy transferring to the bag in that moment. After this visual exercise, breathe on the bag and then keep it close to you at all times. The spell will be activated.

Spell Four: Stay on Their Mind

Purpose: To keep your beloved thinking about you constantly

They say that absence makes the heart grow fonder but sometimes what you need to keep that love going is for you to be on their mind all day. You can achieve this with a very simple home spell. You need:

- Crushed lodestone (1 tbsp)
- Crushed thyme (1 tbsp)
- A scoop of your bathwater

Mix all of these ingredients together in a bowl and find a way to pour it at the entryway of the home of your beloved. Obviously, if you share a home together, that is ideal. If not, you will have to think of an excuse to spill this at their door. Bear in mind at all times the intention that you have for this spell. You do not need to speak it into existence, but your intentions matter.

Spell Five: Follow Me Boy Oil

Purpose: To attract luck, love, wealth, and to make you stand out

- Angelica root
- Catnip herb
- Coriander seed
- Damiana herb
- Fennel seed
- Grapeseed oil (use almond oil for a sweetening effect)

Mix all of these herbs together and pour into the oil. Allow it to sit in a warm place for a few days. Shake every now and then during that time and you are good to go.

10

SPELLS FOR MONEY AND LUCK

A s with every other spell I have described, this type of magic will not create something out of nothing. Instead, it works as a magnet for the thing that you desire. In this case, money. When you are setting your expectations, it is important to be realistic about it so that it aligns with your intentions. If you are hoping that somehow money will fall from the sky or that a tree in your garden will suddenly start sprouting dollar leaves, you will be disappointed. However, a more realistic expectation would be the hope that your business will begin booming or that you will find favor with financially influential people who would be happy to share their wealth with you. In this chapter, I am going to talk about how you can use the elements in our environment to make this happen.

Using the Elements to Attract Money

Attracting money and creating a sustainable source of income is a desire that we all have and is not a wish to be ashamed of. As we all know, wealth does not always go to the most hardworking among us. It goes to those who have the greatest opportunities and know what to do with those opportunities. Hoodoo spells work with this kind of logic. You are not tipping the balance of power by being greedy. Instead, you are bending the elements that guide and control wealth and manipulating them to do your bidding. You receive wealth by ensuring that the right conditions are aligned to deliver the results that you want.

My grandmother used to say that wealth is attained when you are able to fulfill the criteria for it. Sometimes, that criteria could be about attracting favor, being in the presence of the right person at the right time or generally attracting people who are able to fulfill your financial needs. It is hard to describe how it works except to say that, as my grand-mother says, money spells help you create the conditions for wealth. When you are working on a money spell, try not to focus on the "hows." Instead, reflect on the purpose that drives you and use that as an anchor to create the spell.

There are a lot of untruths and misconceptions surrounding the creation of wealth through Hoodoo spells, and while I cannot list all of these or address them right now, I will tell you that there is no spell that can make you rich overnight. There are some spells that increase your chances in games of luck, for instance, if you gamble or play the lotto. But even then, I would discourage you from having grand visions of living in luxury. On the flip side, it is likely that your luck will change because you will suddenly find open doors that had been closed to you in the past, and if you are running a business, you might even have an inflow of clients and customers.

Changing Your Luck

If we consider the concept of luck from a clinical perspective, it is difficult to understand why certain people appear to have more of it than others. There have been many studies conducted to determine why this is so. One particular study showed that people who seem lucky tend to be more outgoing and extroverted. They tend to have a more cheerful disposition when compared to people who are considered "unlucky." If you keep this in mind and think about how Hoodoo works, you will find similarities in the patterns of all the spells, in that they are meant to create the right conditions to bring about the desired results, and that a cheerful disposition is a component in each one.

Hoodoo magic is not about snapping your fingers or waving a magical wand and having everything click into position for you. It is more about aligning the elements in your favor, if you find that you are one of those people who has struggled with bad luck for a long time. This spell is going to condition your mind as well as the universal elements surrounding your situation to bring about the results you want. I have said many times that one of the most powerful ingredients in a spell is your intention, and it is your intention that will help your spell manifest.

When you activate a luck spell in your life, you are conditioning yourself emotionally, mentally and physically to be more aware of the opportunities that are available to you in your environment. But it goes a step further. It attracts those opportunities to you so that you have more chances to attain the life you want. When you have more chances, there is greater possibility that the results you want will manifest. So when you have all of this in mind as you proceed to the next set of spells, you are in a better position to visualize what you want to become a reality.

5 MONEY SPELLS TO ATTRACT MONEY

Spell One: Luck Draw Mojo

Purpose: Increasing luck in the area of money attraction and bringing good fortune

The main ingredient for this spell can be found at a blacksmith's. If you don't have a blacksmith close to you, magnetic sand, which can be purchased in most Hoodoo stores, is an excellent substitute.

You will need:

- A red flannel pouch
- Anvil dust (magnetic sand)
- Garlic (clove)
- Lodestone
- Sugar
- Whiskey

Put the garlic clove and lodestone in the red flannel pouch. Sprinkle the anvil dust (or magnetic sand) and the sugar on the pouch. Sew the flannel shut. As you do this, speak your intentions to the bag. When you are finished, soak the bag in whiskey and you are good to go.

Spell Two: Quick Cash Fire

Purpose: To attract urgent money for those days when you are having an emergency that requires money to solve it

This is one of those spells that is so simple, you might question its effectiveness, but I can promise you that if you are able to put this together, the outcome is quick. Don't expect to become a billionaire overnight, though. This is more about getting urgent cash fast. In addition to your intent, gather these items:

- Bay leaf
- Cinnamon (powdered)
- Nutmeg (powdered)

Mix a generous quantity of these ingredients together. Light a candle to center your focus if you are having problems gathering your thoughts. You need to have a singular intent to which this spell will be directed. If, for instance, you need this money for your rent, focus on the exact amount you need and call for it. Next, burn the mixture. You should get an immediate mix of flavors and scents. Fan the smoke towards you and try to absorb as much of it as possible. It's important that your hands and face absorb the smoke. When you are through, discard the remnants and remain expectant.

Spell Three: The Moneyball

Purpose: To attract cash and fulfill the atmospheric conditions for sustainable prosperity

The previous spell was for petty or fast cash. This one helps to grow your overall wealth. Again, I have to caution you that this is not going to happen overnight. But if you maintain your attitude and intention for the spell, you will find it manifesting in your life sooner than later. To get the money ball spell running, you will need the following ingredients:

- Dry basil
- Green cotton thread
- High John root
- Name paper

Begin the spell by wrapping the basil leaves around the high john root. On the name paper write your name and expectation and wrap the paper around the leaves. Use the green thread to tie this paper. To increase your money attraction, you can coat the thread with fast cash oil if you have it. Wrap the thread around the package nine times and leave some extra thread hanging so you can tie it somewhere and dangle it. Choose somewhere private to hang this and every day afterward, tap it to swing in a circle and recite Psalm 23 as it swings. To keep the spell active, rub it every week or so with fast cash oil or any other money oil.

Spell Four: Debt Dissolved

Purpose: To get rid of debt or create financial report problems that work in your favor by dissolving your debt

If you owe someone money or you find yourself in a predicament where money is being demanded of you, you can take care of the problem by carrying out this spell. All you need is:

- Two medium-sized onions (preferably red onions)
- Piece of paper with your name on it

Write your name on the paper nine times and then turn it over. Write the amount that you owe but do it backwards. Write this number nine times. Now fold the paper and burn it to ash. Cut the two onions in half and rub the ashes from the burnt paper on the exposed side of each of these onions.

Place the onion with the ash coated on it in each of the four corners of your home. Remember to keep your intention in mind as you do this. The problem will be solved.

Spell Five: Lucky Cologne

Purpose: This is used to attract luck and can also be used as spray perfume for candles, mojos and other spells that involve attracting luck

This spell is used as a juice booster for the other spells that you create. You can also put it on you when you go out if you need to attract some luck to whatever activity you are engaging in. It doesn't matter if it is a love spell or a money spell that you want to boost. This particular cologne will increase the chances of that spell becoming effective because of its luck attraction. You just need:

- Orange peels
- Rum
- 9 nutmegs

Put the orange peels into a bottle of quality rum, but do not mix them. Recite the following chant as you shake it: *"**This is a message to all my kin, below and above, I want you to make me very lucky... in wealth and in love.**"* Repeat this chant until you experience a release in your spirit and then place the bottle in the sun for nine days. At the start of each day, shake the bottle and repeat the chant. On the ninth day, your lucky cologne is ready to use.

11

SPELLS FOR SUCCESS

T his is another one of those spells that is going to work actively with the image you paint in your mind. The reason for this is simple; success means different things to different people. For some people, having an abundance of wealth is success. For others, passing exams, getting married or convincing someone to give them a business contract is how they define success. Whatever that definition is to you, it is important to hold that image in your mind. You cannot think of success in a broad and general sense because when your desires begin to manifest based on a spell, it will be difficult to identify what is manifesting as a result of that spell. This is why it's important that you have a clearly defined image in mind before creating a success spell. In this chapter, I want to explore the concept of success and help you figure out ways to fine-tune what you want your spell to do for you. It will have a lot to do with attracting luck, wealth and generally maintaining balance in your environment. When you have balance and harmony in your environment, it is easier for things to align themselves with your will.

Using Hoodoo to Invite Positive Change

In order to grow in life, change is necessary. If you look at things from this perspective, you will agree with me that change is one of the prerequisites for growth, and when you have upward growth, you will most likely experience success. We could even say that change is the precursor to success. Keeping this in mind, one of the first things you should train yourself to think about is the kind of changes that you believe will bring about the success you want to see in your life.

For example, your goal could be to simply become successful at losing that extra 10 pounds you gained in the last year or so. For that to happen, you cannot continue to sit on the couch, eat the same thing over and over and lead a sedentary lifestyle, and still expect that transformation to occur. Success in that regard will mean a change in lifestyle and habits. This will now draw your focus towards your mindset. A proper change in your attitude towards health can be the thing that will trigger your successful weight loss journey. This is just one of the ways you can condition your mind to initiate the changes that will bring about the success you want.

It doesn't matter whether you are studying for an exam or applying for a job or even planning to propose to someone. The transformation process required of the mind is pretty much the same. You need to think of the right condition that will bring about the manifestation of the success you desire. The first step you need to take is to identify what exactly you consider success. The more specific you are about the objective, the higher the chances you have for that spell to work. When you have clearly defined this outcome, the next step is to think of the mental state of mind that you have to be in to bring about this change.

When you focus on other people, you lose sight of the power that you have inside yourself and when you fail to acknowledge this power, how can you hope to power up your spell? Yes, you can draw on insight and strength from your ancestors, but it is your link to them that will fire up the power that they lend to you. This means all roads eventually lead back to you. For this reason, I want you to start thinking of that thing you can do on the inside, as well as the mindset you can develop to create that additional ginger that will drive you towards your success objective. When you have this sorted out, you are on track to creating a powerful success spell.

The Key Ingredients for Manifesting Success in Different Areas

As I explained in the previous segment, manifesting success in any area is linked to your ability to aptly and accurately define what that success means to you. Your imagination is going to be one of the most crucial ingredients, which is why it is advisable that moments before you create your spell, you light a candle and meditate to give yourself clarity on the subject. After you have obtained clarity, write out what you see in a journal or on sheet of paper. Read over and over again what you have written down until it becomes a solid image in your mind. This image should be so strong that it almost feels as if you could reach out and touch it. This is how vivid it should be before you step into the place where you create the spell. Hold that image in your mind when you cast the spell.

There are also external conditions that must be fulfilled for a success spell to manifest. Each spell has its own unique identity, which means that it also has individual terms for the fulfillment of the spell's contract. For example, if you are dealing with finances, you need to invoke the aid of elements such as green colors, plant spirits associated with money, and stones that are known to attract money. For a success spell that involves coercion, your willpower is going to be a required ingredient or condition that has to be met. If your willpower is not strong enough, it will be impossible to coerce the other person to do your bidding.

I remember creating a "cheat no more" love potion mix for a client. Her husband was a chronic womanizer who was known in the neighborhood for his infidelity, and this embarrassed her to no end. She wanted to put an end to this behavior. However, she had a very timid and docile personality, which made it difficult for her to command him to stop this action even in absentia. So I had to work on her intonation, mindset and expectation in order for the spell to become fully activated. The second she got it right, the husband stopped his philandering ways. Understand what the conditions of the spell are and endeavor to fulfill all of them. Remember, this goes beyond acquiring ingredients.

5 SUCCESS SPELLS YOU CAN TRY TODAY

Spell One: Save Me From Poverty

Purpose: To quickly draw you from the brink of poverty by ensuring that quick cash, usually $5,000 and below, locates you immediately

There are times when you find you are completely broke, no matter how well you saved your money. Rather than panic about the situation, draw on the elements in your environment for financial sustenance. Success in this regard is about having enough to take care of your basic needs, so that is exactly what the spell is for. To complete it, you would need the following items:

- 1 green 7-day candle
- Dried and ground ginger
- Black tea leaves
- Peppermint essential oil

Poke three holes in a straight line on the top of the candle. Pour four drops of the peppermint oil into one hole. Mix the ginger and black tea together and put a pinch of this mixture into the remaining two holes on the candle. Next, take a piece of paper and write on it the exact amount of money you need. Remember, it cannot exceed $5,000. Turn the paper and sign your name on it three times. Then burn the paper as you say these words: "Holy ones, help me. Bring me a gift and grant me what I need." Recite these words 12 times over the candle, after which you can put it out. For the next seven days, you must repeat the cycle of writing the amount of money you need on the paper with your signature and burning it while you recite the words. Expect to receive the gifts in the following days.

Spell Two: Golden Luck Bath Oil

Purpose: To activate good fortunes

This is more of a blending type of spell than it is an invocation. In other words, you are merging elements together to create a desired magical condition. So you do not need special incantations or to perform it at specific times. If you have all the ingredients, mix them together and bless it with your intentions and you are good to go. The ingredients needed for this are:

- Citroen chips
- Gold mica powder
- Lavender oil

- Orange oil
- Olive oil

Mix all of these elements together and pour the mixture into a transparent glass bottle and you have your golden luck oil. Every time you take a bath, put a few drops in to attract the kind of success you desire, whether it is in business partnerships, new relationships or money-related issues. It works for me every time.

Spell Three: Golden Prosper Bath

Purpose: To bring and attract wealth and money into your home, business and person

In addition to the bath oil I just described, you can create a bath spell that activates wealth in your center, thus attracting success to you at every turn. The ingredients are very basic but might need to be purchased at a local Hoodoo store. You need:

- Goldenseal root (One or two roots)
- Marigold petals (two large handfuls)
- Sassafras leaves (two large handfuls)
- Water (holy water if you can find it)

Pour all the herbs together into a gallon of water and boil the water. Once it boils, pour it into a strainer to separate the herbs from the water. Recite Psalm 4 as you stir the water clockwise. When you have finished, the spell is ready. Bury the herbs somewhere in the garden afterwards. You can use the water with your bath for purification purposes as outlined in the chapter about purification baths or you can use it to clean your home as described in the cleansing ritual. If you are using it for your place of business, the best practice is to put it into a spray bottle and spritz it all over your work space. Make sure to spray it on fabrics like curtains, chairs and so on.

Spell Four: Big Man Cologne

Purpose: To attract successful relationships in business, friendship and romantic life. Also, to project an aura of power and success

This one is specifically for guys. As a man, it is important that you present your A game at all times. However, this is not always easy. This spell will give you a leg up and set the tone for the life that you are hoping to live. You will need:

- Bay leaves
- Dixie John root
- Juniper berries
- Lemon grass
- Lemon peel
- Your favorite cologne

Pour all these herbs into a bottle containing your favorite cologne. Allow them to soak there for at least 12 days. Store this mixture in a dark place during these 12 days to allow it to absorb the essence of the herbs. At the end of the 12th day, shake it vigorously to stir up everything and then strain it into another container. Bury the herbs and keep the cologne. Use this on your person when you want to attract success. Rub it on your pillow and beddings to attract romance. Spritz a little on your wallet and hands for business success.

Spell Five: Prosper Me Wash

Purpose: To open up new paths and usher in success

Cleanse your immediate environment, whether it's your home or business, and create a new pathway for success with this simple but potent spell. All you need are four ingredients:

- Lemon grass
- Magnolia petals
- Peppermint leaves
- Water

Mix two handfuls of each herb into 3 quarts of water. Boil the water. Meditate and pray on the scripture Psalm 23 while the mixture is boiling. When it is ready, pour it into a strainer and discard the herbs under running water. This symbolizes old things going away. Use the water from the mixture to wash the floors, walls, windows and door frames of either your home or business or the place to which you want to attract success. Do this once a week for five weeks. The best time to do it is on a Friday at dawn.

SPELLS FOR PROTECTION

> *"...You will not fear the terror of the night*
> *Nor the arrow that flies by day...*
> *For He will command his angels concerning you*
> *To guard you in all your ways..."*
> **Psalm 91**

S afety is a priority for everyone, regardless of where you live. Sometimes the danger that we face is a physical one and could threaten our lives. Other times, the danger is spiritual, which can also threaten our lives but starts its damage by crippling us from the inside. A protection spell in Hoodoo practice serves to keep you physically, mentally and spiritually protected and helps to keep out negative energy and ensure that the space you are in is constantly feeding you with the kind of energy that preserves, calms and uplifts you. In this chapter, we will delve into the less common practice of spiritual preservation.

Because of our attachment to logical thinking and reasoning, not many of us understand the pull from the other side. Some of us are spiritually alert and can sense certain auras or spirits around us. But for the most part, people tend to be blissfully unaware of the threats posed by these entities. The impacts they could have on the quality of your life can be felt in physical ways, and this is why it is important to protect yourself at all times. When you practice Hoodoo, you acknowledge the presence of these entities and spirits, and with each step of your journey, the spirit becomes more aware of you. Sometimes, their awareness of your presence could be dangerous for you. I will explain all of this in more detail as we continue.

Protection from Physical and Spiritual Attacks

The practice of Hoodoo is a spiritual one. You are embarking on a journey every single day that connects you with your inner goddess/god and this makes you aware of the entities in your environment. I would love to tell you that the journey is always beautiful and peaceful and full of gentle awakening. However, just as there are good spirits with good intentions, there are also bad spirits with bad intentions. There are malevolent entities whose mission is simply to ruin lives. I have personally had tough spiritual cases that involved individuals who were touched by these evil spirits, even though they had no idea that such spirits existed. They had a lot of negative manifestations in their lives and it felt as if they were simply going from one problem to another. Sadly, these manifestations of evil are not limited to individual experiences.

Inanimate objects can also be touched by negative influences. You have probably watched horror movies where people move into a home where there is an entity that threatens their lives. While entertaining as a movie, the truth is that this happens in real life. There are homes that are haunted by the spirits of people who inhabited them. There are also situations in which people are living under a curse. A curse is not simply negative words spoken against you. It entails the binding of evil forces to a person, so it feels as if that person is always under a negative cloud, no matter where they go. These curses can be incurred both knowingly and unknowingly. You may accidentally come in contact with objects that are cursed and for that singular act you are penalized. You may also have dealings with people who are cursed and through your relationship with them you attract their curse into your own life.

I could go on and on, listing the physical and spiritual dangers that are ever present in our environment, but my objective is not to scare you or cause you anxiety but to prepare you for this journey that you are about to undertake. Being a Hoodoo practitioner means that you acknowledge these things that I have talked about, but rather than feel helpless, you are empowered to banish, or at least restrict their influence over your life and over the lives of the people you love. In this chapter, you will learn how to remove/nullify common curses, sanctify personal spaces and keep negative energy and entities out of your life. The spells, as with all the other spells in this book, are uncomplicated but very effective.

Protecting Inanimate Objects

Transference of energy from a person to an object or from a spirit to an object is a real thing. This is why our ancestors developed the craft of blessing certain objects to help amplify the spells we are creating and also to unify your intents. A protection spell over an inanimate object does not necessarily mean that you are binding powers to that object. What you are doing is transferring energy and intent to that object and using it as a beacon to attract what you want. For example, you could cast a protection spell over your home to attract benevolent spirits, positive energy and create an active force field to keep out anything that wants to cause you harm. This is very important for any Hoodoo practitioner because as you begin your journey, you will find that you are becoming more spiritually enlightened with each passing day and are therefore more open spiritually, which means you will attract both good and bad entities.

It is important that the place where you practice your craft the most, which is probably your home, is fully cloaked and protected, especially in the early stages. You do this so that these malevolent entities do not take advantage of your spiritual youthfulness and invade your space. A protection spell cloaks you from the eyes of evil and wicked men. It also ensures that spirits that do not have your best interests at heart are unable to enter into your space. A protection spell over your home casts out negative energy and creates an atmosphere that enables and empowers your spells. Your home is your first line of defense. It is also your altar and your spiritual launch pad. You would do well to ensure that you are strongest in this place at all times. The spells you create to carry around with you will be an extension of the force you are able to create in your home.

There are purification baths you can carry out to cleanse and protect you physically and spiritually. Then there are objects to which you can transfer spiritual energy and carry around with you when you are mobile. These objects often imbibe your intentions and your reach to ancestral powers, who are very helpful when it comes to building powerful protection spells. As you grow in the craft, you will be able to create runes, marks and spells that alert you the moment you come in contact with a vile entity. The reaction to this warning can be so intense that you experience pain and nausea, or even have a seizure. Creating these powerful spells is not something for beginners. It is something you will learn as you grow. For now, here are some steps you can take to keep you safe as you continue to practice your craft.

5 SIMPLE BUT POWERFUL PROTECTION SPELLS

Spell One: Black Salt Powder

Purpose: for protecting stationary or inanimate objects like your home, jewelry or even the area where you cast your spell. You can also use it as a protection spell for a person

Protection spells commonly use circles. In Hoodoo magic, drawing circles is a form of basic ritualistic practice. You use certain elements to create circles around what you are blessing, cursing, protecting or empowering with your spell. It is no different in this situation. The black salt that you create should be used in a circle around the person object or space that you want to protect. Here is what you need:

- Black pepper
- Charcoal
- Salt
- Wood ash

Put all ingredients together in a mortar and grind them using the same movement as the clock hand. Ensure that everything mixes smoothly and evenly. Empty the contents into a bowl and bless it with a prayer from Psalm 91. Use the salt powder to make circles around anything or any person you want to protect.

Spell Two: Be Gone Fire

Purpose: To remove specific things that you no longer want in your life

Before you initiate this spell, take a moment to sit down and think about something that has been bothering you lately. Concentrate on this singular thing. Form the words that accurately describe this thing. When you are certain that you have it in your mind, you can begin. You will need these items:

- Bay leaves
- Lemon grass
- Peanut shells
- White onion skin

Make a fire in an outside space. When you have a nice fire going, write on a bay leaf exactly what you wish to banish from your life. It could be the one thing you have been concentrating on or it could be a list of things. If it is a list of things, use one bay leaf for each thing. Pour the bay leaves and all the other ingredients into a bowl. Stir it counter-clockwise and repeat these words nine times: "That which I have written, send away forever." When you are finished, burn the mixture in the fire. Do not inhale the smoke. When everything has burned down, let it cool and find somewhere far away to bury the ashes.

Spell Three: Hard Day Cleanse

Purpose: To get rid of negative energy and exhaustion

Energy plays a role in enhancing the atmosphere and making it conducive for your spells to thrive. If you find yourself having a rough day, this spell will wash off the remnants of these negative emotions and set you on a path to healing and restoration. You will need the following:

- Eucalyptus leaves
- Lemon peels
- Peppermint leaves
- Rosemary
- White cheese cloth

All the ingredients should be fresh. Tie them up in the white cheese cloth. Pour a hot bath and steep this cloth with the herbs in the hot water, stirring it counterclockwise. Inhale the steam that comes from this activity and keep at it until the water becomes cool enough for you to get in. Remove the herbs from the cloth and set them aside for disposal later. Immerse yourself completely in the water for a few seconds. As you emerge, visualize a light filling you up on the inside and washing over you on the outside. Get out of the bath and air dry yourself. Throw the remnants of the spell far away from your home.

Spell Four: Protection from Evil

Purpose: To provide active protection against spiritual or physical harm

Regardless of whether or not you practice Hoodoo, there are people you will meet in this life who will immediately set your teeth on edge. All the alarms in your body go off but you don't know why you feel this way about them. This is usually an indication that that person could be dangerous, so this spell is designed to protect you from these kinds of people. You can also activate it to protect someone you care about from these very same people. It is potent but is also something you can do as a beginner. You will need the following items:

- Blue 7-day candle
- Camphor essential oil
- Cloves
- Dried onions
- Name paper

Grind the cloves and dried onions together. Mix them up thoroughly and set aside. Next, poke three holes on the top of the candle. In the first hole, pour four drops of camphor essential oil. In the other two holes, put a pinch of the dried herbs. Next, write out the name of the person you want the spell to protect and place the paper underneath the candle. Pick a scripture of protection that you like. My personal favorite is always going to be Psalm 91. Recite this scripture as you gaze into the light of the candle. The purpose of this is to center your thoughts and your intent. Draw on the energy that you receive and direct it towards the person. You will experience a sense of calm wash over you at the end of the recital. Put out the candle and repeat this process every day for the next seven days.

Spell Five: Reputation Saver

Purpose: to silence the voices of people who may have something evil and negative to say about you and to preserve your reputation

In this day and age, where a single tweet can undermine years of hard work, it is important to ensure that your reputation is able to stand the test of time. This protection spell helps to keep your name off of the lips of people who might say something negative about you. It helps silence gossip and rumor mongers. To initiate you spell, you need:

- Dirt from crossroads
- Paper with your name on it
- Reversing oil/Shut up oil/Stop gossip oil
- Silver dime
- String to tie the spell
- Sunflower seeds

Write your name in bold on a piece of paper with jagged edges. Pour nine drops of your preferred oil on the paper.

Put the silver dime, dirt from the crossroads and sunflower seeds on the paper. Fold it up neatly and tie the string around it to secure it. Hold it close to your lips and repeat these words nine times: *"I bind all that speak evil of me."* The spell is cast. You can place it on your person by putting it in a bag or in your pocket and ensure that is with you at all times.

13

SPELLS FOR JUSTICE

Life, they say, is not fair. You cannot truly understand this statement until you find yourself in a position where you feel as if you have been deprived of justice. And while it is benevolent to sit by and wait for karma to work, sometimes you feel like you have to do something yourself, and the only way to create a balance, or at least tip the scale of justice in your favor, is to intervene spiritually. This is where spells of justice come in. This does not automatically mean that everything is going to be okay. Granted, revenge feels good when your perceived enemy is being made to suffer for the things they have put you through. However, it doesn't always bring about the satisfaction that you seek. With this in mind, it is important to understand the elements at play when you decide to cast a justice spell.

Invoking Ancestral Spirits for Aid

When you practice Hoodoo, one of the things you will quickly come to learn is the fact that we do not actively believe in karma. As you continue to grow in the craft, perhaps you will also come to see things from my point of view. Even so, because of our Christian roots, many of us are guided by strong moral and ethical beliefs. When you decide to cast a spell of justice, you are usually filled with righteous indignation and there is no one who will understand this pain better than ancestors who share your blood and come from the same root as you. Each and every one of us has suffered some form of injustice at some point in our lives, and it is possible that we will not live long enough to get the justice that we deserve.

When you call upon the spirits of the ancestors for spells like these, they are most willing to aid you. Their assistance is relied on heavily for these types of spells because it helps account for that karmic element. In Hoodoo practice, this isn't talked about in general circles, but this is what our ancestors do when they help us. If they offer their assistance with the spell you are creating, they also take up the burden that comes from dabbling in these sensitive matters. In other words, you do the magic that they help you to activate, but they deal with the consequences. So luckily, there really isn't much for you to lose. However, you must ensure that in rendering the spell, you pay proper homage to them by offering sacrifices worthy of their involvement. Every spell, as I have said continually throughout this book, has a condition to be fulfilled. With a justice spell, most of what you need to do is ensure that your ancestors are appeased. They will handle the rest.

Karma, Vengeance and Justice

As I told you earlier, karma is not a concept that we think about in Hoodoo practice. As long as you fulfill the conditions of the spell and ensure that it is rooted and balanced, you are fine. In a case where emotions might be running high, the spell might be unstable, so involving the help of your ancestors can help mitigate the consequences of casting an unstable spell. Again, this really has nothing to do with karma. It is more about retaining balance between good and bad, and ensuring that your intentions are aligned with the properties of the spell that you create.

Vengeance is a powerful emotion, especially when it is motivated by pain. The stronger the pain, the higher the rage and thirst for revenge and this has a way of clouding your judgment. In the introductory chapters of this book, I talked about how important it is to have clarity of mind and centered focus in the delivery and rendering of the spell that you want. Distorting it with emotions can create an imbalance that will have an adverse effect. Much like in cooking, you have to make sure that the salt balances out the other flavors in the soup. If it overpowers the other flavors, the result will not be appealing. This does not mean that karma is serving you, it is simply a consequence of an action or inaction. Keeping this in mind, let us look at 5 simple spells that can help to bring you justice or tip the scales of the law in your favor.

GETTING JUSTICE WITH 5 UNIQUE SPELLS

Spell One: Make it Stop

Purpose: To temporarily hold off people from taking legal action until you are ready to deal with the situation

This is particularly helpful if you find yourself in the middle of a court case for which you are totally unprepared. You know that it can be a time-consuming process, not to mention the amount of money that will be required for legal fees and to sway justice in your favor. So until you are ready to deal with it, you can set the spell in motion. The spell is quick, easy and doesn't require too much. You need:

- A piece of paper
- A transparent jar

Write on a sheet of paper everything you are going through with the court case. Focus particularly on the charges that have been made against you and what your worries are about the case. Insert this paper into a jar of water and put it in the freezer. The spell is done. As long as that water stays frozen, the case or pending legalities will be frozen. However, bear in mind that this is only temporary. It does not stop the problem, it simply puts it on hold.

Spell Two: Hot Sauce Revenge

Purpose: To cause the people who hurt you to physically suffer

Revenge, they say, is a dish best served cold. But sometimes, all you need is a little hot sauce and that revenge will have a rewarding taste in your mouth. The star player in a revenge spell is hot sauce. I would advise that you find the hottest sauce available over the counter if you really want to inflict revenge on this person. Don't worry. The person on the receiving end of this spell will not die or experience anything inhumane, but they will suffer. You should get:

- Hot sauce
- A doll, figurine or candle

Begin by baptizing the candle, doll, figurine or whatever you are using as a physical representation of the person on whom you want to cast a spell. If you do not know the name of the person (often the case when you have been slighted or hurt anonymously), you can simply tag the doll: "whoever did xyz to you." "Xyz" obviously represents the action or hurt that was carried out against you. When you have consecrated the doll in their name, pour hot sauce all over it. Ensure that it is completely covered and leave it out in the sun. As the hot sauce dries on the figurine or candle, the person for whom the spell is intended will begin to experience inexplicable heat and will develop welt marks on their bodies.

Spell Three: Dry Up Their Love

Purpose: To completely break up a relationship without drama or negative consequences

We have all been in the situation where our beloved or someone we care about is having an entanglement with an ex. This spell is designed to put an end to that by simply drying out whatever affection they have for each other and causing them to drift apart. You need:

- Burned matches
- Jar
- Name paper
- Pins
- Salt
- Sand
- Red rosebud

Put a handful of burned matches into an equal part mixture of salt and sand. Write down the name of your beloved on one paper and their object of affection on another. Fold this name paper into the rosebud. Use the pins to pierce this rosebud with the name papers inside. This will quickly end their sexual connection. Pour the sand, salt and burned matches mixture into a jar. Put the rose with the pin piercings into this jar. Seal it and bury it in a graveyard. Put your mind at ease and you will witness the slow, gradual but definite decay of that relationship.

Spell Four: Storm Head Work

Purpose: To torment and torture your enemy

There is no peace for the wicked, and if you really want to be your own angel of vengeance, you can drop this spell to ensure that your enemies have no peace. Just remember to center your energy and emotions before activating this spell. Here is what you will need:

- A black string
- Black marker
- Coconut

First baptize the coconut in the name of your enemy by submerging it in water and chanting these words: "I baptize you (say your enemy's name). This coconut is now your head. Whatever happens to this coconut will happen to you." Repeat this three times and then proceed to activate the spell. With the black marker, write out what you want to happen to this person on the coconut. For example, you could say, "experience incurable headaches" or "move far away" or "lose your wallet." Whatever your petition is, write it on the coconut. This spell is best performed on the eve of a storm, so that as soon as you are finished writing your petition, you hang it on a tree outside. If the coconut is gone after the storm has passed, you can take it as a sign that the spirits have answered your petition. If it's still hanging there, break it down and break it with a hammer. Your intentions will still manifest in the life of your enemy.

Spell Five: Protection from Harm Bottle

Purpose: To prevent against arrest, abuse and injustice

If you find yourself in a situation where any of these three things is bound to happen; an arrest, physical abuse or injustice, a spell like this can activate protection over you that will stop this from happening. This spell is one of the earlier spells my grandmother taught me and its power is still relevant in today's atmosphere. The ingredients are:

- Black feathers
- Hard liquor
- Name paper
- Oregano
- Salt

Write down the name of the person you want to protect. Place it inside the bottle of liquor. Put the oregano, black feathers and salt in the same bottle, then seal the bottle. If it makes you feel more comfortable, you can back up this process by reciting a protection prayer from your favorite verse in the Bible. When you have finished doing that, shake it 11 times and store it outside your back door whenever you sense problems associated with arrest, abuse or injustice. When you are through with it, you can store it in a dry place until you need it again.

CONCLUSION

I have trained many people in the sacred craft of Hoodoo practice, and writing this book gives me the same pleasure I derive from seeing my students thrive. I hope that using this book you are able to get clarity on some of the problems you are experiencing and will become empowered by the spells I have shared. More than this, it is my desire that you become an active part of our small and unique community of Hoodoo practitioners. Even as this book comes to an end, I want to encourage you to keep searching, keep growing and keep learning. There is so much information out there and the more you connect yourself with it, the more our ancestors will reward you.

Being a Hoodoo practitioner is more than just casting spells and changing your destiny. It is about aligning yourself with your spiritual purpose and I am thankful and honored to be a part of your process. As you close this book, meditate on some of the lessons that you have learned here. Especially the ones that deeply resonated with you. From time to time, re-read the book to find clarity on things that may have not offered enlightenment the first time you read about them. If you have friends who are equally curious, share with them the knowledge that you have gained. I believe that our world becomes a better place when knowledge is shared. Unlike the olden days, when Hoodoo was relegated to dark and mysterious corners of the world, today we are openly practicing our craft and we are proud of it.

I want you to share in this pride. If this is your calling, pursue it diligently. You will be amazed by the results and blessings that will come your way as a result. Since the day I took up the mantle of my grandmother, I have never regretted a moment of it. I have been on a rollercoaster of emotions, from joy to anguish to sorrow when I hear some of the things that my clients are going through. But the emotion that stands out above all others is pride. I take pride in seeing people take their place in their community because of the opportunities that have become available to them... opportunities that without Hoodoo magic might not have presented themselves. You are now presented with a unique opportunity. Grab it with both hands and use it to change your world. I hope that one day our paths will cross, and I will hear your story too. Until then, stay blessed.

HOODOO FOR LOVE AND PROSPERITY

AUTHENTIC ROOTWORK & CONJURE MAGIC
SPELLS FOR LOVE, FRIENDSHIP, MONEY,
AND SUCCESS

ANGELIE BELARD

INTRODUCTION

I have been a Hoodoo root worker for most of my life, and in my little corner of the world, I am respected for what I do. People travel to meet me to cast spells and create items that will aid them in their quest for success, friendship, love, and other life issues. I have done more workings than I can count, and I know that I have fewer years in front of me than I do behind me. As the years pass, I feel more and more strongly the urge to ensure that what I know about Hoodoo isn't lost.

My first book, *Hoodoo for Beginners*, was meant to teach the basics about Hoodoo. What it is and what it isn't, where it came from, and how it works. I'm proud of that book, but there is so much more to teach. Hoodoo has a history hundreds of years old, and it can't be taught in just one book.

In this book, I want to teach by doing. I know most people want a book of spells they can cast, but it's important to me that you know why the spells work the way they do. Which root is good in which circumstance, how to use candles, how to make your own conjure oils, mojo bags, spiritual baths and washes. And, most importantly, how to work with your ancestors, because they are the key to Hoodoo.

Don't worry, though, this book does have many spells (in Hoodoo we call them workings or conjures, but I'll bend with the tide on this one). Each spell has one key ingredient that I discuss, so you learn how it fits into Hoodoo. After you've read this book, it is my sincere hope that you will be able to make your own Hoodoo.

Some of the more common spells that people come to me for are love spells or money spells. With love work, they either want to draw love to them, to draw the right person, or to restore passion and commitment to a relationship. With money, people want more of it, or they desire success in business. These are fundamental human needs. The desire to love and be loved is strong and powerful. As humans, we were created to love and we also share the need to provide for those we love. Sadly, these needs are not always met. But it doesn't mean you should resign yourself to your fate. A simple spell can turn things around and you don't have to travel to see me for that. In this book, I share detailed spells designed for different purposes, but all are suitable for manifesting your desires for love and success.

Over the years I've used many of these spells, and many like them, for a client who has become a dear friend. To protect her privacy, I'll call her Maxine. I first met her when I was 27. She was a few years older than me, but we were kindred spirits. She had been through a very rocky patch in life and had just come out of a long relationship that had left her broken, broke, and completely battered.

Her first wish was to sever ties with this man because, on some level, she knew he was not good for her, but she kept going back. So, our first spell together was to break soul ties. After this was complete, she spent a year or two as a single woman, until she decided that she was ready for a new relationship. But things didn't go quite the way she hoped, as men didn't seem to notice her. We cast another spell together, this one to draw love to her. Within a few months, she had all the attention she'd ever dreamed of.

After a while, however, she realized what she really wanted wasn't an abundance of suitors, but rather, that one man who was right for her. As she reflected on her previous bad relationship, she realized she didn't want to waste time with someone who would turn out to be wrong for her. With the help of her ancestors, we designed a working to find the right man for her. A few months later, she met a wealthy widower! He was kind and caring. They connected. It was strong, it was beautiful, and it was passionate.

About a year or so later Maxine came back to see me. She told me that the relationship was great, but she wanted to move on towards marriage, and he seemed reluctant. She thought the loss of his first wife was holding him back, because he was afraid of becoming attached and then losing her. We created a spell to help him see clearly and to cast off his fear. Two days after we did the spell, he proposed. They got married and are still married to this day. Later, when Maxine decided to open her own beauty shop, we did several workings to guarantee her success, which she was, until she sold the business a few years ago.

I mention Maxine's story so you'll understand ahead of time that there's no "one spell" that will fix your life. Your circumstances and needs will change over the years, so if you can learn the "why" of the spell materials in this book, you'll be able to create your own successful workings. I have helped many people with Hoodoo throughout my life, but not everyone can come to see me in person, so I wrote this book because I want to help everyone use Hoodoo to improve their life.

The spells in this book are simple; there is nothing that requires the aid of an elder like myself. Even as a novice or beginner, you can search through the contents of your kitchen cabinets and gather the ingredients you need to create a spell so strong that it creates a doorway for those dreams of love and success to become your reality.

1

AN INTRODUCTION TO HOODOO

B efore you can start using Hoodoo, you need to understand what it is, where it came from, and how it works. I covered this in *Hoodoo for Beginners*, so if you've read that book, feel free to skip ahead to Chapter Four, where the spells start. But if you haven't, I strongly encourage you to read the first three chapters of this book so you will have a solid, if introductory, understanding of Hoodoo.

Without understanding Hoodoo, trying to use the spells will get you nowhere. Hoodoo is a system, not a cookbook. You need to know the "why" before you learn the "how", so that you're not just going through the motions, and so that, eventually, you can create your own Hoodoo conjure.

We'll start with a short explanation of Hoodoo and its history, which will go a long way towards explaining the "why". I'll also share a bit of my own story, so you can understand how Hoodoo has affected my own life and the lives of those around me, and hopefully you'll see how it can affect yours in the same way.

A BRIEF HISTORY OF HOODOO

Hoodoo evolved from traditional African religions brought to the New World by enslaved Africans. The slave owners taught them a new language, dressed them in new clothes, gave them new food to eat, and attempted to "reform" them. Although they were separated from the people and everything they knew, some things were too deeply woven into their very existence to be altered or changed.

Slaves in the New World came from many areas of Africa, but frightened, confused, and abused in a strange land, they sought each other's company, finding comfort there. Gradually, they became a community, in which they shared their customs. The old ways of doing things that they'd brought with them were adjusted, tweaked, and manipulated to match their present circumstances.

Many aspects of Christianity were familiar to the African slaves. They already believed in one creator God, who was helped by powerful spirits to run the world, which they recognized in the Christian saints. They understood the Bible as a powerful spell book, and Hoodoo practitioners still use Bible verses in their work. In other words, Hoodoo is, historically, strongly based in Christianity. My grandmother Estelle, who taught me Hoodoo, was a devout Baptist, and met many of her clients after church on Sunday. We don't see Hoodoo as a separate religion or as being in any way in conflict with Christianity.

The African slaves incorporated more than just Christianity into their spiritual practices. They met Native Americans who helped them learn the power of the herbs and roots in this strange new land, and they incorporated aspects of European witchcraft and hex work. The slaves couldn't be picky about their tools, and the Hoodoo they did often involved life or death situations. If something didn't work, it just wasn't used. If you learn one thing from this book, I want it to be that **Hoodoo is practical**. If something works, use it. If it doesn't, discard it. You'll never see a Hoodoo spell that calls for Pink Himalayan Sea Salt, because slaves didn't have access to that kind of thing. But if there is a spell that calls for salt, and all you have is Pink Himalayan Sea Salt, then by all means use it!

The African religions evolved differently depending on where the slaves landed in the New World. In the larger Catholic plantations of Cuba, for instance, the slave owners had less direct control over the slaves, so they were better able to maintain their traditional practices. Those slaves focused more on the Catholic saints as being aspects of spirits from their homeland, and their practices grew into Santeria. In Haiti, also strongly Catholic, the practices grew into Voodoo, which played a large part in the revolution that freed the island's slaves from the French. In other places, the African religions developed into practices like Candomblé, which was practiced in Brazil.

On mainland North America, there were fewer slaves per slave owner, so the slave owners had more control, which made it harder for the slaves to practice their traditional spiritual ways. Hoodoo evolved in those mainland colonies, which is why Hoodoo is less of an organized religion compared to Voodoo or even Santeria. You don't need to be initiated into Hoodoo, and there's no hierarchy among practitioners. You'll also find that Hoodoo differs from place to place.

HOODOO BELIEFS

Let's talk about exactly what Hoodoo is in practical terms. It shares many qualities with practices like Voodoo and European-based witchcraft, so it's important to know what is different about Hoodoo.

Ancestral Veneration

I think working with the spirits of our ancestors is, perhaps, the key part of Hoodoo that separates it from other spiritual and magical practices. The spirits of your ancestors can be called on for aid and guidance. It's important to develop a relationship with your ancestors, and not simply call on them when you're in need, like a fair weather friend who you only hear from when they need something from you. How long would you stay friends with someone like that? Everyone practicing Hoodoo must have an ancestor altar, and I'll explain more about what that means in Chapter Two.

Rootwork

There is power in roots and herbs, and you can call on that power. In Hoodoo, we call this rootwork, and you'll find roots and herbs in nearly every Hoodoo spell. You can usually understand why an herb is used by understanding the plant it came from, the aspects of the herb itself, or the effects it has on the human body. For instance, cinnamon is a common herb used to speed up drawing work, because cinnamon is both sweet and a bit warm to the tongue. The sweetness will draw things to it, just like a bear being drawn to honey. And the heat will make the work faster, just like in cooking or chemistry.

Sometimes the "why" of a root is biblical. For instance, hyssop is used in purification and cleansing because it is mentioned as being used in the Bible (Psalm 51:7 "Purge me with hyssop, and I shall be clean"), and the Bible is understood to be a powerful spell book.

Devil's Shoestring is often used to "trip up the devil", which in Hoodoo means to keep evil away or end bad habits. Our ancestors knew how to use it because the roots of this plant are a twisted mess and are great at causing things to lose their footing.

Not everything we call rootwork is a root or herb, though. We'll use items like keys for opening new possibilities, or dice for luck, or money for prosperity.

The Power of the Earth

Just as roots and herbs have power, so does the earth itself. The energy around some locations can seep into the dirt, and you can harness that energy by using that dirt. For instance, money flows into and around banks all day, so you can collect the dirt from outside a bank to use in money drawing work. Similarly, the dirt from a church is good for purification and cleansing, as well as helping to bring about marriage. Dirt from a hospital can be used for healing magic, dirt from near a court can be used for justice, and so on.

There are two special cases of using earth that I want to discuss in a bit more detail, and the first is graveyard dirt. Graveyard dirt is special because it can be used in a number of different ways, and also because collecting it is more involved than it is at other locations. Dirt in a graveyard hasn't just collected the energy of a place, it has also collected the energy of the spirits that reside in that graveyard. A graveyard is home to many spirits, like a neighborhood, and you should not enter such a place without showing respect.

First, whenever you enter a graveyard, you should cover your head. This is both a sign of respect and a way to block the spirits from attaching themselves to your mind. Second, always bring with you an offering to leave at the entrance. This can take several forms, but the most common are rum, sweet bread, or three pennies.

After respectfully entering the graveyard, you'll also have to find a spirit whose grave you want to work with. The dirt from graves of different spirits has different effects. The dirt from a gambler's grave can be good for luck work, while the dirt from a murderer's grave is good for crossing. I strongly suggest that the first time you collect graveyard dirt, you do so from the grave of a loved one. And before ever collecting graveyard dirt, you must develop a relationship with the spirit of that grave. Introduce yourself as you would when entering someone's home. Make small talk and ask the spirit about itself. At first, you'll find it hard to hear what they have to say. It may manifest as the blowing wind, a feeling in your stomach, a tingling in your fingers, or just as sudden intuition. And speaking of intuition, always trust yours. If you have a bad feeling about a grave, stay away.

The second location you need to know more about when it comes to using its dirt is a crossroads. In Hoodoo, a crossroads is anywhere two roads meet to form an X. The importance of the crossroads descends from African traditions of the Congo, whose people knew that spirits reside at crossroads. These spirits have different names, but what is important to know is that, like at a graveyard, you must show respect to these spirits. Don't just go to a crossroads and collect the dirt! You have to first establish a relationship and show that you will give something in exchange for what you take. Like at a graveyard, offerings of sweets, rum, or coins will do. I tend to carry some butterscotch hard candies in my purse. The spirits like them, and so do I.

The crossroads is used for many things in Hoodoo, but usually it involves the idea of carrying something away. If you want to sever ties with a person, you can incorporate crossroads dirt into your work. If you need to dispose of the remnants of a spell, you can bury it at a crossroads so the energy will be cleanly dispersed.

HOODOO AND THE BIBLE

As I mentioned earlier, the history of Hoodoo and Christianity in America are intertwined. Our ancestors recognized the Bible as a powerful spell book, and most rootworkers in the past have viewed themselves as Christian. While I admit I haven't been to church as much as I should, my Bible is always open to one page or another. Readings from the Bible are incorporated into many Hoodoo workings, such as Isaiah 55:11 "So is my word that goes out from my mouth: It will not return to me empty but will accomplish what I desire and achieve the purpose for which I sent," which is good for any reading during any working, if you can't find something more specific.

With that said, you do not have to be a Christian to work Hoodoo. Our ancestors worked magic long before they came to this land, and so can you. For some of the spells in this book I'll mention Bible readings that are appropriate, but consider them optional. If you don't use them, it's always good to explain to your ancestors what you want to accomplish. No matter what your beliefs, your ancestors will aid you.

MY HOODOO HISTORY

While Hoodoo has been around me all my life, I never set out to be a conjurer. I was familiar with our ways of doing things thanks to my mother and my father. Neither of them was a typical Hoodoo practitioner, in the sense that they rarely sat down to make up spells for specific purposes. However, they possessed certain eccentricities that made it clear to others that they were connected to our practice. My father, for instance, always went to bed with a herbal mojo bag under his pillow for protection. My mother regularly cleansed the house to clear out bad energy and ward off evil spirits. But my grandmother, Mama Estelle, was famous as a conjurer. People from all over Louisiana came to her for spells. Word of her legendary gifts spread so widely throughout our community that even in school, the boys were afraid to mess with me because there were rumors that she could put a hex on them. Of course, none of that was true. But her reputation was one of the factors that added to my positive experience in high school.

At the age of 13, I started apprenticing under Mama Estelle. Our intention wasn't for me to become a full-time conjurer. She simply felt that my parents weren't adequately carrying the tradition and that someone in the family needed to be given all the knowledge that she had accumulated over the years in order to pass it on to the next generation. When she died, there was a hole in my heart and my life. Through self-reflection, as well as some of the experiences I had at that time, I concluded that Hoodoo was that element I needed to fill up that empty space. It has been more than four decades since her passing and I have never looked back. I enjoy every moment of my life as a conjurer. I don't particularly like being called that, though. It's a name the people outside our community came up with. I am simply Angelie.

I practice Hoodoo because it is who I am. I love connecting with the power within as well as the powers that are around us. I am happiest when I create a spell and watch my dreams or expectations manifest. As you begin to practice, you will find that your connection to Hoodoo is not the same as mine. But it will give you fulfillment as it has given me. The spells in this book focus on love and financial success and I believe that this is something we all have a right to enjoy. Many people come to me with problems that have simple solutions that they could have created in their backyards. I feel it is my responsibility to pass on the knowledge of my ancestors to this generation and perhaps even the one after it.

HOODOO AS A WAY OF LIFE

You can't talk about Hoodoo from a native perspective without going into stories from the motherland. These stories were orally passed on to us by our ancestors. You will not find them on the pages of history books. Even in the books of those who have tried to chronicle our history for us, Hoodoo is not a religion or a belief. It is the way we live our lives.

Our ancestors lived off the land. This meant that when they were sick, it was the land that provided healing. If they needed love, they turned to the land. On the land is where they would find water, herbs, and any other accoutrements that, when combined, could provide solutions to the problems that plagued them. Courage, community, and culture inspired them at every level, and continue to inspire us.

What do I mean by courage, you may wonder? Courage to face problems head-on instead of running away from them. Courage to embrace every part of oneself even though it may not favorably tally up against the opinions of the public. Courage to do what is necessary to achieve the results you desire. This was the kind of courage my people spoke and sang about.

When it comes to community, our practice is a communal one. The energy that we tap into when creating spells is a powerful communal or ancestral energy. We feed on the energy of our past and bind it to our will/intention in the present.

Finally, we come to culture, which is our way of life. Hoodoo is not some secret cult practice that we hide in the back of our closet only to put on a mask to present when we are in public. It is the very essence of who we are. The more you incorporate Hoodoo into your day-to-day living, the more powerful your spells will become.

When we wake up in the morning, there are specific habits and rituals that we carry out to get our day started on the right note. These rituals provide protection and enhance our overall spiritual atmosphere. But this doesn't mean you have to automatically change the way you do everything. Hollywood has portrayed Hoodoo in a way that makes it difficult to picture us 'conjure folk' as normal people. But believe me, the Hoodoo culture is very regular. I believe we're simply more in touch with nature.

Most Hoodoo practitioners are very connected to the earth. You'll find us tending mini herbal gardens that not only serve a practical purpose in the kitchen but also provide easily accessible herbs that we can use to create tinctures and spells. When we take a bath, we don't just use soap and water to wash off the dirt of the day. We make it a spiritual experience by using herbs tied to specific intentions to attract what we want.

When you create spells after Hoodoo has already become a part of you, those spells will be more potent.

2

PREPARATION

Now that we have brushed up on what Hoodoo is, let us look at what goes into the preparation of a spell. You can't just waltz into your ancestral altar with the ingredients, say a few incantations, and hope for the best. There is a ritual that needs to be followed to guarantee the success of that spell and that will be our focus in this chapter.

ENERGY

Your energy plays a very important role in the spells that you cast and that energy is fed by your mind. If your mind is not in the right place, it can influence the outcome of your spell. This is why it's very important to work on your energy before you get into spell-casting. There are a couple of things we will talk about in each spell that we create that enable you to purify your energy and ensure that it remains positive. Think of your spells as a computer. The information you feed into it will be relayed back to you. When your energy is not focused, it creates discord or disharmony in the rhythm of the spell. This is something you may not pick up on as a beginner. But as you continue to practice, you can intuitively detect the mood of a spell and determine the mental state of the person who cast it.

So, before you set out to create a spell, you have to get into the right mindset. I like to take a walk in the woods near my home, which always brings me a sense of peace. I love gardening and humming in the garden while I work takes my mind off whatever is bothering me and puts me in a positive state. When I'm doing love drawing work, I like to listen to romantic music.

You will have to find what works for you, but at the end of the day, the objective remains the same. You want to set the tone for the spell that you are going to cast. For some people, it can be rigorous exercise or watching a few funny videos on YouTube. It could even doing a simple meditation exercise. Do whatever calms your mind and prepares it to create a spell.

People who cast love and prosperity spells are often doing so from a place of desperation. This is not positive energy. It will only give birth to an outcome that inspires the same feeling. If you desire success, you must mirror that successful attitude with your energy. If you want love, mirror those feelings with your energy.

YOUR ANCESTOR ALTAR

One of the most sacred aspects of Hoodoo practice is the space where you carry out your spell. Within our community, this space is commonly known as the ancestral altar. This is where you pay homage to the ancestors who paved the way for you, and then tap into their powers to create and manifest the desires of your heart. An altar is a place of transformation and the starting point of manifestation.

The altar is the space through which your ancestors can give their blessings and pour their power into the spells cast by you. It is where you will feel the most powerful. Your altar is crucial to your Hoodoo practice and is traditionally meant to be somewhere in your home. However, it is not uncommon to place it outside your home, in a location where you feel most connected to your ancestors.

Either way, your ancestral altar does not need to be in a glamorous location. The important thing is to use it to connect with the power of the people who came before us. Long ago, Hoodoo practitioners established this connection by adding items known to have a direct link to their forebears. For example, my grandmother Estelle gifted me the Bible of my great, great grandmother. Even if you don't have something like this, a picture of your ancestors would suffice, particularly if it is of those with whom you have fond memories.

Another thing that must be present in your altar or space where you cast a spell is a glass of water. This is an offering to your ancestors, and a kind of spiritual alarm bell. When something unusual is going on spiritually, it can often be seen by careful study of the water. If the water is evaporating faster than it should, or is bubbling in a strange way, it may be that your ancestors are trying to get your attention.

You should also leave your ancestors other offerings at your altar. If you knew your ancestors, offer them things they liked in life. If not, things like rum, or cigar smoke, or candies are usually well accepted.

INTENTIONS

When you create a spell, you summon powers and then you put those powers to work with your intentions. It is not enough to put the items together for all the rituals, speak some words, and hope for the best. You must be clear on the mission you want those powers to accomplish and clarity of mind is inspired by intention. Again, this is where binding your conjure or chore to a Bible verse makes a huge positive difference. When you know what you want in very explicit terms, you will make it easier for the arrow to find its target. This is especially important when you are creating a love spell. You can't just say you want someone to fall in love with you when you haven't determined what exactly you want to do when they actually fall in love with you. If you shoot an arrow under windy conditions, it will likely miss its mark because of the wind.

The same thing happens when you make a spell. It moves towards the objective but the world outside of the physical plane is very different. There are waves of forces moving at the same time. Always remember that one event can create multiple outcomes. Your spell needs to be heightened by your intention, so that those forces that may conflict with your objective will not be able to deter or slow down the potency of your spell. This way, when it reaches its target, the outcome is a satisfying one.

I had situations in which my clients carried out a love spell efficiently on their own but somehow got an undesirable result. The spell worked... just not in the way they had hoped. It is like cutting down a tree. You sharpen the axe blade, grab the handle, and then swing in the direction of the tree. Experienced tree cutters will tell you that you also need to pay attention to where you cut. If you don't, the tree could fall anywhere, including on top of you.

Your intentions anchor the spell and keep it on the path you want it to go. This way, when it accomplishes what it set out to do, it doesn't turn into an unpleasant experience. Another effective method of strengthening your intention is by strengthening your ancestral connection. Their spirits will not only fire up your spell, in a love spell, they will lead you to the right person for you. Know what you want. Be crystal clear about it. Rid your mind of thoughts that conflict with your desires. During conjuring, it is a good idea to use a candle to center your focus and thus sharpen your intention.

CLEANSING AND PURIFICATION

Before doing any Hoodoo, it's important to perform some kind of spiritual cleansing. Having a regular cleanse is the way of life for people who practice Hoodoo. For us, a cleanse is beyond washing off your body with soap and water. You have to purify yourself and this purification provides fortification.

When you tamper with powers beyond the physical plane, you expose yourself. With or without fortification, there are dark spirits that will ride on the waves of that ancestral connection and enter into your space. A thorough cleanse will ward off their impact and cause them to be powerless. But when you fail to do a cleanse, you will absorb that impact and as you continue to cast spells, they will begin to change form and become darker until the darkness consumes you. If the spell is intended to be a love spell, this darkness will also consume the person your spell is directed at.

My grandmother explained it to me this way: The powers of our ancestors are like the ocean. When you look at the ocean, you see water. But there are strong forces pushing and pulling the water in different directions. A cleansing bath puts a barrier on your body and allows you to swim in the ocean to your target and then return without having the ocean overwhelm you. The water will roll off your back and onto the floor without causing any damage.

In the chapters where I talk about the spells, I include an important cleansing ritual that you must carry out before you cast any spell. Even when you are not casting a spell, it is a good idea to take cleansing baths. Not only are they good for your skin, but they also keep your mind and body in a positive state. They offer an extra layer of protection and also help to maintain a positive aura.

3

TYPES OF WORKINGS

As I mentioned, in Hoodoo we don't usually call it a spell, but I know most people outside of Hoodoo use that word, so I'll use it in this book interchangeably with "working" or rootwork or conjure, which is what we do in Hoodoo. There are several types of work in Hoodoo you should be familiar with.

SPIRITUAL BATHS

A Hoodoo spiritual bath is a way of applying the power of rootwork directly to your skin, the closest kind of contact you can get. There are many types of spiritual baths, but the most common is performed as a spiritual cleansing. You can wipe away any negative energy or spirits, and even bad luck that may have become attached to you. This restores your spiritual balance, leaving you better able to perform Hoodoo workings, and to make those workings more powerful. Also, they can serve as a fortification ritual. If you are seeking to protect yourself from bad energy, bad vibes, or even bad spells; there are types of spiritual baths that give you an added layer of protection.

A spiritual bath can also be used to turn your body into a kind of magnet that attracts the things you desire. This is particularly useful when you are creating a love spell. They are also used to disengage the forces of a negative spell that has been cast over you. In other words, if you have been cursed, spiritual baths are one of the things you have to do to end the power of that curse over your life.

FLOOR WASHES

Just as a spiritual bath is used on the body, a Hoodoo floor wash can be used on your home or place of business. For example, if you move into a new space and you have some bad vibes or you feel the presence of an evil entity, a thorough floor wash can cleanse the energy in that space and build a boundary that will push back any negative vibes hovering around the home. You can also use a floor wash to set up barriers around the house or space so that certain types of energy, spirits or even people are unable to locate or enter that space. This protection barrier will have to be renewed consistently to keep it potent and effective.

Just like spiritual baths, a floor wash can also be used to create a field of attraction. This is particularly useful for businesses. You want to be able to attract the kind of clients that will boost your business profile and also attract wealth and opportunities to it. A floor wash works hand in hand with conjure oils and mojo bags.

MOJO BAGS

A mojo back, sometimes called a gris-gris, is a small pouch that contains rootwork made of herbs, oils, and other items. This creates a small spirit that you carry with you. This little spirit can be directed to help you achieve your aims, whether they be for love, luck, money, protection, or just about any kind of working. Mojo bags work like a power bank to support whatever intentions you have and can be formulated to suit any purpose.

I am a huge fan of mojo bags, because sometimes you may not always have the energy to concentrate your intentions and focus on the purpose of the spell you have created. For example, if a mojo bag was created for love and you happen to be in the place where you have potential candidates, a mojo bag will amplify the power of the spell you created earlier and set things in motion. If it was created for protection, you might find yourself in a situation that appears safe but is unknown to you, and there might be hidden elements that pose a threat to you. A mojo bag will detect this threat and activate the protective layer around you. In short, it is designed to be a portable power generator that ensures your spell stays powered up at all times.

The spirits of the mojo bags must be fed to stay active. You can generally feed a mojo bag smoke or rum, but sometimes you should feed it conjure oils or other things more appropriate to the spirit within. For instance, a mojo bag for luck might be fed Van Van oil, which is good for luck, while one for protection might be fed Florida Water.

CONJURE OILS

Conjure oils are oils that have been infused with the power of roots and herbs, and are useful when directly applying the roots or herbs can be problematic. For instance, it's easier to dress a candle with a conjure oil than it is to dress it with many different herbs.

Conjure oils are made by adding a blend of herbs to a carrier oil, like sunflower oil, and binding them to a purpose. They can be used to dress candles, as I mentioned, to feed mojo bags, in spiritual baths and floor washes, and in just about any Hoodoo work.

Let's say you wanted to create a love spell. Getting a conjure oil designed for love can help increase the potency of that spell. You can put it in your cleansing bath, use it in a floor wash, pour it into your mojo bag mix, or use it to bless the candle that you will be working with.

Conjure oils are created for specific purposes. It is important to understand that there is no conjure oil that works for everything. It has to be created for a specific purpose. When you are buying it from a Hoodoo practitioner, be sure that they know what they are doing because the potency is linked to the intentions and energy of the person who created it. If you buy from the wrong source, the outcome of your spell may not be satisfactory. On the bright side, conjure oils have a longer shelf life than mojo bags. They don't need to be reworked to maintain their potency. When you buy from a good source, it lasts as long as it is available.

ROOT WORK

Of course, at the heart of almost every Hoodoo spell is root work. Plants contain energy that you can use in your magic, and understanding what kind of energy they contain is the key to mastering Hoodoo. When you know how herbs interact with each other, you develop an inner system that allows you to bring these items together to serve you. You will harness the powers that lie dormant within them and use them to channel the power of your ancestors to bring to life the thing that you desire the most.

4

SPELLS FOR LOVE AND FRIENDSHIP

L ove is a beautiful feeling. To love someone and have that person love you back in a way that is wholesome is something we all desire. I am 1000 percent in love with love. I love being in love. I love seeing people fall in love. But more than that, I love to see people going the distance together while in love. Have you ever watched a couple in their 80s or 90s celebrating love after spending more than half of their life with each other? It is pure and beautiful to behold. To find companionship that lasts you on the journey of life is something that most of us want. Sadly, not many of us can achieve that dream.

So, we turn to other means to guarantee our happily-ever-after. One way to welcome lasting love into your life is through a love conjure. But before you dash off to your altar, there is something you should know. Love spells do not make someone fall in love with you. They can draw love to you, make someone new notice you, and even remind someone of a time when they were in love with you in the past. But they will not force another person to fall in love with you.

As I've explained, Hoodoo derives its potency from our connection to our ancestral spirits. These spirits often act as guides. Because they see beyond the physical eye and operate in a different realm, they are able to pull your lover towards you.

My grandmother was fond of saying that there is a cover for every pot. This phrase is what she said to clients who came to her for love spells. For some reason, by the time these people came to my grandmother, they had all but given up on the idea of love. They had even convinced themselves that no one could love them. But she firmly shut them down with that little phrase, and then set to work with a love conjure that showed them how wrong they were.

All they needed was an open channel that draws their beloved closer to them faster. This is where your ancestral spirits come in. They help to locate this person who is uniquely suited for you. Then they forge a circumstance that bridges the distance between the both of you. Know this; your ancestral spirit will never bring someone who may cause harm to you. Nor will they force someone to love you against their will.

If you are having problems in your current relationship, a love spell can make your partner open to suggestions but they will never be manipulated to a point where they are no longer making decisions of their own free will. I have had clients come to me for love spells but when they finally meet someone, they start questioning the authenticity of the relationship because they worry the person is with them against their will. Hoodoo rootwork is nothing like that.

Another thing I should cover before we get into the love spells is your state of mind. I know you have been searching for love. You have probably been hurt by love and maybe even feel a little desperation to find love at all costs. You are going to have to leave all of those emotions outside your door. Feelings of desperation, loneliness, pain, hurt and betrayal do not create the right atmosphere within you for a love spell.

Before you cast the spell, you need to fall in love with the idea of love. One quick way for me is to play some Al Green music. Whatever type of love spell I'm working on, that man has a song for it. His words stir my heart.

You need to find a way to get to this point. Don't make it about the person you are hoping to meet or the spell you are trying to create. It is about activating an atmosphere of love inside of you so that you become the beacon that attracts the love you seek for yourself. This is perhaps one of the most crucial elements when creating a love conjure. Now, let's begin.

LOVE DRAWING OIL WITH ROSE PETALS

Conjure oils are one of the most commonly sold items in any Hoodoo shop, and Love Drawing Oil is probably any shop's best seller. You can use conjure oils in many other Hoodoo workings - in a mojo bag, to anoint a candle, or in spiritual washes and baths. You can also use it directly on your skin like a cologne or perfume. This Love Drawing Oil can be used by both men and women. It is a beginner-friendly root-work that is almost impossible to get wrong.

Before you can make this conjure oil, or any other, for that matter, you need to select a carrier oil. You want an oil that is malleable and easy to work with. Almond oil, sunflower oil, and rapeseed oil are my personal favorites, and I prefer almond oil for love work. In our community, there are a lot of varying opinions on which oil is the best. But one thing we all agree on is that whatever oil you use, it is better to go with a more natural oil than a synthetic one. Olive oil can also work as your carrier oil but I don't use this as a first option because it is very thick. I have friends who lighten the olive oil with natural essential oils. This can be a good option as well.

If none of the options I mentioned are immediately available to you, your good old-fashioned cooking oil will do just fine. If you learn one thing from this book, I hope it's that Hoodoo is adaptable and practical. Use what works.

This conjure oil features rose petals, a common ingredient in Hoodoo love workings. The sweet scent of a rose has been associated with love for thousands of years, so it probably comes as no surprise to find that it's used in Hoodoo. You can alter this oil to suit your needs by changing the color of the rose petals used, or mix and match to combine.

What You Will Need

- Carrier oil - five tablespoons
- Five rose petals (pink for romance, red for passion)
- Jasmine oil (to draw romance) - three drops
- Patchouli oil (to draw love) - three drops
- Dried orange peel (for purity) - a few pieces
- Strainer
- Bottle
- Mortar and pestle

The Work

1. Add the jasmine oil to the carrier oil. Swirl (do not shake) and set aside.
2. Manually blend the rose petals, dried orange peel, and patchouli in a mortar. Be careful not to turn the herbs into a paste! We want to do just a little more than bruise them to extract their essence.
3. Put the oils and herb mixture together and pour into the bottle, then store for seven days.
4. During those seven days, shake the bottle once a day.

5. Pour the mixture through a strainer into a clean bottle. The oil in the clear container is your Love Drawing Oil. You can discard the herbs, or store them away in a dry place to use in future love work.

This oil can be used in many ways. You can pour it on your candle before you light it for work. You can put a few drops in your bathwater or sprinkle it on your vision board or journal/list where you write down the things you want to manifest in your relationship. It can also be useful when preparing your mojo bag for love or friendship.

If you're a Christian, or looking for something to say as you make the Love Drawing Oil, you can pray with Psalm 63:1.

FINDING LOVE WITH HONEYSUCKLE

Honeysuckle is probably my favorite plant to teach people about Hoodoo with because it's useful for many things. If you have ever seen a honeysuckle vine, you might be able to guess why. The sweet-smelling flowers of the honeysuckle are perfect for drawing love. But the majority of a honey-suckle vine is covered with green leaves, not flowers, which is why the leaves of the honeysuckle are for drawing money and abundance. The vine itself, however, grows quickly and can strangle the life out of other plants, which makes it highly suitable for Hoodoo spells of domination or crossing. Understanding how plants grow is vital to being a good rootworker!

Attracting love is one thing. Sifting through the throngs of people who will come to you after you start using the Love Drawing Oil is another ballgame entirely. This work, using the flowers of the honeysuckle, allows you to find the kind of love that you are in need of.

With this simple rootwork, you can find the proverbial needle in a haystack. It is designed to bring you genuine love. This means that you must mirror the type of love you want. Lose the Hollywood romance plot. Focus on real, unfiltered love and you will attract it to you. Plant the seeds of love in your heart as you whip the tools together. It would put your spirit in the right frame to receive this love.

What You Will Need

- Love Drawing Oil
- Red candle
- Honeysuckle flowers

The Work

1. Dress the love candle with the Love Drawing Oil by rubbing the oil on it from top to bottom.
2. Place the candle on a plate on a non-flammable part of your altar.
3. Sprinkle the petals of the honeysuckle flowers around the candle wick and then light it.

4. Center your focus on your intentions (to attract your true love) as you watch the flame burn.

This work draws on your energy and focus. You will focus on the flames, visualize your intentions, vocalize your expectations in the form of the scriptures, and then will them into existence. You must stay at the candle until you can smell the scent of the honeysuckle, and then let the candle burn down naturally. You can speak the Song of Solomon 2:10-13 to aid the work as the candle burns.

LOVE BINDING WITH HOODOO DOLLS

Hoodoo uses dolls as the spiritual stand-in for your target, so whatever you work on the doll manifests physically on that person. You can purchase a doll from a Hoodoo shop, or you can make one yourself. You can even purchase a doll from a toy store, but try to find one that looks like, or reminds you of, your target. For this work, you are simply using the doll to create an opportunity for the two of you to blossom and grow into more than just acquaintances.

The connection between the doll and the person is strengthened by something that represents them, ideally something from their body, such as their hair, their spit, or even their blood. If you can't get any of these, you can use a piece of their clothing or a picture of them. After this item is affixed to the doll, the doll is baptized and brought to life with holy water, which you can purchase online or get for free from a local church.

This working is for when you already know the right person for you, but they don't seem to know you exist. You see them on the street and you exchange a cursory nod, some mumbled greetings, and that's about the extent of your communication. You can change that with this 'Get Noticed' rootwork. It beams the spotlight on you and directs this person's focus to you in the most positive way. You are subtly influencing their emotions or feelings as this root-work leaves them open to suggestions from you.

What You Will Need

- Two dolls (one for you and one for your target)
- Something to represent your intended
- A lock from your hair
- Something to affix the previous two items to the dolls, such as tape or glue
- Two red candles
- String
- Holy water

The Work

1. Affix your hair to the doll that represents you.
2. Sprinkle the doll's head with the holy water and say, "I baptize you in the name of the Father, and of the

Son and of the Holy Spirit." Then give the doll your name. "I name you Angela." Repeat this three times.

3. Repeat this process with the doll representing your target. Use one of the items of theirs that you were able to get (picture/clothing/hair).

4. Light the candles at your altar.

5. Place the dolls on each other and bind them together with string.

6. Speak your intentions (for example, "Notice me, Eric") three times and blow out the candles.

The person whose doll is bound to yours is now bound to you. You can tell them to notice you and they will. As you gain more experience in the craft, you can learn to make the dolls yourself instead of purchasing them.

TURN A FRIENDSHIP INTO LOVE WITH LODESTONES

The most sustainable relationships are those born out of genuine friendships. When you find couples who have been together for decades, one of the secrets to their lasting relationship is their friendship. However, we often find ourselves in situations where we are stuck in the friend zone. When you are in the friend zone, it means that when you talk about the potentials of that relationship, the other person is unable to see beyond friendship. This usually results in one party pining over the other.

This conjure work, to turn friendship into love, requires the use of a lodestone. Lodestones are magnetic rocks. They occur naturally and are particularly useful in attracting what you desire, whether it is a love spell or a money conjure. These mineral stones have gender. So it's important that when you buy a lodestone, it should represent the gender you are interested in converting from friend to lover. Stones with pointy edges are considered masculine, while those with curvier edges are regarded as feminine. Also, every time the stone is able to attract or bring you closer to something that you asked it to do for you, you must feed it with magnetic sands to continue to boost its energy. Whenever I am recommending rootwork for beginners, I like to use conjures that involve lodestone because it is very simple to work with and difficult to get wrong. Despite its simplicity, it is very effective at getting the job done.

This working also uses vervain oil, which is useful in both love and domination spells, as well as in Anointing Oil, making it perfect for this work in which we will use it to anoint the lodestones and compel your intended.

What You Will Need

- Two lodestones (one to represent each person)
- Magnetic sand
- Whiskey
- Vervain oil (to attract love) - a few drops
- Transparent jar

The Work

1. Pour the whiskey into the transparent jar. Ensure that the jar is at least half full or contains enough whiskey to completely submerge the lodestones.
2. Place both lodestones into the whiskey and seal the jar, leaving it overnight.
3. In the morning, take out the lodestones and place them on a flat surface in your altar, letting them dry for a few minutes.
4. As soon as they are dry, take a few drops of the vervain oil and consecrate the lodestones. Do this by rubbing the vervain oil on the lodestone and telling each stone its name, one for you and one for your intended.
5. Tell the lodestones in clear terms what you want them to do for you. For example, "I want Mary to see me as someone she could fall in love with."
6. When you are done, take a pinch of magnetic sand and sprinkle it on the lodestone. Repeat this process at least once every week.

When the stone is completely covered with sand, gently toss the sand off and reinsert the lodestone into the whiskey jar to repeat the process. When the stone is no longer able to attract sand, that means its energy has expired. The best way to discard a lodestone with dead energy is to bury it.

MAKE SOMEONE CALL YOU WITH CIGAR SMOKE

We have all been put in this scenario: you go out to a party or an event and you meet this amazing guy or girl. You exchange numbers and then for days you hear nothing from them. Waiting for this call can be a crushing and devastating blow to your self-esteem, as it projects the perception that this person does not really care about you and probably doesn't want to be with you.

With this rootwork, you don't need to fold your hands and wait. You can stimulate that person's memory of you and get them to pick up the phone and call you. We can also use this work to get that business call we need to come through. It is really that easy.

This spell that I am going to teach you involves the use of cigars. Ancestors love cigar smoke, so we use it to draw their attention to the work and thank them for their help. When we use a cigar in Hoodoo, we light it and get it going, then turn it around and put the lit end into our mouth and blow the smoke out the other side. Please, please be careful with this or you'll end up burning your tongue.

What You Will Need

- Your cell phone
- One white candle
- Cigar
- Chalk

• Salt

The Work

1. Place the cell phone on something you can draw on with the chalk. A wooden table, a driveway or a sidewalk will do.
2. Using the chalk, draw a straight arrow pointing towards the phone.
3. Draw a small circle below the cell phone.
4. Carve the name of the person you want to call you on the candle, then place it in the center of that circle. You can drop a bit of the candle wax into the center of the circle and put the candle on top of the wax to help it stay in place.
5. Use the table salt to draw a line underneath the circle and then light the candle.
6. Light your cigar and get it burning well. Turn the cigar around and put the lit end into your mouth. Avoid your tongue and clench it with your teeth, blowing the smoke out in a circular motion around the candle and the phone arena you have created.

The arrow will draw the person's energy to your phone, as will the light of the candle. The line of salt below the candle will make sure they can't get around you - their thoughts will have only one place to go.

RESTORE PASSION MOJO BAG WITH DAMIANA

One of the things that keeps a relationship sizzling hot is passion. Remember the days when your partner would walk into a room and you would feel your stomach drop because of all the butterflies in there? Well, as time goes on, these feelings fade and boredom begins to set in. You won't experience the same hot and bothered flushes you had when you first started dating each other.

But this doesn't have to spell doom and gloom for your relationship. You can restore passion. To do that, there are a couple of things you can do, including this rootwork that involves the use of damiana. This is a plant famous for its aphrodisiac qualities (among other things). Some people dry it, grind it into a paste, and put it in their tea. In this work, we'll use the petals in a mojo bag so you can keep it with you.

What You Will Need

- Dried damiana leaves - one tablespoon
- Red rosebuds (to draw love) - one tablespoon
- Lavender buds (for luck in love) - one tablespoon
- Mixing bowl
- Red flannel bag

The Work

1. Put the rosebuds, damiana, and lavender buds in a mixing bowl.
2. Stir the mix thoroughly.
3. As you stir, focus on your intention to bring back passion into your relationship.
4. Pour your mixture into the red flannel bag.
5. Dress the mojo bag with Love Drawing Oil once a week and keep it close to you at all times.

When focusing your intention, you can use these Bible verses to support your cause. For use on a man, read Songs of Solomon 1:2-4. For use on a woman, use Songs of Solomon 7:6-8.

SWEETEN A RELATIONSHIP WITH A SWEET POTATO

There may come a time in your once upon a time 'can't-get-enough-of-each-other' relationship where everything comes to a standstill. You are both stuck with each other but also find that you cannot stand each other.

Relationships often go through different stages and the stage where everything gets boring can last for a very long time. If you are unable to get things back on the sweet track, you risk losing the relationship, and this is something we want to avoid at all costs. The work I am going to share here should only be used for a relationship that you feel has the potential to be something more, and the key ingredient is a sweet potato. Sweet potato is an old Hoodoo staple, and as it grows, so will the sweetness in your relationship. This isn't a spell for someone you're just passing time with, it's for a long and meaningful relationship. If you are sure that the person you are with is worth the work, then let's get some romance cooking.

What You Will Need

- One fresh sweet potato
- A jar
- Brown paper
- A small knife
- Water
- Four toothpicks
- Twine

The Work

1. Write down the names of yourself and your partner on the brown paper.
2. Fold the paper in four and set it aside.
3. Use the knife to make a small incision in the sweet potato somewhere in the middle. Make the incision just big enough to fit the folded-up paper.
4. Insert the folded paper. Ensure that it goes in completely.

5. Wrap the twine around the area of the sweet potato with the insertion and tie it closed.

6. Use the toothpicks to pierce the sweet potato below the twine so that they form an X and can be used to support the sweet potato at the top of the jar, so that half is positioned above the top of the jar and half is inside it.

7. Fill the jar with water.

8. Place the potato in a drawer with the toothpicks serving as a support base to keep the potato upright. Watch for the development of roots at the bottom of the potato and the first signs of growth on top.

As the potato takes root, your relationship will begin to evolve into something sweeter. It may not be exactly as it was in the beginning, but it will be something new and sweet.

REMOVE OUTSIDE INTERFERENCE WITH CANDLE MAGIC

In my experience, when a person exits their current relationship, they are often leaving for another person. This means that many of our relationships come to an end because of external interference. This external interference could manifest in many forms. Sometimes, it is because of an affair or a romantic interest in someone other than you. In other cases, the other person's family may be actively trying to break up your relationship simply because it does not meet their standards or expectations.

The work we are going to do here will be to focus on external interference of the romantic sort. Regardless of your gender, you can put together the items for this work to get rid of this interference so that your true love can keep 100 percent of their attention on you. This will probably be the first advanced candle work you are going to do. Candles are a form of representation magic in Hoodoo work. The color of the candle can set the tone for the spell. Red for passion, pink for romance, and so on. For this kind of work to do its job, you need to have a couple of details on hand before you proceed. Those details include, but are not limited to, the interfering person's name, their date of birth, and (if you can get them) some personal items from your love, such as their hair or nail clippings.

As soon as you have secured the information required for this kind of work, you can proceed. One more thing; the candles that you purchase for this work should be personalized to represent both of you. There are different ways to do that, but the easiest is to buy each candle in the same color as your respective birthstones. If you can't get ahold of those, two white candles will do. Make sure the candles are in glass for this spell, because they will be wrapped in twine or string and we don't want that to catch fire.

What You Will Need

- Two candles in glass to represent you and your love
- A black candle to represent the person interfering
- Twine or string
- Partner's hair or nail clippings (if you can get this)
- Paper bag

The Work

1. Carve your names into the candles that represent you and your love.
2. Carve the name of the person interfering into the black candle.
3. Sprinkle your partner's hair or nail clippings around the top of their own candle.
4. Cut the twine a foot or so in length.
5. Tie each end of the twine around the candles that represent the both of you.
6. Light the two candles. Do not light the black figure candle.
7. As each candle burns, slowly turn both candles inwards. As you do so, the twine will force them to grow closer together until they touch.
8. Meditate on your intentions until you experience contentment.

The light of your candles, and the ever-shortening twine, will draw you and your love to each other, while the unlit black candle will cause your love to stop noticing that other person. After the candles have burned down, place the black figure candle in a paper bag and toss it in a river, to be carried out of your lives forever.

TO BRING A SECRET LOVE INTO THE OPEN

Relationships that are cultivated in secret can be exciting, but as time goes on the excitement wears out and you start to feel like you are trapped in a cage. You are in the relationship of your dreams but you can't tell anyone about it. Being with someone who is afraid to let the whole world know that you are together can quickly turn into a problem. It can be especially difficult when you're ready to tell the world, but your partner is not, and doesn't seem to understand why the situation is so painful.

You don't have to endure that kind of torment alone. With this work, you can make your partner feel the same anguish that you feel, making them ready to bring your love out into the light.

This work uses calamus root, also called sweet flag. A flowering calamus looks like, well, let's just say a man who isn't thinking with his head. Our ancestors noticed things like that and were able to decipher what herbs could be used for which spells, and now calamus is a common herb in Hoodoo love and domination spells.

What You Will Need

- Calamus root powder - three teaspoons
- Salt
- Piece of paper
- A pan

The Work

1. Write both your names on the piece of paper.
2. Put the calamus root on the name paper and fold it closed.
3. Place the folded name paper in a pan and cover it with salt.
4. Place the pan on a stove on medium high heat.
5. When the pan is hot enough that the mixture starts to crackle, call out your lover's name three times.
6. Announce to the spirits that you want your lover to reveal your relationship to the world.

The heat and calamus root, along with the help of your ancestor spirits, will pick at your lover's mind until they do what you want. You can let the mixture cool and then bury it in the ground.

REMIND YOUR PARTNER ABOUT YOUR INITIAL LOVE WITH A PHOTO

Love is a beautiful thing and the first three months of love are the most amazing. You feel as though you are floating on clouds and living in this bubble where nothing can touch you. It is incredible. But as time goes by, over-familiarity seeps in. You hang out together and see the bits and pieces about each other that are not so pleasant.

As a result, the rose-tinted glasses come off, and reality sets in. And when this happens, love does not always stay in the picture. Things get boring. You take each other for granted and the relationship becomes shaky. It is a typical love story in the real world. Everyone goes through it, but if you feel this is the relationship of your dreams and you want to keep things hot and spicy, one way to do that is to return to the way things were in the beginning.

Sometimes, sitting down and reminiscing about the good old days can help reignite those feelings. But what would make this even more effective is if you could put your lover under a spell to make them feel as if you are both back in the early days. A picture freezes a moment in time and captures the emotions. This spell will use that trapped energy to remind your partner of what you once felt for each other.

What You Will Need

- Love Drawing Oil
- Red candle
- Picture of you both together at the start of your relationship

The Work

1. Place the picture on your altar.
2. Soak your mind in the memory that this picture inspires.
3. Dress the red candle in Love Drawing Oil.
4. Carve the initials of your beloved on the candle, light it, and place it next to the picture (be careful not to catch the photo on fire!).
5. Allow the candle to burn out.

This spell picks up on the energy created by a previous memory and the picture that you put on the altar anchors that energy. The spirits of your ancestors will focus on this energy and use it to redirect it back at the person you want to remember how they felt about you in the early days. This is one of those Hoodoo conjures that we have to do at least once a month in order to keep things feeling great.

INCREASE COMMITMENT WITH ORANGE PEELS

Orange peels are very good in control work, especially those spells that beginners do. They have a way of mentally and emotionally clearing blockages. If you have a partner who enjoys being with you but finds it difficult to actually commit to you, conjure work involving orange peels can help push their mind in the direction that you want it to go.

For this spell, we are going to combine orange peels and candles to help illuminate the path for your partner and lead them to the conclusion that they want to spend or invest more time with you. This is the kind of work you do for someone you are serious about. It would be unfair to require a commitment from someone you have no intention of committing to.

While rootwork does not exactly deal with karma and the consequences of one's action, I still like to advocate good will generally when carrying out these conjures. So, before you initiate the rituals that go into this conjure, be absolutely sure you are ready to be committed to this person.

What You Will Need

- Dried orange peels
- White cloth
- Twine
- Tall white candle
- Piece of paper

The Work

1. Set up the white candle at your altar.
2. Write your name and your intended's name on the paper.
3. Place the cloth flat in front of the candle.
4. Put the orange peels and the paper at the center of the cloth and wrap it up with the twine.
5. Let the candle burn for one hour a day.

This work is meant to clear any doubt your partner may have about committing to you. It also puts you in a positive light so that they are more inclined to see all the amazing qualities you have. When they sleep, their mind and thoughts will be imbued with images of you, making them desire to be and connect with you on a deeper level. You can enhance the work by praying Psalm 31.

SPEED UP A RELATIONSHIP WITH GINGER

Relationships go through different stages, and while there is no fixed method of getting from friendship to marriage, it is also necessary to make sure that you are moving forward. You start out as strangers and then become friends. Then you become physically intimate, which makes you lovers and then you usually move to the engagement phase, where you become the fiancé(e). Finally, you become a wife or husband.

The period of time between the stranger phase and when you become a legal spouse varies. I know of couples who went from being strangers to being married within weeks and I have heard of people who took decades to finally marry. You don't have to lean on the other person's sense of timing in order to get to the stage you want. With this spell, you can quickly move through these phases and get to where you want. For this conjure, we are going to use ginger. Ginger has a way of infusing energy into whatever it is added to.

Even when you take it for health purposes, any drink or herbal concoction that has ginger in it has a way of lifting your spirits. In Hoodoo, it energizes the person for whom the rootwork is intended. Remember to put your mind in the right place before you initiate the spell. Going into it with desperation and frustration can alter the course of the spell and possibly render it ineffective. Put your mind in a positive state before you begin.

What You Will Need

- Ginger - one tablespoon
- Dried yarrow flowers (for love) - one tablespoon
- Dried lady's mantle (for faithfulness) - one tablespoon
- Black cohosh extract (for dominance) - five drops
- Licorice root powder (for courage) - one tablespoon
- Red candle

- Jar

The Work

1. Inscribe your partner's name on the candle and light it at the altar.
2. Assemble the herbs and mix them till they become powder.
3. Add the black cohosh extract.
4. Place the powdered herbs in a transparent jar.
5. Speak your intentions clearly and concisely into the flames.
6. Seal the jar when the candle burns out and use it as instructed below.

If you want your partner to propose, sprinkle the herbs in their shoes. This would prompt them to hasten up in their decision to marry you. If you are in a friends-with-benefits situation, the next time you two meet for a tumble, sprinkle the herbs onto the sheets. You can also put a little bit of the herbs in your perfume or laundry detergent to attract serious relationships or hasten commitment if you are single and searching.

BRING SOMEONE TO THE ALTAR WITH CEMENT

We all have that amazing love who checks all the boxes for us when it comes to long-term commitment but the problem is getting them to that point where they actually commit. They might hang out with you and your family often enough to be considered family. They might even know all of your friends and have charmed every single person in your circle. But for some reason, they just don't take the step that shows their commitment to your relationship. This conjure is designed to cement that person in this relationship and get them to be 100 percent in.

It is particularly helpful if you are in a relationship in which you feel you're one of several in their life. In other words, maybe they are looking for other partners while they are actively in a relationship with you. If you want to get them to fully commit by taking that step to the altar, this rootwork is perfect. All you need is some of their hair.

Now, if you are harboring anger or resentment, do not start on the spell, since the energy you are projecting can influence it and misdirect the spirits of your ancestors. Remember the love that brought you to this point where you want to be committed to this person? Focus on it. Enjoy the beautiful aspects of being in love and let that fill you up as you do this work.

What You Will Need

- Foil tray
- Cement
- Red candle
- Partner's hair

The Work

1. In the foil tray, mix the cement according to instructions. It should be almost at the brim.
2. While the cement is still drying, place the red candle in the center of the tray and light it.
3. Roll your partner's hair into a ball and singe it twice with the flame.
4. The third time, allow it to burn. You can drop it into the cement if the flame is getting near your fingers.
5. As the smoke rises and spreads out, speak your intentions into the flame.
6. Leave the candle to burn and melt into the wet cement. When the flames burn out, your work is done.

Inability to make it to the marital altar is a form of commitment phobia. The cement hardens their resolve and the candle wax at the center represents where that resolve is directed; love. To back up your intentions, pray with Ruth 1: 16-17.

FOR CONTROL IN A RELATIONSHIP WITH LICORICE

Sometimes, it is easy to get what you want out of a relationship if you are more in control. You can dictate the terms as well as the direction of the relationship when you have superior power, and that is what the love work here is about. It allows you to exercise total dominance over your partner without demeaning them or causing them any harm.

This love sweetening jar uses licorice to add an element of control. If you've ever taken a whiff from real licorice root, you'll have noticed how strong the smell is, which is why licorice is used for sweetening and compelling.

I've seen a lot of people on the internet use honey in their love sweetening jars, but I usually use sugar water. The problem with honey is that it's slow, so it's good for long-term love work, but if you want something to happen faster, sugar water is the way to go.

What You Will Need

- Dried licorice root - just a pinch
- Damiana root - just a pinch
- Cinnamon stick (to speed the work)
- Small jar
- Piece of paper
- Sugar
- Water
- Small tea candle

The Work

1. Write you and your partner's name on the piece of paper and place it in the jar.
2. Fill the jar about halfway with sugar.
3. Place the licorice and damiana into the jar.
4. Fill the rest of the jar with water.
5. Close the jar and shake it. This will dissolve the sugar.
6. Place the jar on your altar, and place the tea candle on top of the jar.
7. Light the candle and let it burn down.

You can discard the candle after it's burnt out. Shake the jar daily to gain and keep control in your relationship. You can read Hosea 6:1-2 to enhance the work.

END A PARTNER'S BAD HABITS WITH DEVIL'S SHOESTRING

Devil's shoestring is primarily used in protection spells. The goal is to trip the devil so that his mission is never accomplished. For this work, you want to trip your partner up so that they stop their bad habit pronto. When you are in love with someone, it's almost as if they can't do anything wrong. But as you spend more time with them, you start noticing those micro details that you were oblivious to in the initial stages of the relationship. And then there are those glaring bad habits that irritate you.

A proper conjure work can help them overcome these habits and create an environment where love can thrive. When you are constantly irritated and annoyed by someone, it's difficult to enjoy their presence. Also, getting rid of bad habits can help set them on the right path when it comes to their health. But most importantly, it can put your mind at ease. This conjure work is also recommended for people with spouses who find it difficult to keep their pledge to be faithful. It applies to both womanizers and man-ivores.

It is an easy conjure. I used it on someone who struggled with smoking, and also to help a woman rein in her errant man, so he was only committed to their marital bed. There are specific spells that can cripple a person sexually whenever they want to commit sexual acts with anyone other than their significant, but this one is more generic.

What You Will Need

- Two white candles (for the banishing)
- One black candle (for the bad habit)
- Four purple candles (for your willpower)
- Devil's shoestring incense
- Piece of paper
- Picture of your intended

The Work

1. Place a picture of your intended on your altar.
2. Write your petition down on the paper and place it behind the picture.
3. Position the white candles directly in front of your ancestors (or their possession), on a line that spans the width of your altar.
4. Put the black candle at the center of the altar.
5. Place the purple candles around the black candle like a cross.
6. Light the incense and put it between the purple candle at the top of the cross.
7. Leave until the black candles burn out.

When the black candle burns out, bury it in your backyard. This is not a one-time spell and only works to remove the things that might tempt your partner into that specific bad habit. It does not necessarily stop them from doing the thing. It just cuts off their supply, making them more likely to quit in the long term. When the time comes to renew the spell, make sure you use a new set of candles. You can enhance your work with Titus 1:11-12.

PINNING YOUR PARTNER DOWN

Wayward partners are the worst. First, there is the physical betrayal and trauma that comes with that behavior, not to mention the risk of contracting STDs, among other things. Then there is the emotional pain of knowing that someone you love is disregarding the love you have for them. In marital homes, this disregard becomes complete disrespect for the vows that they took at the altar. I take cheating spouses seriously because of my own experiences and also because of what my clients have been through.

But you know what? If you love that idiot so much and you think that your relationship is worth saving, you can use conjure work to keep their sexual organs only functional when it comes to you. For this rootwork, we are going to use dolls and pins. This is one of the most common forms of keeping a straying partner at home. I like it because it is simple, effective, and can be turned on and off. So, if you have a partner who you are sure is cheating, you can make a doll and fix it in a way that whenever your partner goes to have sexual relations with someone other than you, they will not be able to perform as expected.

What You Will Need

- Hoodoo doll
- Tailor pin (for a man)
- Candle (for a woman)
- Holy water
- Pubic hair of the target

The Work

1. Place the pubic hair of the target on the doll for potency. The pubic hair should be placed on the corresponding genital area of the doll.
2. Bind the doll to the target by sprinkling the doll's head thrice with holy water and repeating these words, "I name you (insert target's name). You are now this doll and this doll is you."
3. For a man, pierce the genital area of the doll with the pin, but make sure it doesn't go through the doll. Then tell the doll what you want.
4. For the woman, place the genitals of the dolls over a burning candle. Call her name three times and speak your intentions to the flames. Don't let it burn. The result might be permanent.
5. Keep the doll in a safe space.

Whenever you want to have intercourse with your partner, take out the pin for the man. For the woman, place a ball of wet cotton wool on the doll's genitals. Relations should proceed as usual. When they go out and you suspect their intentions, simply run through steps 3 or 4 and then repeat step five.

BRING A LOVER BACK WITH TWINE

The spell we are going to use in this rootwork is designed to work on partners who are indecisive and have a habit of breaking things off and then returning to you, only to repeat that again and again. To save yourself the heartache, it's better to simply pull them in and ensure that they stay in. This conjure is different from getting a person to commit, as it is more about returning them to your arms.

Twine is used like bindings in many Hoodoo workings. It symbolizes the bond between things, or can be used to prevent an enemy from making any moves. If you only have plain string in your home, that's completely fine - use what you have.

I remember doing this for a client who had been in and out of a relationship for more than half a decade. It got to a point where she was done with the constant heartbreaks and wanted to seal the relationship once and for all. This was a particularly poignant situation for her because he had abandoned her and their one-year-old daughter. She decided she wasn't ready to have her daughter go through the same thing she had been going through. I understood her concerns, so we set to work.

Through this work with candle and twine, you can reel your lover back in and, in the process, hopefully remind him of what he's missing at home.

What You Will Need:

- Two white candles (to represent you and your target)
- Twine

The Work:

1. Assign the candles to both of you by inscribing your names on them. One for you and the other for your significant other.
2. Cut about a foot of twine and tie each end to a candle.
3. Light the candles and speak your intentions into the flames.
4. Turn the candles inwards toward each other until they meet.
5. Put out the candles when you experience closure. Store the candles in your closet.

This conjure is similar to the one for blocking out interference, except that you are not using black figure candles and the candles that you lit can remain at the altar. To empower your spells, I suggest doing a cleansing bath before you start this work.

END CONFLICT WITH SUGAR

Sugar has a restorative quality and can sweeten almost anything. Lemons, coffee, a sour relationship… it is excellent for conjure works focused on removing bitterness and conflicts. Conflicts are inevitable. Even in a relationship that is considered perfect by all accounts, the parties are bound to have a disagreement at some point. The hallmark of a healthy relationship is not the absence of conflict but the ability to resolve things amicably without degradation or abuse. Sadly, there are times in a relationship when both partners behave like cats and dogs - arguing constantly, divided at every turn, and seemingly unable to reach a satisfactory compromise on anything.

When conflict goes on for too long, it leads to a breakup. If you find that dialogue, as well as other means of communication (including mediation by external influences), has not brought you and your partner any closer together, and you are certain that this relationship is what you want, a spell to end conflict might be what you need.

This spell tears down walls erected by pride, suspicions, poor communication, and so on, giving both parties an opportunity to bury the hatchet and make an attempt to know and understand each other better. Burying your work is a very symbolic act. You use it to put an end to something, close a chapter or keep something out of sight.

What You Will Need

- Sugar - one teaspoon
- Vanilla extract (to calm troubles) - one teaspoon
- Lavender essential oil (for luck in love) - a few drops
- A small blue candle
- A jar filled with water

The Work

1. Poke three holes through the top of the blue candle.
2. Pour a few drops of lavender oil, vanilla extract, and sugar into each hole.
3. Place the candle at the center of your altar and light it.
4. Speak your intentions as the candle burns.
5. When the candle burns out, put the candle ends inside the jar of water.
6. Seal the jar tightly and bury it in your backyard.

Blue candles are used for bringing healing to relationships. When your relationship is gripped with strife, putting an end to the conflict is one way to put things back on track and restore peace. When the sealed jar goes into the ground, so does the conflict. When you cover it with dirt, the conflict is as good as gone. Do not break this jar. You can enhance the work with Psalm 32.

SMOOTH OUT RECONCILIATION WITH WORMWOOD

Wormwood is a powerful spiritual herb. It is used in powerful protection spells and to promote mental and spiritual healing. Sometimes, you need a little help to get you to a place where you can smooth things over with your partner.

Let's say you've gotten into a serious conflict but have done your best to bring it to an end. You don't just want it to be closed and never spoken about again, but you want to make sure you both have closure and the healing you need to move forward. This conjure work can make that happen. You need a pink love candle and wormwood. The most important ingredient for this spell, though, is your state of mind. You have to let go of any residual anger or resentment. You must put yourself in a forgiving mood.

To make things even better, put your mind in a love trance. Listen to some good love songs. Remember the days when the love was super sweet between you and your significant other. Don't make this conjure work about the situation or source of conflict. Your focus should be on smoothing out your relationship. Ask yourself, if it works out the way you want, how do you plan to enjoy your relationship going forward? The answers might give you some extra incentive and a spirit boost to your spell power.

What You Will Need

- Wormwood powder or dried leaves - a few teaspoons
- Honey (to sweeten)
- Pink candle
- Eight pins

The Work

1. Carve the name of your beloved on the candle.
2. Dip all eight pins in honey.
3. Stick each pin into the base of the candle to form a halo.
4. Scatter wormwood at the top of the candle and then light it.
5. As the smoke rises, pray for swift reconciliation. If your beloved is mad at you, they will be visited with dreams about you that will turn away their anger and change their mind.

Give this spell an hour before putting out the candle. Repeat it every day for nine days. If a candle finishes, bless a new candle and repeat the process. On the ninth day, thank your ancestors for a successful job. Pack all the burned candles, wash them under running water and dispose of them.

MAKE THINGS FUN AGAIN WITH RINGS

The spell we're going to work here is two-fold. The first is for people who are in relationships and would like to strengthen them and move towards marriage. The conjure works by igniting the spark that was there in the beginning. The second use is for couples who are already married and would like to heal whatever rifts have taken place during their marriage. Both works require the use of rings.

It doesn't matter if you are not engaged and therefore have no ring in the first category. You can use an old ring to carry out the spell. For the married couple, you will use your wedding ring to activate the spell. Two ingredients, basil and mint, will be used for this spell. You can use both of them together or separately. I like them together because while mint refreshes and invigorates, basil works with what you already have. This means that mint can be used when you are trying to bring something new into your life, while basil grounds the work in the love you already have.

In essence, if you have a relationship that is already ongoing, basil will make sure that those new sensations and feelings you want have been activated in that relationship. It is pretty straightforward and very simple. Just grab a ring and we're ready to go.

For unmarried couples

What You Will Need

- Old ring
- Mint leaves (to refreshen)
- Basil leaves (to enhance)

The Work:

1. Place the ring on the altar.
2. Wrap the ring in fresh basil and mint leaves.
3. Leave the ring on the altar overnight.
4. Put the ring under your lover's pillow on the bed that you share.

For married couples

What You Will Need:

- Your wedding ring
- Jar
- Sugar (to sweeten)
- Mint
- Basil

The Work:

1. Pour sugar generously into the jar.
2. Put your ring inside the jar.
3. In a small bowl, crush the mint, sugar, and basil together. You want the flavor of the mint and basil to be absorbed into the sugar.
4. Pour the mixture on top of the ring in the sugar jar.
5. Leave it overnight in the kitchen of the home you share.

In the morning, you can take the ring out and toss the remnants of the spell. Repeat this routine once a month to maintain a constant flow of the fun and invigorating power that this work brings to your home and marriage. However, if the arguments are getting too frequent and you keep creating spells to end the conflict, you might want to think about the source of the issue and see if you can fix it.

PUT AN END TO STUBBORNNESS WITH ORCHIDS

This conjure work is particularly suited for females. So, if you are a woman with a partner who is extremely stubborn, this is the conjure work that you can use to end their stubbornness. It establishes your dominance over them in a relationship and puts the control in your hands. Through this spell, you will be able to get your partner to become docile and submissive towards you. And when you are more in control of the relationship, you can put an end to a lot of the things that cause problems, because your partner will be more willing to follow your wishes and live by your principles.

The most important ingredient for the spell is a live orchid. Orchids are a beautiful flower associated with femininity. If you can find a wild orchid, great, but if not, you can plant one somewhere and it will work just as well.

What You Will Need

- Live orchid
- Piece of paper

The Work

1. Write down the name of your intended target and their birthday three times.
2. Fold the paper towards you.
3. Clearly voice your intentions and bury the name paper at the foot of the live orchid.

The growing orchid will cause your man to be more compliant with your wishes. Where he was previously ferocious and stubborn, he will become gentle and docile. Where he was adamant and unforgiving, he will become receptive and agreeable. This does not turn him into a doormat. Far from it. It merely puts an end to those unnecessary arguments.

END OVER-POSSESSIVENESS WITH BURLAP

When a burlap sack is thrown over a person's head, their vision is immediately restricted. They become oblivious to what is happening around them. As a result, their perception of control becomes altered. This is exactly what you want to do to an over-jealous lover. When I was younger, I have to admit I found a little bit of possessiveness attractive. I liked the idea of my man going crazy at the very thought of another man attempting to flirt with me, even though I had no intention of following through. Jealousy can give off those romantic cowboy story vibes.

That said, when you are in a relationship someone who takes things too far when it comes to possessiveness, it becomes a huge issue and is time to check that trait. Normally, I would encourage you to walk out of any relationship that causes you to suffer any form of abuse. But if you feel that, apart from being overly possessive, your partner has other redeeming qualities, a spell like this can shut down that jealous nature, allowing those other wonderful qualities to shine through.

What You Will Need

- Hoodoo doll
- Burlap cloth (small piece)
- Twine
- Target's hair
- Holy water

The Work

1. Sprinkle the doll's head three times with holy water, and say "I name you (your target's name)."
2. Attach some of your partner's hair to the doll.
3. Place the burlap cloth over the doll's head.
4. Tie the cloth at the back of the doll's head with a small piece of twine.
5. Speak your intentions. For instance, you can tell the doll to stop being paranoid, or to not focus on you so much.
6. Place the doll in a dark place.

With this work, your partner becomes blind to your actions and therefore has no reason to suspect you of anything, much less be jealous. They are oblivious to your flaws and will never hold your shortcomings against you. Understand this, the spell does not rid them of their possessive nature. As I said earlier, it simply shuts them down by turning off their triggers. If their nature causes them to be volatile, get them to seek help, or better still, quit the relationship while you can. You can enhance the work with Psalm 39.

END A RELATIONSHIP WITH A POTATO

Did you know that new potatoes can grow out of old ones? It is symbolic that something new can be born out of the end of something else. Breakups can be painful but this spell ends an existing relationship in a way that lets each person move on to a new phase of their life. And it doesn't have to be the breakup of your own relationship. Perhaps the person you are with is still holding on to an old relationship. We can use the spell to break things off so that he or she can focus fully on you.

It is inevitable that if you have done everything you can to help your relationship thrive and have still failed, you reach a point where the only way forward is to go your separate ways. You must embrace this reality and let go. But breaking up is easier said than done. Telling another person that you are about to sever the connection you have with them can be devastating.

It's important to acknowledge that even though you are the one initiating the break-up, that doesn't mean you are not hurting. Another benefit of the spell we are going to create is that it will try to smooth things over and make the break-up process easier. This is why we are using a white potato as the base for the spell; unlike the sweet potato rootwork that is supposed to sweeten a relationship, here we are breaking things up as delicately as possible.

What You Will Need

- A piece of paper
- Green onion
- White potato
- Twine

The Work

1. Write the names of the couple on the paper. One name should be written horizontally and the other vertically to form a cross.
2. Fold the paper. Lay it forward once. Turn it counterclockwise and fold it away from you once again. Repeat this two more times. Set it aside.
3. Cut the potato from the bottom to the top but not all the way through. The gap should be wide enough to house the green onions. Set it down.
4. Hold the green onion in your hands and focus on your intention.
5. Call the name of your partner and the name of the person you are breaking them apart from, whether it's you or someone else.
6. Split the green onion into two vertical halves.
7. Insert the name paper in between the split onions.
8. Insert the onion and paper in the potato.

9. Tie the potato and onions with twine to secure everything in place.

10. Bury it somewhere the potatoes and onions can grow.

Breaking up a couple other than yourself is a bit of a controversial topic. But I prefer to look at it on a case-by-case basis. Every relationship has its own 'DNA', so the story differs from person to person. The only ones qualified to judge the situation are those involved. So, when you dabble in conjure work that breaks other people apart, try as much as possible not to latch on to the negative judgment of other people. It can create an energy that works against your intentions. Be confident in your decisions.

GET RID OF UNWANTED ATTENTION WITH LEMONS

Lemons are used for spells to turn things sour. If a person is giving you too much unwanted attention, a little lemon can turn things sour and cause them to back off. Nobody wants to be at the receiving end of attention that they do not want.

I had a client who struggled through years of harassment from someone who was totally obsessed with her. She moved to four cities and changed jobs even more than that to escape his attentions. But somehow, he would always find her. She was so psychologically and emotionally damaged by the experience that she could barely function in society. By the time she came to me, she was a complete emotional wreck. Even though she had changed her number more than ten times, this stalker would find her number and resume calling her.

She had reached the end of her rope when she came to me, so I did this conjure for her. This was a man who had harassed her every single day for more than two years. But within nine days of the conjure, the man had vanished from her life, and for the first time she was truly free. If you want someone to stop thinking about you and showering you with unwanted attention, perform the spell and your problem will be solved.

What You Will Need

- Four burned matches
- Empty jar
- A piece of paper
- Lemon cut in half
- Onion peel
- Black feather
- String

The Work

1. Write the name and birthday of the target on the paper.
2. Fold the paper.

3. Wrap the name paper around the black feathers and tie it with string.

4. Place the lemon face up inside the jar.

5. Put the onion peel on top of the lemon.

6. Arrange the matches on top of the onion peel like kindling.

7. Poke the feather into the middle of the pile and leave it standing upright.

8. Fill the jar with water and close the lid tight. You may have to push the feather down to get the jar to close.

9. Shake the jar vigorously and call the name of the person whose attention you want to end. Say this, "Leave my life. Take your strife. In this life and in the next, may our paths never cross." Do this nine times.

10. Take the jar far away from your home. The farther away, the better. Bury it in the ground and the job is done.

When you want to cut off the attention of someone, you have to do it mentally just as you have done it physically. In other words, you also have to cut them off in your mind. Reminiscing about the attention they gave you can weaken the energy you put into the creation of the spell. You see, your ancestors latch onto your emotions and intentions when helping you to fulfill the purpose of the spell. When they sense that you are thinking about this person, it weakens your hold on your spirit guide and might also weaken the spell. Bury the jar in the ground and bury this person in your thoughts at the same time.

STOP LOVING SOMEONE AT THE CROSSROADS

It is important to understand that there are spirits at crossroads. If you are going to be practicing crossroad spells, you must familiarize yourself with the spirit by frequently bringing offerings to it. Don't wait until you need to do a conjure before you give that offering. This would make the spirit more inclined to help. Also, when you speak the words in step 3 below, be mindful of two things: Do you want the spell to be permanent or temporary? For a permanent outcome, give an impossible condition, like "until the sun rises in the west." For a temporary outcome, the condition could be something that is fulfilled by the other person, such as, "until he/she loves me unconditionally."

The heart wants what it wants. People say that love is just a chemical reaction in your brain or that it is the stirring in your loins that inspires love. But when you look at it objectively, people in love can seem very stupid at times. A person who is normally perfectly logical will start making seemingly irrational decisions in the name of love. In itself, this can be quite harmless, unless the object of their affection turns out to be ruthless and takes everything they have to offer. In this case, love becomes poison.

You have probably heard stories of people who were completely ruined by love. The problem is not that they fell in love. The problem is the person with whom they fell in love. They probably know that this person is no good for them, but try as they might, as I said, the heart wants what it wants. There is no reasoning or logic to this type of love. If you are in that situation and you want to stop being in love with someone, this is what you should do.

What You Will Need

- Charcoal powder (for banishing) - one tablespoon
- Red rose petals (to tie the banishment to love) - a handful
- Salt (for purification) – half a tablespoon
- Three pennies

The Work

1. Put the rose petals, charcoal, and salt in a mortar and grind the materials until they become a paste. You can add a bit of water to help.
2. Say these words, "My love for (insert object of love's name), I banish you. Never to return until… (insert a condition)."
3. Take the mixture with you to a crossroads.
4. Bury the pennies in the dirt near the crossroads, and thank the spirit for its help.

5. Using the mixture, at the center of the crossroads draw a circle and four arrows pointing away from the circle.

6. Spit in the center of the circle. Turn around and walk away.

Before we move on, I want to point out something. By admitting that the love you have for this person is destroying you, you have made progress. Don't block out the pain. Give yourself time to heal and then move on.

SPELLS FOR MONEY AND SUCCESS

Money is a necessity that we cannot do without. It is virtually impossible to get from point A to point B without some form of financial assistance or transaction along the way. The world we operate in today speaks a universal language and that language is money.

Some people have wrongfully ascribed the word 'evil' to money. I am sure you've probably heard the phrase, "money is the root of all evil." It is this kind of thinking that has caused a lot of people to develop an unhealthy relationship with money. This unhealthy relationship feeds their attitude towards money, and when you don't have the right attitude towards money, it is difficult to attract it into your life.

Money is manifested through energy. The most common form of energy expended to manifest money is physical energy through labor. This is the one we are taught from birth to use. But what many don't know is that you can also focus your mental energy to attract money to you through conjure work.

With the combination of that dark Hollywood narrative on Hoodoo and the many cautionary tales passed on to us by parents and guardians, we see money obtained through conjures and rootwork as tainted. It is almost as if we find it hard to accept money unless we labor for it. But here is the thing with rootwork: it is not limited to specific functions. In fact, I believe we have not even tapped a quarter of the financial resources that the powers of our ancestors have made available to us. If you can sit in your house and create a conjure work that attracts a man to your doorstep, how then is it difficult for you to accept that you can invoke the spirit of money and demand it to work for you?

I always have ongoing money work on my altar. I like to use the green candle with honeysuckle leaves (I'll talk about that spell later on). This conjure work ensures that I have an abundance of money. You see, I don't just want to get by. I want to thrive and enjoy my life. I know that money can play a role in this dream that I have and I'm not ashamed of it. Neither should you be ashamed of your financial ambition. People associate poverty with piety, not realizing that wealth is a birthright and when you channel your ancestors to access what is rightfully yours, you will unlock the keys to a life without lack.

Before you begin any rootwork in this chapter, I want you to do a little reprogramming exercise to rid yourself of any negative perspectives you have about money. Accept that money is neither your friend nor your enemy. You must also train yourself to have discipline when it comes to money. If you don't have discipline, you will burn through money faster than you can make it and not even your ancestors can help you there.

END BAD LUCK WITH AN ORANGE

Oranges are associated with success in Hoodoo work. If you have been having a bit of a bad run lately, this conjure work is the first place to start. It will reverse any bad luck you have had and usher in positive energy that will activate good luck going forward. I recommend it as an excellent starting point for all your money spells.

First, it invites success into your space. Then it ensures that the success you achieve is accompanied by joy. In my opinion, orange has an incredibly positive vibe and I always love working with it. If oranges are not your thing, you can try to substitute them with some other sweet citrus fruit, like tangerines. Do not use grapefruit or bitter lemon. Those can turn things sour and that is the last thing we want for this spell.

What You Will Need

- One whole orange
- Piece of paper
- Knife
- Salt

The Work

1. Write your full name vertically three times on the paper. Beside each name, write your birthday.
2. Fold the name paper towards you
3. Make an incision in the orange.
4. Insert your name paper into the incision and put the salt on top of it to close off the cut.
5. Hang the orange over the main door of your home. If you live in a shared apartment, hang it over your room door. Leave it there for eight days.
6. On the ninth day, bury the orange. Your work is done.

You can enhance the work with Psalm 90 and verse 91 while the orange hangs over your door.

MONEY DRAWING OIL WITH PEPPERMINT

After a bad luck reversal spell, the next step is to create Money Drawing Oil that will attract money to you but can also be used in the development of some of the other spells that will ensure money freely comes into your home. There are many recipes for Money Drawing Oil, but for this conjure work, I decided to develop something very simple, straightforward and effective. The key ingredient for this work is peppermint.

In Hoodoo, peppermint is a harbinger of good fortune, and it opens up the path for wealth and prosperity to flow into your life. When combined with dried thyme leaves and pyrite powder, it creates a potent money attraction spell, and that's exactly what we are going to do.

What You Will Need:

- Peppermint leaves (for good fortune) - two tablespoons
- Dried thyme leaves (to increase money) - one tablespoon
- Pyrite powder (for abundance) - one teaspoon
- Ground cinnamon (to speed the work) - one teaspoon
- Base oil (Sunflower, almond, even regular cooking oil)
- Green jar

The Work:

1. Bruise the peppermint leaves gently to activate the scent.
2. Pour the peppermint, thyme, and pyrite powder into the jar.
3. Top up the mixture with your base oil.
4. Shake the container to mix the ingredients and then allow the bottle to sit at your altar overnight.

Use generously in your other conjures to speed up answers to your money requests.

ROAD OPENING RITUAL

Sometimes you'll know where you want to get, but find yourself blocked from getting there. Maybe you're blocked by circumstances, or blocked by a person, or maybe you've even put roadblocks in your own way. In Hoodoo, we perform a Road Opening to clear the way. You can do a Road Opening at any time, but in the South, we do one at the start of every new year. As you'll see, many Southerners are doing Hoodoo Road Openings on New Year's without even realizing it's Hoodoo. Sometimes there isn't much difference between what's "Hoodoo" and what's just "Southern"!

One important item on your to-do list is to prepare and eat a meal that involves cornbread, black-eyed peas, and collard greens. The golden cornbread symbolizes great wealth.

Collard greens, with their color and texture, symbolize prosperity. And the black-eyed peas represent abundance.

You'll also take a spiritual bath with sunflower and yellow rose petals, to cleanse your spirit and get ready for a fresh start. Sunflowers absorb all that sunlight and represent joy, happiness, social and material wealth and integrity. Yellow roses represent new beginnings and abundance. Each of the things that they represent are key elements that you want to manifest in the financial aspect of your life when you are opening a path for yourself.

You'll also be burning something from your past. It can be almost anything you're willing to part with - a pay stub from a bad job, a bill you can't pay, a photo of an ex-lover, or even just some old clothes that are holding onto the energy of the past.

What You Will Need:

- Something from your past to burn
- Two white candles
- Offering (food that your ancestors are known to be fond of)
- Sunflower petals - from eight flowers
- Sunflower seeds - one cup (including the seeds from the eight flowers)
- Yellow rose petals - one cup

The Work

1. Start the day by burning white candles at your altar.
2. Present your ancestors with an offering of their favorite food. If you're unsure what to use, go with cake.
3. Thank them for their guidance in the past and express gratitude for their presence in the new year.
4. Sit with them at the altar till the candles burn out.
5. Prepare the meal for the day that includes cornbread, black-eye peas, and collard greens.
6. When you eat, include an extra place setting for your ancestors.
7. In a pot, add the sunflower petals, rose petals and sunflower seeds.
8. Pour water in the pot and leave to boil for about 15 minutes.
9. Strain the petals and seeds from the water.
10. Bathe with the water and use the petals as a sponge. Air dry when you are done.
11. Take the item from your past, along with the used petals, and toss it all into a fire. It can be in your fireplace or a charcoal pit.
12. Allow everything to burn into ashes and let it cool.
13. When it has cooled, gather up the ashes and blow them into the four different directions of the earth; north, south, east, and west.

14. Take the sunflower seeds and speak all your troubles into them.

15. Put the seeds in a bird feeder or throw them where birds are sure to eat them. When they do, all your troubles will be eaten away. Do all of this before midnight.

You can do this at the start of a new month, or the start of a new week. But it is most powerful when you do it at the start of a new year. Please note, the offerings to your ancestors and the additional plate setting can be thrown away the next day.

THE GREEN MONEY MOJO BAG WITH PINE NEEDLES

It was my grandmother, Mama Estelle, who taught me that money is a type of energy. All that work that people do to get it, all that time spent accumulating it, all that emotion that goes into holding onto it - it's all energy that you can draw to yourself. But Mama Estelle also taught me that money also has a spirit - a hungry spirit - and if you spend too much energy trying to get money, it will consume you. You need to draw it to you and control it, not let it control your life.

There are many roots that work with money - drawing it, protecting it, and growing it, but one of my favorites is pine needles. The pine tree is "evergreen", just like you want your money to be. It can grow in harsh conditions, and it survives even in the cold of winter. All that makes it perfect to use in a money mojo bag that you can keep with you.

What You Will Need

- Pine needles
- Iron pyrite (to draw wealth)
- A piece of paper and a pen
- Three pennies
- Green cloth bag
- String or twine

The Work

1. Write down your name and birthdate on the paper three times on three different lines.
2. Use a hard object to crush the pine needles to let out their scent.
3. Rub the crushed needles on the coins and iron pyrite.
4. Tuck the coins, needles, and iron pyrite into the name paper and fold to completely conceal everything.
5. Put the folded paper into the green cloth bag and tie it all closed.
6. Leave it on your altar overnight.

You can carry this mojo bag around with you, so it can be working on you all the time. Feed the mojo bag three drops of rum once per week to keep the spirit active. Or, if you're taking it gambling, feed it ahead of going out.

QUICK MONEY WITH NUTMEG

Emergencies, whether they are health-related, or due to a failure in business dealings, or even death, are things that you cannot properly plan for. You may be able to save up some money in your emergency account but that will only get you so far. This spell is designed to help you call forth quick cash when you are caught in such situations.

The star ingredient for this spell is nutmeg. Nutmeg is known as a spice that hastens the spirit's response to money requests. With this spell, you can ask your ancestors for help and they will respond swiftly. The amount of money that you can petition for has a limit, though.

You cannot ask beyond what you need at that moment. That is why it's called a quick money spell. It won't make you so rich that you don't need to work ever again. It simply takes care of whatever problems you need to solve immediately.

What You Will Need

- Nutmeg powder - one tablespoon
- Fresh bay leaves (to bring success) - five leaves
- Cinnamon powder (to speed the work) - one tablespoon
- Green candle

- Bowl
- A fire

The Work

1. Gather all the ingredients together in a small bowl.
2. Inscribe your name on the green candle and light it.
3. Speak over the ingredients with your intention. Be clear, concise, and straight to the point when making your petition known.
4. Toss all the ingredients into a burning flame.
5. Hold the candle in front of you and stand in the direction where the smoke from the flames is going. Let it wash over you.
6. When the fire burns out, the spell is done. Put away the candle and be expectant.

The key to this work is to be specific. It helps to focus on the exact amount of cash you need.

ANCESTOR MONEY TREE

When you need some money help from your ancestors, you can leave money on your ancestor altar. That alone helps direct the spirits to provide you financial aid, but you can take it a step further, too. Money doesn't normally grow on trees, but in Hoodoo, it can.

Money that has been left on your altar (I recommend at least three days) can be used to make a Hoodoo Money Tree. Take that ancestor money and combine it with the vitality of a living plant to bring prosperity. When you are in need of cash or are looking to improve your financial health, this money comes in very handy. Of course, your ancestors do not take the physical cash away. Instead, there is an exchange.

Your offerings and prayers are accepted and their essence is poured into the money. When this happens, the money takes on the ability to grow literally and it becomes a conduit through which they (your ancestors) can offer you more.

What You Will Need

- Ancestor money
- A leafy indoor plant
- Transparent tape

The Work

1. Position the indoor plant where it can receive the maximum amount of sunlight that it needs to thrive.
2. Take a few bills from the money at the altar. Cut a small piece of tape, stick one end on the money and the other end on the leaf of a plant. It should look like money is growing off the plant.

3. Say something along the lines of these words, "I am experiencing abundance this season. Whatever I spend, double returns."

4. When you need cash urgently, take a single bill from this tree and spend it.

Feed, water, and care for the plant the same way you would a normal house plant, but, in addition, you should feed it some holy water at least once a month. Do not over-trim the plant, and whenever you take money from the tree, endeavor to replace it when you get a bill that matches the one you took. This new money should first sit on the altar, though.

FAVOR COLOGNE WITH RUM

I love a good conjure that works with rum. Whenever I use it in my works, the energy I get from my ancestors is excitement. There is a certain fervor and willingness that I sense during these works. It's as if they are more than happy to answer my petition. And, I admit, I take a little nip of rum for myself!

In Africa, rum and dry gin are frequently used to get elders to do favors. I am guessing that being in the afterlife increases their fondness for it. This cologne we will create here is perfect for days when you have an interview or you are giving a presentation for a finance-related project.

If you are in the contract business, you can spray a little of this over any written material that will be used in your communique. Also, dabbing this cologne on you before you leave your house can attract financial favors to you.

What You Will Need

- One long strand of orange peel from an orange
- A small bottle of rum
- Your own perfume or cologne
- Nine whole nutmegs

The Work

1. Put the orange peel inside the bottle of rum.
2. Place the nutmegs inside the rum one at a time, each time speaking to it before dropping it. You can say, "Bring me financial favor from far and wide. Let wealth and abundance dwell by my side."
3. Seal the bottle and shake vigorously.
4. Set the bottle in the sun for nine days.
5. At the end of the ninth day, mix some of the work with your perfume. Use whenever you need it.

Another way to use this work is to rub it on money candles for petition. Just make sure that you don't light the candle until it is dry. Rum is flammable!

DISSOLVE DEBTS WITH ONIONS

In Hoodoo, onions are excellent for dissolving, unblocking or dispelling curses. In situations where your life has been under a powerful generational curse, you will use onions in combination with other herbs to break those free. But for a simple money or relationship fix, an onion on its own will do the job.

If you are in a relationship with a person who is trying to put up walls and prevent you from getting into their heart, an onion spell will break down those walls and give you passage. If you are suffering from a mountain of debt, using onions in your conjure can reduce that mountain to rubble. On your journey to financial freedom, you want to break out of the prison of debt.

Whether it is school loans, loans that we have taken from other people, upcoming bills, credit card debt or anything else, this conjure can make it dissolve and offer you the freedom to start fresh and create a new template for a life of wealth and abundance.

What You Will Need

- Two red onions
- Piece of paper
- Pen
- Knife
- A fire

The Work

1. Write down the name of the person or business to whom you owe money nine times.
2. Turn the paper a quarter of the way counter-clockwise.
3. Write the amount that you owe backwards nine times.
4. Fold the paper in two away from you.
5. Put the folded paper on fire and burn it to ash.
6. Gather and set aside the ashes. It's okay if they contains ashes of the wood used to make the fire.
7. Use the knife and cut the two red onions into two equal halves from top to bottom.
8. Smear the insides of the four halves of the cut onions with the ashes from the name paper.
9. Position each half onion in one of the four corners of your house with the insides facing the wall.

As the onions disintegrate and rot, so will the debts linked to the conjure. You will have to do a separate conjure for every debt.

PAY ME BACK WITH HOT PEPPER

For the most part, pepper is used in Hoodoo work to create discomfort in the life of your target. This is very useful if your intention is to cause a breakup, or to irritate or frustrate someone for reasons best known to you.

In this case, if there is someone to whom you loaned money or perhaps carried out a business transaction but they have refused to pay you, throwing some hot pepper into the conjure work will make their life difficult until they fulfill the condition, which is to pay you back. One thing you should know about using hot pepper in conjure work is that it doesn't last very long (thankfully).

The suffering that the person is going to endure will not be indefinite. There is a timeline to it, which is perfect. The idea is not to make them suffer; just motivate them to pay you faster. If your intentions are concise and clear, they will understand that their current predicament is as a result of their failure to fulfill their debt to you. Quick tip; the hotter the pepper, the more fiery the spell will be.

This work also uses a wooden box, which is often used to trap the spirit of someone in an uncomfortable situation. If you don't have a wooden box, a cardboard box or even a shoebox will do.

What You Will Need

- A picture of the target
- Two extra spicy peppers
- Turmeric - one teaspoon
- Ginger - one bulb

- A small wooden box

The Work

1. Place the picture of the person in the wooden box.
2. Mash the peppers into a paste. You may want to use plastic gloves, and be careful not to touch your eyes until you've washed your hands.
3. Put the turmeric, ginger, and pepper on top of the picture.
4. Cover the wooden box and say something along these lines, "<name of your target>, feel the heat and pain until you pay me back."
5. Place the wooden box in a prominent location where sunlight can hit it during the day. Leave it there until the person responds to your demand.

As long as the person has not paid the money, whenever you see the box, imagine them suffering or experiencing physical discomfort. Your ancestral spirits will convey your thoughts and put them into action. But as soon as the person pays, make sure that you empty the box. Throw away the tools for the work, tear the picture or burn it, and thank the ancestors for their work.

PROSPER ME WASH WITH LEMONGRASS

This simple version of a floor wash is something you can do to bring prosperity to a home or business. I recommend doing it once a week for five weeks. What this does is attracts people to your business, bring excellent opportunities your way, and create an environment in which you can thrive financially.

To set up the tools for this conjure, we are going to use lemongrass. In Hoodoo work, lemongrass is used to open the road and attract opportunities. To supplement its work, we are going to use the magnolia flower and peppermint, which help sweeten and radiate positive energy, respectively.

What You Will Need

- Magnolia flowers (handful)
- Lemongrass (handful)
- Peppermint (handful)
- Water (three quarts)
- Pot

The Work

1. Put all the herbs and the water inside the pot and bring to a boil.
2. Stir the contents of the pot until it is boiling.

3. Think of the results that you want as you stir and communicate that to your ancestors.

4. After about half the water has boiled away, strain the herbs from the water.

5. Bury the herbs or wash them away under running water.

6. Use the water to wash the floors of your home or business. Be sure to wash the doors, walls, windows and frames, as well.

As always, your mindset plays an important role in this conjure work. Try to maintain a positive attitude as you do the wash.

GET INSPIRATION WITH CLARITY OIL

Sometimes what you need most is clarity about a situation, but in business it can be hard to separate yourself from the situation. This work will bring you the inspiration you need, and uses Clarity Oil to clear the way, and candles to bring new ideas.

A spell like this will train your intuition to act like a hound hunting down a specific scent. It will follow the trail that will lead you to what you seek. It is also useful for setting specific goals and creating the right mental atmosphere that will allow you to achieve those goals. This Hoodoo work requires absolute focus.

For this work, you will have to do things one goal at a time. When you have successfully achieved your first goal, you can move on to the next on your list. Don't worry, the process for setting the spell is quick, so you should be able to achieve your goals within a reasonable timeline.

First, you must make your Clarity Oil. This recipe is a small batch, good for just this one working, but you can scale up the ingredients if you'd like. For this you need essential oils of the following herbs:

- Pine (three drops)
- Rosemary (three drops)
- Sage (three drops)
- Carrier oil (one teaspoon)

Mix all of this together under the light of a yellow candle a day before you start the work. Leave it overnight and your oil is ready.

What You Will Need

- Yellow candle
- Piece of paper
- Clarity Oil
- Pen

The Work

1. Write down on the piece of paper one goal that you want to achieve for your business. Be very specific. Statements like "I want to be rich" are not helpful. Instead, try something like, "I want to develop a profitable business idea."
2. Add a few drops of Clarity Oil to the paper.
3. Position the candle at the center of your ancestor altar and light it.
4. Place the goal paper in front of the candle with the goal facing up.
5. Fold down the top third of the paper, and the bottom third of the paper up.
6. Fold the left third of the paper to the right, and the right third of the paper to the left. You've created a simple envelope.
7. When the candle has burned for a bit, drop nine drops of wax onto your envelope to seal it closed.
8. When you are done, express your gratitude to the spirits and then put out the candle.

Carry the paper with you at all times until you have achieved the goal.

DRAW MONEY WITH BASIL

The color green symbolizes wealth, abundance, and prosperity. The green in basil is the perfect shade for a rootwork that is designed to attract money, which is why basil is used often in Hoodoo for money and prosperity work. Also, the rich scent plays a very important role in fulfilling all your intentions for this spell. It leads the money spirits to your door and keeps your path to financial success clear.

For this spell, we are going to combine strong elements linked to money spirits and put them in a location that will act as a beacon for money. These funds that you are expecting can come through business transactions, generous friends or luck in your financial endeavors. You must feed it consistently to keep its power strong.

This work also uses high john root, an incredibly important root in Hoodoo. Explaining high john requires its own section, but for now, know that it brings success through cunning and luck. Honestly, carrying a high john root in your pocket is probably the simplest Hoodoo you can do to bring success and luck into your life.

What You Will Need:

- Green thread
- Basil
- High john root
- Piece of paper

- Pen
- Money Drawing Oil

The Work

1. Write down your name and birthdate three times on the paper on three separate lines.
2. Place the high john root in the basil and wrap it. Ensure that you have enough basil to cover up the root.
3. Use the name paper to wrap the basil.
4. Dip the thread in the Money Drawing Oil.
5. Wrap the thread around the name paper to secure it.
6. Tie three knots in the thread, and leave a little extension so you can use it to hang the conjure.
7. Hang this work over the entrance door of your home or business.
8. Every day, rotate it in a circle and speak your intentions. You can say something like, "Money, I command you to come to me. I command abundant wealth to come to my business."

Feed this ball every day with the three drops of Money Drawing Oil. You can also pray Psalm 23 every time you feed it. Focus on the part that says, "I shall not lack."

PROTECT YOUR MONEY WITH THE ROSE OF JERICHO

Sometimes it isn't about drawing money to you, but keeping what you have. I've certainly been in the position where money seems to be flowing out of my pocketbook faster than it goes in. Now, sometimes that's a person's own fault for spending money on frivolous things. But sometimes unexpected costs pop up - a car breaks down, your child needs a doctor's visit, your landlord increases your rent.

To help protect your finances, you can use the wonderful Rose of Jericho. This amazing plant looks like a tumbleweed from an old cowboy movie, all shrunken and curled up. It appears quite dead. But add a bit of water to it and it unfolds and turns a dark green: the color of abundance. That's why it's also known as the resurrection plant. When it dries out, it curls back up and can hold onto something, like a closed fist. That makes it special in Hoodoo for protection, though it can also be used in crossing work.

What You Will Need

- A Rose of Jericho
- Ancestor money - any denomination
- A piece of paper
- A white tea candle
- A small bowl of water

The Work

1. Write down what you want protected on the piece of paper. In this case, you can write "Protect my money." If you need something more specific, write it down.
2. Place the Rose of Jericho into the bowl of water. It should be submerged about halfway.
3. Wait for it to open, usually in a few hours.
4. Place the petition paper and the ancestor money into the open Rose.
5. On your ancestor altar, light the candle, and place the Rose.
6. Ask your ancestors for help protecting your money.
7. Let the candle burn out.

The Rose of Jericho will slowly close as it dries out, holding tight to your money.

SWEETEN MY BUSINESS WITH HONEYCOMB

Rootworks that are created with the intention of sweetening are designed to establish stability. When used in a relationship, it means you want your partner to be more reliable and more committed. When used in a conjure work for business, you want to create financial stability that will guarantee a steady flow of income.

Honeycombs in Hoodoo work represent stability. If you look at a honeycomb, it's a pattern that repeats and repeats, designed by nature over millions of years to be efficient and stable. And of course, it's covered with honey, which is both sweet (to draw) and sticky (to keep that money stuck to you). Now, honey is a slow sweetener, but that's fine for a long-term working. Honeycomb aids in building and positioning you for success. So, when you use a honeycomb to do your rootwork, you are building a solid foundation that will ensure your business is not a one-hit wonder. Instead, it grows, thrives and expands, all the while keeping you financially happy. It is a simple rootwork with a long-lasting impact.

What You Will Need

- A small piece of honeycomb (to sweeten and stabilize)
- Lodestone (to attract)
- Three basil leaves (to draw money)
- Piece of green cloth
- String or twine

The Work

1. Place the green cloth at the center of your altar.
2. Put the honeycomb at the center of the green cloth.
3. Put the lodestone and basil leaves on top of the honeycomb.

4. Wrap the green cloth to cover everything and tie it closed.

5. Bury the bundle close to your business or home.

This spell can also be used if you are uncertain about your job. Repeat the process mentioned here, but in the last step, bury it close to your place of work.

PROTECT YOUR BUSINESS MOJO BAG WITH DEVIL'S CLAW

The Devil's Claw is an herb with a very strong protective energy. Despite its name, it doesn't have any diabolical properties. It draws its name from the claw-like shape of its seed pods, which are long and hooked.

While the Rose of Jericho is good for general protection, I find Devil's Claw more useful when you need protection from something specific. Think of the Rose of Jericho like a shield protecting you, while Devil's Claw is more like a sword swiping at any who would harm you. For a business, that could be something like losing employees, preventing theft, or keeping customers coming back.

What You Will Need:

- Devil's Claw root, dried or powdered - one tablespoon
- Dried five finger grass - to ward off evil - one teaspoon
- Goldenseal root - for protection - one teaspoon
- Money Drawing Oil
- Piece of paper
- Pen
- Green cloth
- Twine

The Work

1. On the piece of paper, write down your business's name along with your intention. Something like, "Stop people from stealing from me."
2. Pour 7 drops of Money Drawing Oil on the paper.
3. Put the herbs on top of the petition paper and fold it closed as best you can.
4. Wrap the paper with the green cloth.
5. Secure the green cloth with a twine.
6. Put it in a safe location in your business.

A mojo bag is a small spirit, and must be fed. You should feed the mojo bag regularly with either rum, Hoyt's Cologne, or holy water. A few drops once per week should do. Each time you feed it, remind the spirit inside what you want it to do.

REPUTATION SAVER MOJO BAG WITH SUNFLOWER SEEDS

In a career or business, your reputation is everything. A single piece of gossip can burn down all you have worked hard for. To prevent that from happening, you need a binding spell that will shut the mouths of anyone who speaks ill of your reputation. Another way this work comes in handy is to help socially awkward people from saying things that could land them in trouble.

If you are the type of person who speaks inappropriately when you are forced into the spotlight, a binding spell like this will ensure that you don't say anything that will damage your integrity. I would recommend using this conjure work right before you give a presentation. This will help you focus on what you have put together for potential clients and remove or shut out anything you might say that could backfire negatively.

The key ingredient for this work is sunflower seeds. The sunflower represents light and integrity, and using it in this conjure work will help you to project yourself or your business in a positive light that other people will find appealing. In doing so, your reputation will be kept intact.

What You Will Need

- Sunflower seeds - one tablespoon
- Rosemary essential oil - to protect - three drops
- Chia seeds - to stop gossip - one tablespoon
- Crossroads dirt - to carry off any bad things that people think about you - one tablespoon
- A piece of paper
- Pen
- Silver coin (or substitute three pennies)
- Cloth bag
- Twine

The Work

1. Write down your name and birthdate three times on three different lines on the paper.
2. Put three drops of rosemary oil on the paper.
3. Place the sunflower seeds, dirt from a crossroads, and silver coin in the paper.
4. Fold up the paper, and say this nine times: "Let no one speak ill of me."
5. Place the paper into the cloth bag and tie it closed with the twine.

Take this bag with you whenever you go to work, or before you give a presentation. If you are going to be pitching your services to a client, you can have this bag in your pocket while you do so, especially if you are worried about saying the wrong things.

SEAL THE DEAL WITH PANCAKE SYRUP

Are you trying to make a sale? Have you just concluded an interview with a hiring manager and you want to seal the deal on that job? Are you still in the process of negotiating your salary in the new firm where you are hoping to work? What you need is a Hoodoo work that will seal the deal for you, and we are going to do that with pancake syrup.

Pancake syrup is a good sweetener, and it's sticky like honey, making it good for sealing a deal. I find it works faster than honey, but the effects don't last as long. So it's good for when you want something to stick, and stick soon, but don't need it to last a long time. For example, if you are going to sell something to a client and it is a one-off deal, a pancake syrup can deliver that to you.

If you are negotiating your salary with the HR person and you are sure that you will not be working with them in the future, this is also what you want to use. Do this before you conclude that deal and everything will move in your favor.

What You Will Need

- Pancake syrup
- Jar
- Brown paper

- Pen

The Work

1. Write down the name of the person you want to seal the deal with on the piece of paper three times.
2. Put the syrup in a pan and leave it to boil. Syrup may be faster than honey, but boiling it will speed it up.
3. When it is bubbling, pour the syrup into a jar.
4. Put the person's name paper in the jar.
5. Store in a dark place and then go ahead with the deal.
6. Dispose of the jar in running water as soon as the deal is done.

To give more power to the spell, you can substitute something personal from the target instead of using a name paper. Things like pieces of their clothing, their handwritten signature, and so on would work just fine. Just swap out their name paper and follow the rest of the instructions.

GET A PROMOTION MOJO BAG WITH MUD DAUBER NEST

Mud daubers are a type of wasp that build their nests out of mud. You can often find their nests on the side of houses or trees, where they make little columns protected from the rain. I'm not a fan of wasps, but I do respect mud daubers.

Carrying that mud from the ground up to where they want to build is no small feat for such a tiny creature!

In Hoodoo, we use their nests when we want to inspire diligence and hard work, which is what you'll need if you want a promotion. This work isn't for your boss, it's for you. It will make you into such a good worker that your boss will have no choice but to promote you! Of course, you can also give the mojo bag to someone else who may need a boost.

In addition to the mud dauber nest, we are going to work with gravel roots and calendula. Gravel roots are for attracting jobs, so when you put this inside of a petition, it binds your petition to the thing that you desire. Calendula, on the other hand, is good for luck. So, let us get to work.

What You Will Need

- Mud dauber nest powder - three teaspoons
- Gravel root powder - one teaspoon
- Calendula powder - one teaspoon
- Dried Peppermint leaves - five leaves
- Green thread
- Green cloth bag
- Twine or string
- Pen
- A piece of paper

The Work

1. Write down your name and birthdate three times on three different lines on the piece of paper.
2. Put all the herbs and mud dauber nest powder on the name paper.
3. Spray with the Favor Cologne from a few spells back.
4. Wrap the paper around the herbs and put it all into the cloth bag.
5. Tie the bag shut with the twine or string.
6. Spray the mojo bag with the Favor Cologne again.
7. Place overnight on your ancestor altar and petition your ancestors for the job you want. Be realistic but don't be afraid to go for what you really want.

Put the packet in your pocket and take it everywhere with you until the job you petitioned manifests. When that happens, you can gently discard it or bury it. Until then, spray it once a week with Favor Cologne.

BANISH A TROUBLESOME COLLEAGUE WITH PEPPERS

For this work, we are trying to get rid of that annoying colleague who gets on your last nerve. I know that sometimes we meet people with whom we have disagreements every other day. This is normal, as long as neither of you feels disrespected. But once in a blue moon you come across that person who simply takes delight in running you down. They seem to have made it their life's mission to torment you. For this work, we are looking at that nasty colleague but it can also be used for relatives, neighbors, or anyone else you encounter who causes problems for you.

This is a variant of hot foot powder, which causes irritation to the target when they cross over it. There are many ways to make hot foot powder, and you can vary the ingredients to change the effects. For instance, the hotter the peppers used, the more irritation the person will feel. You can use banana peppers for a mild effect, or jalapeno for a quicker and more dramatic result. Be careful which you choose. At work, a slower, more subdued affect may be better than a quick, dramatic one.

What You Will Need

- Dried hot peppers (your choice) - one tablespoon
- Black pepper (for extra irritation) - three teaspoons
- Mustard seeds (to cause confusion) - three teaspoons
- Dirt from a busy road (to compel them to leave) - three teaspoons
- Yellow candle
- A pot with a handle
- A jar
- A fire or stove

The Work

1. Light the candle.
2. Mix all the ingredients together in the pot.
3. Speak your intentions in a clear and concise way. Say something like, "Our path will now be separated. You will go your way and leave me be."
4. Hold the mixture in the bowl above the flame. Turn it around counter-clockwise as you say the words.
5. Put the pot above the fire or on the stove. When it feels hot, remove it to cool. You only need it to become hot to the touch.
6. Take the mix with you and sprinkle it inside your colleague's shoes, or on a road that you know they will walk on, or else at their seat at work.

This spell is not intended to bring harm or calamity to the target. It simply removes them from the immediate environment where they cause conflict for you.

BOSS FIX PACKET WITH TOBACCO

I'm sure we can all agree that life is easier when we have the favor of the boss. Many times, people go to extremes to get the boss's attention, in the hopes of securing their favor. You don't need to go down that route and stoop beneath your station in the process. With this work, you can fix it so that you become your boss's favorite person.

Tobacco leaves, which are the focus of this conjure, have many uses in Hoodoo, stemming from African slaves' knowledge of it from working on the plantation. It is most often used for protection or domination. In this case, you want to dominate your boss, but not in a way that makes it obvious to everyone that you are in control. You want to be the one who they favor above all others.

You can get the tobacco for this work by cutting open a cigarette. Also, if you are a woman with a boss who is harassing you for sexual favors, adding a few drops of your menstrual blood in the work will stop the harassment, and greatly increase the power of the spell. However, that's only effective if your boss has a sexual interest in you.

What You Will Need

- Tobacco - one cigarette's worth
- Calamus root - for domination - one teaspoon
- A piece of paper
- Pen
- Black cotton string
- Black cloth bag
- Favor Cologne

The Work

1. Write down your boss's name and birthdate three times on the paper. If you don't know the birthdate, you can skip that part.
2. Spray a few drops of the Favor Cologne on the name paper.
3. Put the calamus root and tobacco in the name paper.
4. Put the bundle into the black cloth bag.
5. Tie the bag closed with the black cotton string.
6. Tie nine knots when you are done. (If you are a woman trying to control your boss, put one drop of your menstrual blood on each knot).
7. Call your boss's name nine times and tell him/her to freely give you whatever you want.
8. Place the packet in the space where your boss works.

You can enhance the work by reciting Genesis 39:2-4 during the preparation of the conjure.

RESTORE PASSION FOR YOUR WORK BATH WITH SAFFRON

Saffron is an herb that infuses passion into whatever you are using it for. When you work at a job, the general expectation is that every few years you will advance to the next stage in terms of skills, your position, and your financial compensation. However, many people find themselves stagnating in their jobs.

They spend longer than they should in the same spot. In time, whatever passion they have for their job fizzles out, leaving them both mentally and physically stuck. With this particular Hoodoo work, you can activate genuine passion in a job situation. Patchouli promotes wealth and progress, while gravel root is focused on bringing blessings to your job.

So with these three herbs working together, you are immersing yourself in a situation in which your passion for your work is reignited and then blessings over that job are activated. With all of these elements in play, you are strategically positioned to stand out to your superiors, and they see you as a prime candidate for promotion.

What You Will Need

- Saffron - one cup
- Patchouli (to move forward) - one cup
- Gravel root (to bring blessings) – one cup
- A pot of water
- A stove
- Spray bottle
- A strainer

The Work

1. Pour the ingredients into the pot.
2. Bring the water to a boil.
3. Let half the water boil away, then set the pot aside to cool.
4. Strain into a spray bottle and dispose of the herbs in running water.
5. In a bathtub or shower, wash the water over yourself. Take your time, and think of the parts of your work that you actually like, or liked when you first started.

You can enhance the bath by reciting Psalm 23 while you wash. Before leaving for work, spray on some of the Favor Cologne to help bring you good fortune.

LANDLORD FIX WITH PEANUT BUTTER

As renters, the joy you experience at home depends on the relationship you have with your landlord. If your landlord is only interested in collecting the rent, you could end up with numerous situations where broken items and fixtures around the house are abandoned, leaving you somewhat handicapped.

Then if you want changes, the costs have to come out of your own pocket. You can fix that situation by preparing this work with peanut butter. I enjoy most Hoodoo works that involve peanut butter. Peanut is a powerful restrictive element. It is particularly useful if you have lost a relationship, money, or a job.

A good conjure work that involves peanut butter can restore these for you. In this context, we are trying to restore balance to the relationship that you have with the landlord because your landlord is not only there to collect rent. They are supposed to maintain the home so that your stay there remains comfortable.

What You Will Need

- Peanut butter
- Three pieces of paper
- Pen
- Twine

The Work

1. On the first paper, write down your address.
2. On the second paper, write down the name of your landlord.
3. On the third paper, write down the task you want them to carry out. The instructions must be short and clear.
4. Take a little bit of the peanut butter and rub it on the landlord's name paper.

5. Stick the address paper on top of it.
6. Rub a little bit of peanut butter on the address paper and stick the instruction paper on top of it.
7. Roll all three papers to form a cylindrical shape.
8. Tie it up with twine.
9. Hang it in front of your house. Your landlord will do as the instruction paper commands.

You must be clear on what you want them to do. Your instruction on the paper should be short and straight to the point. Something like, "fix the plumbing" or "don't be mad at a late payment" would work.

DREAM HOME PURCHASE WITH SHOES

The ability to buy the home of your dreams is a luxury that not many can afford. And even those who have worked hard enough to raise the funds to afford this dream could find themselves in a market that is currently inflated, making it almost impossible to achieve this goal. But with a little help from your ancestors, all the elements you need to manifest your dreams can be brought together in your favor.

This conjure will help the owners of the property favor your bid above all others, so you'll have to have a specific house in mind first. The offer you make for the house will be appealing to the seller and any circumstance or roadblock that will hinder the process will be eliminated.

Hoodoo uses foot tracks and shoes in a lot of workings. This type of magic comes directly from Africa, where our ancestors knew tracks were connected to the animals and people who made them. Sometimes foot track magic works by crossing a person's path with a working like hot foot powder, so that when they cross the powder, the spell takes effect. Hoodoo also works with shoes as representing both a person's tracks and as a personal item attached to them.

What You Will Need

- One green candle
- One yellow candle
- Two pieces of paper
- Pen
- Favor Cologne
- A pair of shoes (yours)

The Work

1. Write down the address of your dream home on each of the pieces of paper.
2. Dress the papers with the Favor Cologne.
3. Insert each of the pieces of paper in each shoe.
4. Walk around the building you want to buy nine times, then return home.
5. Remove the paper from each shoe and set it aside.
6. Light both candles at your altar.

7. Burn the papers in the flames of these candles, one piece of paper per candle.

8. After you've finished, dispose of the tools for the spell in running water.

Please note that this spell is meant to be carried out before you place the bid on the house. You can put the papers into your shoes before doing a walk-through, and then walk around the house nine times as part of that process.

THE GAMBLER'S CHARM WITH IRON PYRITE

Wherever anyone used to go in the world, throughout history, if they had gold, they were rich. The allure of gold drove the Spanish and Portuguese to explore the New World, and to exploit it they began importing slaves from Africa. Those slaves, separated from everything they knew, did everything they could to hold on to their spiritual traditions. Eventually, those traditions, mixed with what they learned in the New World, grew into Hoodoo.

The African slaves, of course, never got any of that gold. But they did occasionally come across iron pyrite, also called fool's gold. Iron pyrite has nearly the same luster as gold, and our ancestors realized that luster was wonderful for drawing abundance. And iron pyrite has a quality that makes it even better than gold for Hoodoo workings - it's magnetic, just like a lodestone. That combination of looking like gold and drawing like a lodestone makes it wonderful for drawing money. When combined with bay leaves and a pair of dice, you get a very handy lucky charm for gambling.

What You Will Need

- One iron pyrite crystal
- Three fresh bay leaves (to bring success)
- A pair of dice
- White candle
- Red cloth bag
- String or twine
- Van Van oil (for good luck)

The Work

1. Light the candle.
2. Place the iron pyrite crystal, bay leaves, and dice into the cloth bag.
3. Tie it closed with the string or twine.
4. Feed it nine drops of Van Van oil.
5. Tell the spirit inside what you want to do. Something like, "Help me roll the dice well" would do.

Carry this mojo bag with you before gambling to improve your odds. You should feed it Van Van oil before each time you gamble, or at least once a week to keep the spirit inside alive and happy.

272 | ANGELIE BELARD

ST. JUDE FOR A MIRACLE

The saints play a very important role in Hoodoo conjure. When the African slaves arrived in the New World and were forced to adopt Christianity, they recognized many of the saints as manifestations of the same spirits they venerated in their homeland. Over time, Hoodoo incorporated beseeching the saints for aid as a powerful way to help a conjure. Now, I want to note that not all Hoodoo workers work with saints, since many Hoodoo workers come from predominantly Protestant areas and Protestants don't venerate the saints as Catholics do. But, as I've tried to make clear, there is no one "right" way to practice Hoodoo, and it varies from one place to the next. Louisiana, where my people are from, was predominantly Catholic back then, so we incorporated those elements into our Hoodoo. A similar thing happened with Voodoo, but that's a whole other book's worth of discussion.

Different saints are called on for different needs. Saint Jude, for instance, is the patron saint of lost causes. At a point in your life where faith is hanging in the balance and you are unsure of what the next moment will bring, a miracle might be the only thing that can pull you back from the edge of destruction.

There are different types of miracles that you can request from Saint Jude. But for the purpose of this conjure, our focus is going to be on finance. If you are desperately in need of financial favor… and I'm talking about the kind of financial favor that only a miracle can deliver to you, this is the conjure for you.

You should always give an offering when working with a saint. For Saint Jude, water and bread are appropriate.

What You Will Need:

- Statue or picture of St. Jude
- Piece of paper
- Cup of water
- Bread (any type will do)
- White candle

The Work

1. Place the statue or picture of Saint Jude on your altar.
2. Place the bread and water on your altar as an offering to St Jude.
3. Light the candle.
4. Ask Saint Jude for help. Speak from your heart and tell him what you need.

After the candle has gone out, leave the bread and water overnight. The next day you can remove the bread from your altar and dispose of it in your trash without worry. St. Jude will already have received your offering by then.

This work may seem like a simple prayer, but remember that you're doing it on your ancestor altar. That way it's not just you asking, it's all your ancestors crying out on your behalf!

CONCLUSION

There are no words to describe the feeling you get when you successfully complete a spell. To know that you can reach into the spiritual world and get help feels like such an incredible relief - you know that you're not alone. Your ancestors are out there, and they want to help you.

However, your first few workings may not turn out the way you intended. Hoodoo is a skill, and like any skill, it takes time to become good at it. You can't get off a couch and run a marathon without a lot of practice, and you can't master the spiritual world the first time you approach your ancestor altar. You will become better with practice, I promise. When I was a young girl just getting started, I was a mess. But my grandmother, Mama Estelle, encouraged me to keep going. I want you to do the same.

Also remember that some spells take time. Expecting to get an immediate result after you carry out a conjure is not realistic. Some spells work very fast, but most of them require at least a few days' interval in order to be effective.

Give it time to marinate and get going. For the most part, you are working with the help of the spirits. Your first foray into Hoodoo work is an introduction to your ancestors. They will be interested in working with you, but you have to establish a relationship with them. This is why I always recommend putting offerings on your altar. Coffee, rum, and even sweets are little gifts that the spirits of our ancestors often enjoy.

Think of it this way: when you want to ask someone for a favor, you don't just walk up to a complete stranger and recite your list of petitions to them. Your first instinct is to try to establish some kind of relationship with them so they are more inclined to listen to you and then respond. It is the same way with spirits. Get to know them. And don't worry, it won't take long for spirits to warm up to you, especially if they are your ancestral spirits.

If anything, they will be delighted to have the opportunity to be involved in the affairs of your life. Enjoy the opportunities that conjure brings your way. Embrace your roots and your identity by connecting with your ancestors. This connection will empower your spells and turn you into a powerful Hoodoo worker in no time. Most importantly, enjoy yourself. Learn. Grow. Evolve.

It is my fervent hope and desire that your dreams and aspirations will come true and that you live a life that brings you genuine happiness and contentment.

HOODOO FOR WAR AND PEACE

WORKING MAGIC SPELLS FOR JUSTICE AND PROTECTION

ANGELIE BELARD

INTRODUCTION

"Hoodoo is a curse." "It is unnatural." "It is people tapping into things they don't understand in order to play God." "It is a manipulation of the natural order of things." These are a few of the phrases I have heard people use to describe Hoodoo over the years. Interestingly, almost no one with this perspective has ever practiced Hoodoo. I, on the other hand, have been a practitioner of Hoodoo for decades and this is not how I perceive it, either in my own life or in the lives of those I have encountered over the years.

When I wrote my first book on Hoodoo, it was born out of a sense of urgency. I had a burning need to pass down the knowledge that had been passed on to me by my grandmother, who'd learned it from her mother and so on, back through generations. While I still have this desire, this third book in the Hoodoo series is born out of gratitude.

The title, though you might find it somewhat misleading, comes from a place of reflection. When I look back at my life, I have much to be grateful for. For starters, I am rich, though I am not referring only to financial wealth or social success. I am talking about the life I have lived and the wealth of experiences I have curated over time. Hoodoo has been an integral part of these experiences.

I wasn't always a Hoodoo practitioner, but as far as I can remember, Hoodoo has always been present in my life in some form. My mother hung mojo bags in specific places around the house to ward off evil spirits. I was given small spell packets to carry around with me for protection. And if I had bad dreams that included certain things, I was given a cleanse at midnight in the woods near our home. To others, this probably sounds strange. But for my family, it was simply the way we lived, thanks in large part to my roots.

My grandmother was well known for her Hoodoo skills. Her conjurings saved marriages, established businesses, and helped to create a community that thrived, both mentally and emotionally. But she wasn't all sugar and rainbows. She could do a mean crossing as well. People often make the mistake of believing that Hoodoo is mainly used for love, wealth, or health purposes. But life is about more than love, money, or health.

My grandmother used to say that even the sweetest and mildest dog will bare its fangs if pushed into a corner. There are dark times in life. In those times, you may be forced to bare your fangs, and the fangs that nature gave you might not be enough to keep the wolves at bay. During such times, a little help from beyond is exactly what we need. My grandmother helped people get the help they needed in such times.

In my early 20s, I became a full-time hoodoo practitioner. I took over from my grandmother in preparing conjures for people who came to us for help. One of the more popular requests had to do with curses… or crossings. A curse is a terrible choice of words used to describe what rootwork is. If you have read any of my books, you know by now that Hoodoo is neither inherently good nor bad. The outcome and your level of satisfaction with it are what makes it good or bad. However, curses have a way of hitting the intended targets with the full force of your will and intention. For people who like to discuss ethics, this may be the area where they draw the line.

But before you jump to conclusions, let me tell you about a client who I worked with to perfect a crossing for her ex. Before she came to me, she was in a long-term relationship that was very abusive. Thankfully, she was one of the lucky few who got out with her dignity intact. Unfortunately, her ex refused to let go. He didn't approve of her leaving or even living, so he became a threat to her life. He harassed and hounded her at work, at home, and at every opportunity he could find. When she came to me, she was a wreck. She felt as if she was losing her mind. As if that wasn't bad enough, her family, who were supposed to be her primary support unit, were opposed to her leaving the relationship. They pressured her to reconsider her decisions and treated her terribly for standing her ground. Basically, she was being hit from within and also from all around her. She was mentally unstable, emotionally traumatized, and had no physical support whatsoever to help her find her bearings.

To fix things, we had to remove the one element that was at the center of the whole crisis, which was the offending ex. I used the hot foot powder (a personal favorite) to make life a living hell (literally a burning-up) for him every time he came within a few feet of her or members of her family. Within weeks he dropped his obsession over her and moved out of town. The next step was to mend the broken relationship she had with her family. We did that with a healing conjure. Finally, the last piece of the puzzle was to help her find inner strength and courage to move past her trauma. This is typically what a conjure looks like that's designed to protect your peace and wage war against those who want to take that peace away from you.

Beyond this anecdote, this book is dedicated to explaining what Hoodoo is for those who have never tried it out and also to re-educating those already familiar with the core pillars that guide our practices. Building the life you desire using a little spiritual help from the practice of Hoodoo is not limited to boosting your wealth or attracting love into your life. That is what this book will show you. Many of my clients also want to protect the life they already have and I can teach you how to do the same. We fight with enemies both seen and unseen. And sometimes, no amount of love or money can rid us of that enemy. But with the right conjure using roots and herbs, you can ensure that everything you have worked hard to build is protected and that you are able to reap the rewards of your labor. We all deserve to enjoy in peace what we've worked hard to achieve.

The knowledge I share with you here is not meant to show you the dark side of Hoodoo.

In fact, there is no dark side. Instead, it is intended to help you realize that you have everything you need to take the life you are living and make it your own. Through your intentions and help from your ancestors, you can manifest the life you want and ensure that you come out on top no matter how bad the situation becomes. Your intention is key, though, so in the next chapter I will elaborate on all of this.

For now, I want you to know that you are not alone. That you are capable and you are strong. Everything I share with you is knowledge that has been passed down to me through generations. I hope it brings you peace and it helps you find your path on this crazy journey called life. I hope this becomes a turning point for you, where you can look back decades from now and proclaim, "Yes, I am rich. Not just in wealth and love but in experiences that helped me be the person I am today." Now, let us begin.

1

While it is tempting to immediately delve into spells, conjures and all the other fun stuff you're waiting for, the foundation for that kind of power is knowledge and understanding. Without this knowledge, you only focus on what you want and, more often than not, that method leads to a dead end. When you know what you are doing, you equip yourself with the necessary tools needed to ensure the success of conjures. I became a full-fledged Hoodoo practitioner in my early twenties but I started my education long before that, without even realizing that I was being trained for the role I will take up later in life.

My mother, father, and most especially, my grandmother, taught me what Hoodoo truly is. If you consult the internet, you'll see a lot of dark images and dark thoughts associated with Hoodoo and will also find a lot of information that doesn't add up. So even when you're given a formula for a spell, you're not able to complete it. This is because your foundation is not right. This is why I begin every book I write with the proper foundational knowledge.

Don't worry, we won't delve too deep. I simply want to make sure you understand key aspects that will make a difference in the success or failure of the conjures you learn. In this chapter, we will learn what Hoodoo is, where it comes from and why we practice it. I will also touch on some of the general misconceptions people might have about Hoodoo. Keep an open mind as you learn. Be patient as you go through this chapter. Patience is a key ingredient in any Hoodoo conjure.

Think of your journey to the end of this chapter as a good starting point for a lesson in patience. Before we begin, I want you to pretend you don't know anything. Let go of any preconceived notions or prior research you may have done on this subject. Forget the pressing need that brought you here. Make your mind a blank slate so you are not fighting the information I share with you. Instead, sit back and allow your curiosity to lead you to explore beyond the confines of what you think you know.

THE HISTORY OF HOODOO

The story of Hoodoo cannot be told without talking about the many slaves who were forcefully taken away from their homes in Africa and forced to work on farms for their masters in a new country. Their strength wasn't the only thing demanded of them. They were made to learn the ways of their masters; the way they talked, the way they dressed, and the things they believed in were imposed upon these slaves. In a strange land surrounded by cruelty and hatred, they had to learn a new language, and believe in a new god. On top of this, they had to do everything they could to survive the hardships that plagued their daily existence. But these resilient people did more than just survive. They created a community for themselves. They didn't leave their motherland behind - not completely. They embraced the new faith and merged it with knowledge from their mother-land. Then they acclimatized this new thing they had created to the land that had now become their home, and that is how Hoodoo was born.

The whips of their masters became the sword through which these slaves earned their freedom. The faith passed to them became the anchor that linked them to their identity as they practiced Hoodoo. The strange plants and leaves in this new land in which they found themselves became the channel through which they accessed healing, love, wealth, and protection for their community. Hoodoo was never about faith. These people already had that in Christianity. It was never about where they had come from. This was a new life and they learned to make something new for themselves in it. It was about honoring the journey that led them to that point. It was about acknowledging the people who had started this journey long before they did. It was about ensuring that they maintain a connection to their ancestors.

Hoodoo is a way of life. It is what we do when we wake up in the morning, the thoughts we nurture, and the intentions we carry around with us as we perform our daily tasks. Hoodoo is about access. As we continue through this chapter, as well as the rest of the book, you will understand what I mean. For now, know that Hoodoo is not the dark magic that Hollywood or non-practitioners would have you believe it is.

RELATIONSHIP TO VOODOO

One of the first things to know is that Hoodoo and voodoo don't have much in common beyond the rhyming of their names. For starters, Hoodoo is simply a way of life, while Voodoo is a religion practiced predominantly in the western part of Africa, although its presence here in America is pretty strong too. People often think Hoodoo is the African American version of Voodoo. While there are shared principles between the two practices, in truth they are more like distant cousins. For example, both seek help with the use of roots and herbs. There is also a shared belief in using our link to our ancestors as a conduit for the power that we call upon whenever we perform a conjure. But that is as far the similarities between Hoodoo and Voodoo go.

To practice Voodoo, you need to be initiated. To practice Hoodoo, you simply need to know the right recipe or formula for a spell and put your intentions to work. Voodoo is a religion while Hoodoo is not. Voodoo practices require paying homage to not just your ancestors but to specific deities associated with the voodoo faith. Hoodoo, on the other hand, while predominantly practiced by Christians, does not require any form of tributes to be paid to a specific deity. You can freely practice whatever faith you identify with and still practice Hoodoo. The only requirement, which is more of a suggestion rather than being mandatory, is to occasionally put offerings on your altar to appease the spirits and ancestors who help you with the conjures you make. This brings me to the next point.

USE OF THE BIBLE

My grandma Estelle was a devout Christian. She never missed a church service and she always bundled me up and took me with her even when I didn't feel like going. For her, faith was not something you ever compromised. Although I didn't understand what I considered at the time to be her obsession with church activities, I gradually developed a personal relationship with God, and this has been a strong force in determining how I express myself as a Hoodoo practitioner. I feel more powerful when I use Bible quotes in executing a spell. Some of my favorite scriptures for conjures are subconscious ways for me to connect with my grandmother whenever I perform those workings. But for some people, it goes even deeper than that.

The words contained in the Bible are important to every Christian. For those Hoodoo practitioners who also happen to be Christians, using quotes from the Bible helps them identify the practice with their faith. But it's less about religious than it is about firing up their intentions. As mentioned earlier, intention plays a very important role when it comes to creating a successful conjure. You can have the best ingredients assembled to put a spell together but if your intentions lack charge or energy, it will not be enough to power up the spell. The scripture for many Hoodoo practitioners provides conviction, and conviction empowers intention. This is the main reason many use the Bible when they practice Hoodoo. For non-Christians, however, using the Bible to activate a conjure might not be effective, since the conviction is not there.

The key thing to remember is that Hoodoo was created and then adapted, meaning it is not fixed or rooted in a specific religion. The first people who started working with Hoodoo created something that harmonized the things that were important to them; the Bible, their traditions, and their way of life. But you can be a Buddhist and even an atheist and your belief will not automatically cut you off from benefiting from the practice of Hoodoo. Hoodoo is for everyone, regardless of their gender, faith, or skin color. The foundation of Hoodoo was intended to help people who felt marginalized and helpless. As I mentioned earlier, Hoodoo is about access. If you need to access the powers that lie beyond the world of our physical senses, you are welcome.

Using faith to obtain that access is way down on the list when it comes to the tools that can help make your conjures more powerful.

ANCESTRAL ALTAR

The ancestral altar is sacred for everyone who practices or intends to practice Hoodoo. It is a space dedicated to communing with your ancestors. While it is possible to carry out this communication anywhere, having a dedicated space creates a concentration of power that can now be diverted into whatever conjure you are working on. An ancestral altar, as the name implies, is an altar that links you to your ancestor(s). You create that link by placing on it an object of value that belonged to someone in your lineage. The closer you were to this person, the stronger the bond or power will be. The more objects of value you have on this altar, the more beneficial it is. In addition to the objects of value belonging to the ancestor(s) you want to connect with, you can attract their spirit with offerings based on the things they liked, such as their favorite drink or favorite sweets.

Your ancestral altar doesn't have to be a large space. A small table will do. It is not something you should be ashamed of, so hiding it away in a closet is not necessary. I am not suggesting you be blatant about it, but it is something that identifies you with your roots, so be proud of showing off where you come from. If you are more of a private person, however, it is okay to put it somewhere that people do not readily have access to. You don't want someone to tamper with your conjures and spells. We don't always know everyone we let into our homes or what their intentions might be, so keeping your altar on display but not easily accessible might be the best option.

For me, one of the things I am most proud of is our ancestral bible, which sits proudly on display on my ancestral altar. Unlike the conventional Christian Bible that focuses on the words of God, this is a genealogy of my family tree that dates back over 100 years. I like to look back at where I come from and this inspires pride in me. something I believe I share with my ancestors. You might want to find an object like this that you identify with but that you also share as a link to your ancestors.

Apart from the link to your past, having a glass of water at your altar is also a good idea. Think of this as a spiritual alarm that lets you know if your spell is working or not. When you perform a spell and notice bubbles on the surface of the water in the glass, it could be an indication that a malicious spirit might have interfered with the working of your spell. And water evaporating faster than normal could be an indication that your spell is proceeding as planned. Candles are also beneficial to have on your altar, as they provide illumination for your conjure. If you have your ancestral link, some type of offering, a glass of water, and some candles, you are good to go.

SPIRITUAL CLEANSING

Our bodies carry around energies and auras that can sometimes put us in a bubble that manipulates experiences we have without us realizing it. These auras or energies can repel good things from coming into our lives or attract the wrong kind of things. And it is not just our bodies that influence the experiences we have in life. The spaces we live in also have this ability. This is why in Hoodoo, a cleanse is often carried out to enhance the effectiveness of whatever conjure we are trying to work. Cleanses serve different purposes in Hoodoo. Some of them are designed to purify you physically, emotionally, and mentally. The same purification rite can be carried out on the spaces we live in or on objects that serve a special purpose for us. For example, if you are going to perform a spell that involves love-making with your spouse or significant other, carrying out a cleanse on the bed where the event is going to occur can make the love-making ritual even more successful.

Cleanses can also be done for protection. If you suspect that you (or your loved ones) are in danger, a protection cleanse can place invisible and impenetrable barriers around your body so that even when someone casts an evil eye or spell on you, it won't work. The same thing applies to your home or business environments. Speaking of business, there are also cleanses you can perform to attract more customers to your business. Then there are cleanses that act as openers for the conjures you are creating. These cleanses ensure that the intentions coming from your mind and the energy put into the conjures are in sync. This is very important for attracting the right kind of spirit to help you. For most of the spells I will share with you here, a cleanse must be performed beforehand. This will remove any negative aura or energy that might tamper with the conjure you make. Here is a simple but effective cleanse.

The Door Opener

This cleanse is to help you create a door that opens up your spiritual senses and allows you to be more receptive to the gifts that your ancestors offer you. It opens up the portal that allows these gifts to flow to you. It thoroughly cleanses your aura and energy and prepares you for whatever conjure you are about to work on. Carry out this cleanse right before you perform the spells I share with you in this book.

The key ingredient in this spell is mint. Mint is a plant you can easily get from your garden or grocery store. In Hoodoo, it opens paths that are blocked and cleanses your mind and spirit. It is perfect for soothing a mind that is troubled by doubts, fears, and anxiety. Mint can also be used to attract success, aid communication, and help with healing... all of which are necessary for any conjure to work.

You Will Need

- Fresh mint
- Rosemary

- Cloves
- Large pot

The Work

1. Put all the ingredients in a large pot of water and boil it
2. When it boils, add the mix into your bathwater and adjust until the temperature is right. The more steam, the better.
3. Soak in the water for a few minutes. Allow the mixture of scents to envelop you.
4. Step out of the tub and air dry. Proceed with your normal activities, but avoid mirrors until you have completed the conjure you have in mind.

Before draining the tub, scoop out of the water the leaves and anything else that might clog the drain. Wrap the leaves in foil and toss them in the trash or dispose of them in a flowing creek or body of water. This conjure, though simple, can also lift curses.

I had a client who was cursed with a skin disease by a woman who considered her a rival. One day she woke up itchy and this soon turned into sores and blisters. She was put on medication for skin allergies, which is what it looked like on the surface, but none of the medications worked. The odor from the blisters accompanied by her dark dreams were indications that this was a curse. She needed to sort this out spiritually before the medications would be effective. We performed this cleanse once and I asked her to resume her medications. Within two days, the blisters began drying up.

UNDERSTANDING THE POWER OF ROOTS AND HERBS

Roots and herbs are very important tools in preparing a conjure in Hoodoo. Traditionally, spells or conjures are referred to as rootwork because we work with plants to help create the kind of results we want to manifest in our lives. A deep understanding of herbs and what they represent plays a crucial role in putting these sacred tools together to work. In Hoodoo, we believe that our world was created by a supreme being who left their essence on earth. The plants around us embody this energy, and the earth, which is directly linked to the plants by their roots, also has this imprint.

Most plants have masculine or feminine energy, though some are neutral, and these are the ones more commonly used in general spells. This detail is important because when you cast a spell you have to factor in the gender of the target as well as your own gender as the spellcaster. The energy you put into the spell should be able to bind well and help you find your target. The energy of a plant is especially important in conjures that have to do with love and romance. They also are required in spells that are intended to manipulate the will of another person.

Plants are divided into various parts: the flowers, the fruits, the stem, the leaves, and the roots. No part of a plant is wasted in Hoodoo. For example, in a lot of spells that involve candles, leaves and flowers are used. The same goes for spells that involve cleanses. For something more potent, the root is often employed. The state of the plant is also something to note. Some spells, such as love spells, require you to use fresh leaves or flowers while others call for dried leaves and flowers, which you find in cases that involve mojo bags.

Sometimes the leaves, roots, or stems are dried and then ground for use at the time and also for future purposes. So if the fresh herbs you acquired for your conjure are too much, you can dry up the excess and use them in a different conjure later. There are some cases where you are expected to ingest the conjure. This is mostly when the spell involves healing. You have to be careful in such cases because not a lot of research has been conducted to find out how our body interacts with all these plants. To stay on the safe side, avoid conjures that require you to ingest them without first talking to a specialist.

TYPES OF WORKINGS

The way you perform a conjure in Hoodoo is known as working. Each 'working' is carried out in a specific way. Sometimes, you work with wet ingredients and sometimes you work only with dry ingredients, but there are cases that call for both. Mojo bags, for example, are workings that require dry ingredients. Occasionally, you can add a little bit of oil to it, but oil is not considered wet. For a cleanse, more often than not the tools required are wet, which means fresh plants.

It's okay to alternate fresh plants with dry ones when you are carrying out your cleanses because all of them will be immersed in water. What you use doesn't significantly impact the outcome anyway. Below, we are going to learn about the different types of working I have mentioned. The recipes I share here are excellent templates to follow and if you do everything right, you can achieve the results you desire. You can also create your signature style by personalizing it, or adding a little bit of yourself into the work to make it uniquely suited for you.

My signature in any rootwork I do is the plants I use, because I harvest them from my small farm. Homegrown plants are not a requirement but I like to grow mine because I am intimately familiar with planting cycles according to the phases of the moon and how they can influence the energy in a plant. As I mentioned earlier, all plants have energy, and if you can cultivate these plants according to their cycles, you might be able to pick them for use when the energy is significantly higher. This is why even when you buy roots and herbs from other people, you should make sure they are from Hoodoo practitioners who know what they are doing. Their plants tend to be more powerful than regular ones. If you're interested in following up on this concept, I created a detailed plant manual in one of the books in my Hoodoo for Beginners series. But the point is, the more you practice your rootwork, the more adept you will be at it. Your adeptness will help you figure out some of the little nuances that add your signature to the recipe. For now, let's look at the different types of workings.

Spiritual Baths

Spiritual baths are cleanses for the body. A spiritual bath can cleanse you, your energy, and your aura. It can also serve as a tool through which you manifest a protective layer over your body, thereby keeping you safe from harm. People who feel they have been cursed also take spiritual baths to break free from whatever has latched onto them. Then there's my personal favorite; spiritual baths that can be used to create an aura of attraction. This is perfect for attracting love, wealth, or favor into your life.

Floor Washes

Floor washes are cleanses carried out for buildings. This could be your house, apartment or place of business. You use a floor wash to cleanse a space, either for yourself or for someone else. Just like the spiritual baths, a floor wash can be done for protection and also for attraction. I have done floor washes that fortify the space of my intended client. Spaces that are fortified by floor washes cannot be penetrated by evil spirits. There is a way to ensure that even people who wish to do you harm will not feel comfortable anywhere near the space. This comes in very handy, particularly if you intend to wage war on those who stand against you and also protect your peace at the same time.

Mojo Bags

The best way to describe a mojo bag is like having your own personal genie to carry around. You don't need to make a wish because the spell is already tied to a specific desire. Also, you don't need to renew it after every time it performs for you. However, mojo bags have a shelf life. You need to reactivate them from time to time. There is no consensus about how long a mojo bag remains powerful, but when you carry one with you consistently for a long time, you develop a sixth sense that allows you to detect when its potency is waning. For now, I can only offer an estimate, which is anywhere from three to six weeks, depending on the type of ingredients that were used and the intention of the spell. Some mojo bags are created to protect and some are supposed to attract. Whatever the intention is, a mojo bag is easy to carry around to ensure that you have access to whatever it is you desire.

Conjure Oils

Conjure oils are like fuel to a fire. They tend to amplify whatever it is you are trying to create. Let's say you are doing a spell for love. A few drops of conjure oil suited for what your expectations are will raise the potency of that working from 50 percent to 150 percent. Conjure oils work well with cleanses, mojo bags, and your good old-fashioned rootwork.

A shortcut I recommend to beginners is to buy conjure oils from well-known Hoodoo practitioners. You can do this for the long term or at least until you have a handle on your craft. In many cases, conjure oils are added to rootwork, but there are also times when the conjure oil is the rootwork itself. If you are going for a job interview, for example, dabbing a little attraction oil on the pressure points in your body can make you more attractive to your potential employer. The same effect can be achieved when you are going out on a date. Command oils dabbed on your lips can make the listener do exactly what you want them to do. That is how potent conjure oils are.

Rootwork

Rootwork is the traditional name for spells or conjures. Since you will be working with many plants and roots (hence the name), there's a lot of emphasis on having a good understanding of the various types of spells, as well as the spiritual significance of plants. As much as plants figure into the development of a conjure, they are not the only tool required to make it successful. You need to be clear on your intentions. The spells you create summon spirits, but it is your intention that helps direct the spirit on what to do. If your intentions are not clear, the spirit can only do so much.

The timing of the day can also matter. Some rootwork needs to be carried out at night and some during the day, though of course there are spells that can be performed regardless of the time of the day. The duration of a spell also matters. These details are included in the recipes I will share with you in this book so you know how long you should allow a conjure to cook. This time allows the tools you use in it to release their energy into the conjure. Finally, the disposal of the tools after you are done with them also matters. I will talk about this aspect in more detail later on.

Now that we have familiarized ourselves with some of the basic concepts in Hoodoo, the next step is to look into the two main subjects of focus for this book, namely war and peace. I will explain why I chose this title and what I hope to achieve with it. It is provocative, but the explanation is simple and clear. Remember what I said about knowledge and how it helps you build a foundation for whatever spell you want to work on? Since you are obviously interested in spells relating to war and peace, it's important that you understand my intentions. This will ensure that your mind and the intentions that come from it are aligned with the objective of the spells I will share with you.

2

When the ancestors of African Americans first set foot on this land, they did so in bondage. Whatever life they had before they came was to be forgotten. But this didn't mean that they didn't have a community. In this community, they tried as much as possible to settle disputes amicably. But what happened when their dispute was against outsiders and the battle was unfairly stacked against them? How did my forefathers find a measure of justice when society had built a justice system meant to deny them that? They turned to Hoodoo for help. More than a century later, the system has been overturned and transformed into one that is more equitable and inclusive, but the battle for justice and fairness rages on.

In Chapter One, I talked about how life is balanced because we have good and bad on a scale together. It is impossible to go through life without experiencing both. Most of us know that it goes against the laws of nature to have a life filled with so much good that there is not a single tragedy or sad moment in it. Of course, we can't ignore the fact that these labels of good and bad mean different things to different people, so the burden of interpretation lies with each of us. I cannot tell you what success or a good life looks like for you. I cannot determine what grief, sadness, or pain means to you. But I am going to help you find a way to channel the emotions that these experiences might cause into something creative and empowering.

I am generally a very positive person, but my outlook on life is a little stoic, in that I never presume I have control over everything. Thankfully, my heritage has blessed me with a gift that ensures I am not completely helpless, no matter how hopeless a situation might seem. When life takes a dark turn -- and I am not referring only to tragedy, but to our day-to-day struggles with addiction, dysfunctional relationships, social injustice, and so on -- we need tools to help us come out on top. That is what the title of this chapter means. The goal is not to wage war on the rest of the world just to be declared the next dark king or queen. That is not my intention. My hope is that when you come to these dark times in your life, you have knowledge of the resources you can use to turn things around in your favor. Now let's focus on four critical aspects of war as they relate to Hoodoo practices.

CROSSING

When I hear the word cross, one of two things comes to mind. First, the cross on which Jesus was crucified, and second, the state of mind that every child fears their parent will become because of something they've done. Maybe this is just a black household thing, but if your mother or grandmother was cross with you, it meant you were in big trouble. Depending on the gravity of the offense, it could mean a slipper expertly thrown at your head, or harsh words poured deep into your soul. I usually prepared for the slipper to the head because my grandmother had a way with words that would have me thinking about my existence for weeks.

In Hoodoo, however, someone being cross with you is not an emotional state of mind. It is an action word; 'a crossing'. It means someone has taken offense to you and decided to act on their feelings. This offense might not be inspired by anything you have done but simply because you exist. Traditionally in Hoodoo, a crossing is a type of spell positioned on the path of the intended target so that when their foot crosses this path, the spell is triggered in their life.

A crossing in practical terms is a curse, and a curse in this context is not necessarily what Hollywood's depiction of black magic has shown us. It is usually intended to teach the target a lesson. Remember the client I talked about earlier who had been in an abusive relationship with someone who had no intention of letting go? Well, the spell I performed that drove him out of town like a bat out of hell was a crossing. I instructed her to put it on a footpath that she was certain he would take. There are other ways to implement this type of curse and I will share some of them when we get to the spells proper. But the general idea is that the foot of the target treads on the curse itself before it is activated.

In the old days, when a footpath was made of actual dirt, it was much easier to initiate a crossing. In modern times, though, conducting a crossing on asphalt and concrete requires a little bit of innovation or thinking outside the box. Crossings can be placed in the shoes of the intended target or mixed with dirt and spread across a path that you are sure they will follow. Certain precautions must be put in place, however, if you are going to do the latter, especially if that path leads to the front door of your house. Don't worry, these details will be ironed out in any spell I teach you that has to do with a crossing. For now, you merely need to understand what it means to cast a spell of this nature.

DIVINATION

My grandmother used to say "just because you know how to perform a spell does not mean you should do it." I pass that knowledge on to everyone who starts their Hoodoo journey through me. There are certain things you do in life that bring you to the point of no return. The moment you set yourself on that path, you activate a string of consequences that could have a negative impact on your life. If care is not taken, that singular decision to perform that spell might result in life-changing results that you did not anticipate… and I don't mean that in a good way. Most of the spells that you should not cast without thinking it through fall under the category of a crossing. This is my perspective on the subject and I believe my grandmother shared my feelings.

The question of casting a spell like a crossing is not about whether you are doing good or bad, but about karma. We know that some laws cannot be broken. These are natural laws that help to keep the scales balanced. If one side tips over, it will affect us all. When the motive behind your spell is to exact revenge on the target, apply caution. Don't just follow your emotions. Find out from your ancestors and the spirits that help ensure that your conjures are successful if this is something you should tamper with. They see things you cannot see. They are set on a path you cannot follow. This makes them wiser, especially when you consider that what you do might have a ripple effect that could come back to bite you.

Finding out if your ancestors approve requires divination. To divine the things of the spirit world is not as complicated as it sounds. You simply ask a question and wait for a yes or a no. It is that straightforward. The simplest way to divine is through a deck of cards. Shuffle it as best you can and concentrate your thoughts on the question, then when you're ready, ask. After asking, you simply turn over the card on top of the deck. If it is red, the answer is yes. If it is black, the answer is no. If you are skilled in the art of tarot reading, then you can try that too. However, for a beginner, a deck of cards is very simple and effective. Whatever response you get, respect and accept it. Give it seven days before trying again to see if their answers have changed. After all, it could simply be a question of timing.

JUSTIFICATION FOR WAR

The question of ethics when it comes to practicing Hoodoo is something I have received a lot of pushback on. Some people are curious about my opinions while others exhibit righteous indignation based on what they think should or shouldn't be done. I will simply share my opinions based on my many years of experience. The laws of the universe are not the same as the laws of humanity. The laws of humanity suggest things are black and white. There are a set of rules and you must obey them. The problem with that system is that some people are left out when it comes to justice. Race, social status, gender and even sexual orientation might put them at a disadvantage against their opponents. In such cases, would you say that the system is fair in addressing the problems of everyone?

The laws that guide the affairs of the universe, both on our physical plane and spiritual one, are quite different. Of course, there are still rules that should be obeyed. But in Hoodoo, the only enforcer is karma. The issue of right or wrong is treated on a case-by-case basis and the judge is not me or whomever helps you to set up a conjure. It is the person who is carrying out the spell. Hopefully, we all have an adequate understanding of what is right and wrong. Your conscience is there to keep you in check and it is your conscience that judges you. If you knowingly decide to do something wrong just so you can satisfy the spiteful spirit you have allowed to grow inside of you because of an offense you think someone has committed, that's on you.

You may find some of the spells shared here to be ethically compromising, but as I have tried to make clear, no spell is inherently good or bad. It is your intention alone that earns it that quality.

PERSONALIZING SPELLS

The final piece in this chapter explores the personal element in any conjure. A spell is made up of roots and herbs. The plant provides the energy that acts as a bridge that connects you with your ancestors. Your intention provides direction for the spell. However, personalizing the spells helps them successfully reach the intended target. To add a personal touch to a conjure is to link it directly to the target. You can do this in several ways.

Names

Our name is part of our identity and our identity is a strong part of who we are. So if someone attaches it to a conjure, we automatically become the intended target. There are many

312 | ANGELIE BELARD

ways to use a person's name in a conjure. For example, you can carve it if you are working with candles, or you can write it on a piece of paper.

Body fluid

Blood, saliva, semen, vaginal discharge, urine, and sweat are examples of body fluids that can be used to personalize a spell. Body fluids when used in conjures are more potent because they create a stronger bond with the intended target. Body fluids are especially powerful in perfecting conjures that involve Hoodoo dolls.

Pictures

A picture is worth a thousand words. When it comes to doing a conjure, the picture of your target is a direct link to them. In the early days of photography, some people feared having their picture taken because they worried their spiritual essence would be captured in the image. I won't suggest this is true, but when you place a picture of your target in a spell, you bind them to it.

Personal belongings

We leave an imprint on items that belong to us. Items of sentimental value anchor us to memories attached to them so that even when we exit this world, anyone in possession of one of these items can still feel connected to us. To work a conjure, items of sentimental value might not be terribly effective, but pieces of clothing they have worn are perfect.

Underwear and intimate items are highly recommended. Shoes and socks can also be used for crossings.

Body clippings

A Hoodoo doll comes to life when you use body clippings such as nails and hair. Stitching the hair of the target on the head of the doll and stuffing the belly with nail clippings binds the doll to the target. Naming the doll completes the task. Burning body clippings when doing rootwork that involves candles is another way to use them.

Everything I have discussed so far forms the basis of your foundational knowledge of Hoodoo, though there is much more you need to learn. You can conduct additional research on the internet or look for a local Hoodoo practitioner to teach you the ropes. But you also need to practice. The point is that you need to keep learning so that you can keep growing. It is not just about the spells. Knowing the recipe and having the ingredients, as well as the know-how to carry out the conjure is just a fragment of your journey. As you continue to practice Hoodoo, you will develop intuitive abilities that help make you more effective. This skill can only be acquired through practice. Now that we have covered Hoodoo for war, let us look at Hoodoo for peace.

3

Rootwork for peace is more about protection than anything else. When we're young, our parents have the primary responsibility of protecting us. I was the 'apple of my parents' eye' and they did everything to keep me in a bubble, protected from the chaos of life. But as I grew, that bubble burst, and I was left to face the reality that the world can be a harsh place. Whether we're coping with everyday issues and problems or managing what can be turbulent relationships with those around us, whether we're reclusive or social butterflies, we can't escape the occasional socially awkward situation.

Learning to perform protection spells is not about creating a bubble that keeps you safe, but about silencing the voices of people who have made it their priority to harm your reputation. It is about setting up a barrier around yourself to keep out negative energy or bad vibes. It is about blocking access to you for people who might wish to do you harm. Protection is keeping you and everything you care about safe from anything and anyone who might have bad intentions.

One major area where we experience a lot of turbulence is in relationships. Regardless of the nature of these relationships, one common thread is that they are not perfect. We fight and argue and then try to make amends. But this does not always go smoothly. Our pride, our pain, and in some cases, our reluctance to see the other person's point of view become a threat to the success of that relationship. A Hoodoo spell of protection can help to put an end to these feuds and mend what has been broken. In this chapter, I want to expand your awareness of the types of protection available to you and explain why you need them.

THE NEED FOR PROTECTION

There is a direct relationship between peace and protection. When you are protected financially, physically, mentally, and emotionally, you have peace of mind. While life comes with its fair share of challenges, sometimes the biggest challenges come from people. Strangers, friends, foes, and even family will not always have your best interests at heart. No matter how amazing a person you are, evil will find a way to worm itself into your life. So your best defense is to diligently guard your peace and happiness. But that protection or peace that you are looking for will not be handed to you.

One of my favorite Bible quotes says, "...the kingdom of God suffers violence and the violent take it by force." Essentially, we live in a world filled with strife, so being a mild-mannered nice person will not always earn you your peace. You have to be bold and strong to claim it and I will give you five reasons to do so.

1. You need protection to thrive

A person whose life is plagued with troubles that rob them of their peace of mind cannot function at their best. Their ability to reach their full potential in life is compromised because they are in a constant struggle to survive. In some instances, your peace of mind may not be threatened by natural causes but by curses/crossings directed at you. One clear sign that you are being hunted lies with the types of dreams you have. If you are spiritually sensitive, your intuitive abilities will tell you what's happening. Much like when the hairs on the back of your neck rise, you just know something is off. Hoodoo conjures that are designed for protection will help to remove those things that threaten your survival. This will help your mind focus on other important things.

2. You need protection to keep a home

A contentious spouse or partner will nag you and look for opportunities to start fights. This is a recipe for disaster in any relationship. There are also other things that threaten the peace of a home. External forces such as in-laws or infidelity can damage your relationship. A little Hoodoo spell can ensure the faithfulness of your partner, tame harsh tongues, and even help your partner find a new reason to fall in love with you. Protection spells can avert a crisis and help you maintain a home where everyone feels safe and loved.

3. You need protection for positive energy

Negativity creates a dark pool of energy around a person, and anyone who comes in contact with them will almost immediately feel drained and exhausted. Some spirits are made from this dark energy, so anything they touch becomes corrupted. A chance encounter can cause you to cross paths with such spirits, and when that happens, your life can become a living hell. Even beyond this, latching on to negative energy might cause you to experience a long string of bad luck.

A Hoodoo conjure for protection will ensure that such dark entities have no access to you and have no chance to perpetuate any nefarious intention. A simple spiritual cleanse is an effective way to rid yourself of this problem. When it comes to people with negative energy, avoiding them completely works well too. But since that is not always possible, you can build a spiritual barrier around your home, office, business, body, and even the bodies of those you love.

4. You need protection to settle scores and obtain justice

Disputes can be settled in or outside of court. But sometimes, the process of helping you earn a favorable settlement can take time and many of us don't have time to wait. Perhaps people owe you money or creditors are breathing down your neck. A quick conjure can drive debtors to your doorstep with the money they owe you, which could buy you time with your creditors. And if you have a case in court that you feel is being manipulated to your detriment, you can turn the tide and claim victory, as many did during the slave trade era. Are you having drawn-out custody battles with an unreasonable ex? Hoodoo can provide you with a solution that shortens this process and initiates the kind of peace needed among all parties involved to bring about a happy ending.

5. You need protection to maintain good health

The gift of life and good health is something that people are rarely grateful for until it is taken away from them. When our minds are constantly troubled by stress, worry, and anxiety, our health can deteriorate. Too often, we prioritize our problems over our health. When the mind is in distress, the first place the impact is felt is in the body. Hoodoo might be a spiritual path, but it also has very strong physical impacts. Whenever you find yourself struggling, use a quick spell to unclog your mind, provide clarity, fire you up with inspiration, and most importantly, restore your peace. Trust me, your body will thank you.

TYPES OF PROTECTION

Protection spells are designed to service a variety of needs that we will get into later. However, these spells are presented in different packages. The knowledge of the types of protection available at this level will help you be more efficient at creating advanced spells as you grow in the craft. Protection spells are very tricky, especially when you are trying to reverse a curse or hold off the attack of a dark spirit. But mastering the basics will give you a great start.

1. Bodily protection

You are the center of your universe. If anything happens to you, your whole world crumbles. This is why you need to prioritize protective spells. Rootwork for body protection can be made in the form of a talisman or amulet. A talisman is designed to ward off evil eyes and makes you invisible to those seeking to do you harm. When my grandmother taught me this, she explained that it allows you to thrive right under the noses of your enemies.

There are also mojo bags made for protection. A protection mojo bag based on the intention can provide you or the person you created it for with physical protection, spiritual protection, or even both. You should have them on you everywhere you go. And finally, there are cleanses. If you suspect you have been cursed with a physical ailment, a cleanse is a great way to wash it off. The best part is that, unless it is specified otherwise, you can use a simple recipe for a cleanse to rid yourself of almost any curse that is manifesting as a physical ailment.

2. Protection for spaces

The most common protection conjure for spaces is a floor wash. The simplest method is to prepare the wash the same way you prepare a cleanse, and then wash the floor with it. The major difference is how you dispose of the leftover wash. We tend to dispose of the remnants of body cleanses in a stream or under running water. Washes, however, should be disposed of it under the dirt.

Speaking of dirt, because a space is anchored to the earth, you might be required to collect earth from specific places in order to include it in the preparation of a protection spell. Depending on what you need it for, you might need to collect dirt from a church, a police station, or a courthouse. In cases where you are dealing with nasty spirits, graveyard dirt might be required. The dirt might be used with other tools and either put in a jar or sprinkled across a doorway.

3. Travel protection

Travel is how some people earn a living, while many simply love doing it. But regardless of your means of travel, there are risks. A travel protection spell can help put your mind at ease and allow you to enjoy the journey rather than obsess over fears. Travel protection comes in very handy if you are going to places that may pose a threat to you. A mojo bag is best for a travel protection conjure, but you need to add an oil that attracts positive energy and spirits to you. This will ensure that no matter what happens, you will find favor every step of the way.

With that, we have come to the end of your foundation lessons on the art of rootwork in Hoodoo. In the next section, we will roll up our sleeves and get our hands dirty. Be patient. You may be anxious to resolve your situation or feel discontent because of self-doubt and low self-esteem, but your emotions must take a backseat. You need a clear mind, focused intentions, and above all, to believe in yourself. What you are about to do might seem impossible, but you have the knowledge and resources to do great things. And remember, you are not alone. Hoodoo is about putting the powers of your ancestors at your disposal. We will start with a spell for justice and war.

4

As ambitious as the subheading seems, the reality is less extreme. Even so, spells to get you justice and turn things in your favor should not be treated casually. The consequences of dabbling in something like this could have a significant ripple effect. Remember, karma is not something to mess with, because it will come back to haunt you.

I do understand, though, that waiting on the sidelines can be difficult, which is why I recommend the use of these spells, but only when you can't see any other way out. When you have exhausted every legal means to find justice but aren't making any progress, perhaps turning to help from the other side can give you the results you seek. While the hurt that others may cause us can make us feel an anger that needs to be pacified, we cannot use conjures every time someone does something that upsets us. As Gandhi said, "An eye for an eye makes the whole world blind."

Don't get me wrong - you deserve justice. Just don't make it a routine. But think of using Hoodoo as pressing the panic button. And now that we understand the gravity of utilizing Hoodoo, let's consider what should happen when you fight circumstances that seem bent on harming you. The first rule is to not allow yourself to be governed by your emotions. To have reached this point, chances are your emotions are all over the place. I understand this. But a good conjure requires focus. I am not saying that you should ignore what you feel, but make sure you are in charge of your emotions and not the other way around.

Second, do not allow yourself to be driven by the need to see the other person suffer. It is a long, treacherous ride if you choose to go down that path. Your focus should be on getting justice for yourself, nothing more. Frankly, there are people I wouldn't mind seeing suffer in this life, like an ex who mistreated me during our time together. We had a tumultuous breakup and I was strongly tempted to put a curse on him because he stole from me. But instead of allowing that pain to consume me, I focused on getting him to return what he owed me, which he eventually did. That for me was justice enough, though to be honest, if I saw him today and he was bald and pot-bellied, I would smile happily. But that is karma's job (along with poor life choices on his part), not mine. When doing a conjure of this nature, focus on getting justice over anything else, no matter how tempting that something else might be.

25 Spells for Justice and War

The spells here range from simple spells to more complex ones. They cover cleanses, washes, conjure oils, mojo bags, and candle work. There are spells to bring your enemies to ruin and spells to stop people who are robbing you behind your back. We have spells to put a homewrecker in their place and spells to ensure that a cheating partner is physically unable to continue doing so. Got a neighbor who is making your life miserable? I have a spell that will get them evicted and out of your life. The list of spells here covers a myriad of troubles. One word of caution: don't let the names of the spells fool you. Most of them have a bit more bark than bite, but they are nevertheless guaranteed to help you achieve satisfactory results.

DOMINATION OIL

Domination oil is a very important tool for preparing conjures that demand the manipulation of someone's emotions. You can use it to trigger guilt, inspire love, initiate obsession and much more. You can also use it to curse someone, get revenge, or force a situation to shift in your favor by using coercion. There are a few different ways to make this oil but we are going to use the one my grandmother taught me when I was just starting my training. This particular domination oil can only be used on the person that this conjure is prepared for.

The major ingredient in any domination spell is calamus root. It is used in any controlling or domination type of conjure. It has an appealing sweet scent that compels your intended target when infused with the other ingredients we will use. Calamus root is also known as sweet flag, and the amount of control it allows you to exert over a person's will is mind-boggling. If done right, it can turn even the most powerful people into your personal minion.

You Will Need

- Calamus root
- Sweet almond oil
- Licorice
- A personal effect from the target (hair, nail clippings, body fluid, etc.)
- Jar or bottle for storage

The Work

1. Put the person's effect in a bottle. Make sure it sits at the bottom.
2. Crush calamus root and licorice and pour them into the bottle.
3. Recite Psalm 35, which is a plea for judgment, as you prep the ingredients.

4. Pour the oil on top and allow the bottle to sit under the light of a waning moon.

5. Shake the bottle on the third night and return to the moonlight.

6. It is ready to use on the third day but if you started on the night of a full moon, wait until seven days have passed for maximum potency.

This oil can be applied to your skin if you are meeting the target in an intimate setting. You can also dab it on your hands just before a handshake if the target is someone you are having a business meeting with. In addition to adding it to another conjure, you can also apply it to a doll replica of your target and use it to control them.

CURSE YOUR ENEMIES

Knowing exactly who your enemies are is a rare privilege. It is very common for them to operate in the shadows or under the guise of friendship, so they have access to you and can do more damaging work. From here, they can also ensure that retaliation is difficult for you. However, when their identity is revealed, all bets are off. When someone has made it their life's mission to torment you, returning the favor is only natural and this conjure is perfect for doing so.

Vinegar has a sour taste and smell. In a conjure, it can ensure the target can no longer taste or enjoy the good things in life. It condemns them to a life of misery. It does the opposite of

328 | ANGELIE BELARD

what a sweetening jar is supposed to do. I love its deceptive simplicity. Easy to make but when it takes effect, the impact is devastating. On a more positive note, vinegar in a conjure can also be used to break addictions. But not in this one. This is a curse for your enemies.

You Will Need

- Vinegar
- Hot pepper
- Ashes
- Name paper
- Pieces of broken glass
- Jar

The Work

1. Write the name of the target on the paper nine times.
2. Place the name paper in the jar with the written side facing up.
3. Put the hot pepper, ashes, and pieces of broken glass into the jar.
4. Pour in the vinegar almost up to the brim.
5. Cover the jar tightly and shake it vigorously.
6. Take the jar to a dark place in your house that receives no light. Your work is done.

As you prep your ingredients, pour all your anger and malice into it. For maximum impact, you can bury the jar in a graveyard. My students often ask me what brand of vinegar to use for this recipe, but my answer is always the same: It doesn't matter what brand you use, the outcome will be the same. The cheap white vinegar will do a fine job. You should focus on finding a high-quality jar that has a tight lid. When you shut it, you want it to stay shut.

NAIL THEM DOWN

If you worry that your competition is getting ahead of you, a conjure like this one will stop them in their tracks. People may employ all kinds of dirty tricks to get one over on you. You have earned the right to even out the score and put yourself in the lead. This crossing is without malice or misery. However, it can frustrate those who are used to being on top or winning. This is why it is perfect for court cases.

The main tool for this conjure is nails. Nails have a very strong significance in Hoodoo. They are made of iron and their shape, particularly the square railroad types, represent durability, permanence, and the inability to bend. Rusty nails are preferred in rootwork. The older they are, the more potent. Old railroad spikes have a dark spiritual energy that makes them particularly suitable for crossings, curses, and banishing spells. They also work in protection spells.

You Will Need

- Rusty old nails
- Honey
- Name paper or personal effect

The Work

1. If you have hair or other intimate items, skip to step two. If using name paper, write the name of the intended target on the paper three times.
2. Completely cover the item (name paper or personal effect) with honey.
3. Under the cover of darkness, nail the honey-covered item into the ground next to an active anthill.
4. Let nature run its course and your work is done.

It is a simple conjure but by the time the sun rises, your conjure will have initiated a sequence of events that will hinder your target. It is a neat and effective trick. As long as the nail remains where you put it, the spell remains active. The day the nail comes out, the spell is broken, so keep that in mind.

HOT FOOT POWDER

This spell holds a place in my heart because of the first proper banishment case I handled for a client. Remember the conjure I prepared for my client with the abusive ex? Well, this is the conjure I prepared with the help of my grandmother. It is perfect for those who are just getting their feet wet in rootwork. Of course, you could buy a pack of ready-to-use hot foot powder at a good Hoodoo store, but where is the fun in that? Besides, the ingredients for this conjure are simple tools you can find in your kitchen… except for sulfur, which I want to talk about before we perform the conjure.

Sulfur has some cosmetic purposes and is used in the treatment of skin issues. In spiritual rituals, however, sulfur is a powerful neutralizing tool designed to render harmful energy useless. When you create a conjure like this and intend to use it on someone, chances are they have hurt you greatly. Before you curse this person, the sulfur used in this conjure will ensure that what they have done to you is neutralized. Whether the harm they committed against you was a crossing, wickedness that came from their malicious heart or just pure negative energy, you need to use this to sever their hold on you as you send them away.

You Will Need

- Black pepper
- Habanero powder
- Cayenne pepper powder
- Black salt
- Charcoal powder

- Sulfur powder
- Red sandalwood powder
- Glass jar for storage
- Mixing bowl

The Work

1. Set your mixing bowl on your ancestral table with the tools assembled around it.
2. Pour the ingredients one at a time into the bowl. The order doesn't matter.
3. Meditate on your intentions and ensure that you are clear about what you want to achieve.
4. Mix the ingredients in the bowl.
5. When they are thoroughly mixed, pour the mixture into a glass container and seal it tightly.
6. Open it whenever you want to use it and pour its contents into the shoes of the target. Sprinkling it on a path they walk on is also effective.

This powder can be used again and again for multiple purposes. The ingredients (except for the sulfur) should be measured out equally and the quantity depends on how much you want to make. The sulfur should be measured one pinch to each tablespoon measurement of all the other ingredients. In other words, if you measure out one tablespoon of each ingredient, the sulfur should be one pinch.

Increase this amount in direct proportion to the measurement I have provided here. This is important.

CONFUSION MIST

When people plot against you, there is reason to fear because there is strength in numbers. However, a little confusion in their midst can turn the tide in your favor. Ants band together but toss some ant powder on that bond and they will scatter and abandon their mission. This conjure works like ant powder, except it doesn't matter if it is a group of people or a single person plotting against you. The effect is the same. It will plant confusion in their hearts and cause them to falter in their plans for you.

The star of this conjure is the poppy seed. Opium is a mind-numbing drug and it is made from poppy seed. In rootwork, poppy seed numbs the mind and creates confusion. It can also be used in conjures for protection and for attracting luck. Poppy seed is excellent when you have court cases. Throw a little bit of confusion in the camp of your opponents and watch the team and their case against you fall to pieces and crumble from within. That is the beauty of this conjure. You don't need to do anything else other than the conjure. The confusion in the enemy camp will be triggered and you'll be able to swoop in and claim your victory.

You Will Need

- Poppy seeds
- Charcoal
- Personal effect of the target
- Incense burner

The Work

1. If you don't have a personal effect of the target, write their name on a piece of paper.
2. Light the charcoal.
3. Place the burning coal on the incense burner.
4. Toss the personal effects and poppy seeds into the incense burner.
5. As the smoke comes out, speak your intentions concisely and clearly to the smoke.
6. Wait until everything burns out completely and then toss the contents into a small hole in the ground and bury it.

For this conjure to work, your intention must be very clear. You cannot switch from one intention to another and you can only do one thing at a time. Smoke conjure can be very fickle, so it needs your strength and focus to direct it diligently. I suggest a cleanse like the one I shared with you in Chapter One. This will help you clear your mind. A little bit of meditation also helps to settle your emotions and iron out any confusion or doubts you may have. A scripture verse to calm you as you meditate might also be helpful.

SOUR LOVE LEMON SPELL

Marriage, and even relationships in general used to be between two people. But as with most things in today's world, that has changed. Sometimes it seems as though monogamy is a thing of the past. Even before I was born, relationships often involved a third party. My most common conjures related to relationships, in fact, are not about finding love but about getting my client's partner to give up a mistress or side dude.

I've seen men and women who have devoted themselves to their partners and, in many cases, helped in their partner's positive transformation, only to have someone else butt into their relationship and reap the rewards. This seems completely unfair and that is where a spell like this one comes in.

Lemons are bitter and sour but they are very medicinal, both for physical and spiritual purposes. They are used in simple conjures to sour things up for people and to throw some bitterness into the mix. The usual objective is to drive romantic couples apart. But these conjures can also be used to sour up business partnerships, dissolve friendships, and even break up marriages. If you have a third party plaguing your relationship and you suspect that things are becoming more serious, a quick souring spell would put a wedge between the love birds. A client couple who were under a souring curse felt like they could only see the worst in each other. This continued until they could no longer recognize who they were. In the end, they could barely stand the sight of each other. Thankfully, I was able to reverse it, but I'm telling you about it so you know what to expect.

You Will Need

- Paper
- Lemon
- Vinegar
- Hot pepper
- 9 pins

The Work

1. Write the full name of one half of the couple on the upper part of the paper.
2. Turn the paper upside down and clockwise and write down the full name of the other half.
3. Sprinkle a few drops of vinegar on the name paper and let it sit.
4. Cut the lemon in half.
5. Split the name paper down the middle.
6. Pour dried pepper flakes generously on one of the names and then place the other name on it.

7. Slowly lift both names and place them directly at the center of one half of the lemon.
8. Put the other half of the lemon on top and use the pins to hold the halves together.
9. Place the pinned-up lemon at the back of your freezer.

Keep your intentions clear as you prepare the conjure. You can add a little poppy seed to the conjure just to throw a little confusion into their situation. Keep the work there until what you want to happen has manifested. When it does, take out the lemon and bury it as is deep underground.

STOP A CRAZY BOSS

Most of us have had that crazy boss at one time in our careers who made our lives miserable. This person worked you to the bone but made you feel horrible every second you spent at the office. They pushed you past your limits and never gave you the credit you deserved for the work you put in. I had one of these in my younger years and I used this particular curse to ensure that they lost their job in the most painful way possible. Looking back, I don't feel bad about it. It was my revenge for everything I had been put through. If you have a boss like this, a conjure can help you get revenge, and it exacts it quickly.

The secret to the success of this conjure is a dead wasp. The sting of a wasp is not deadly but it can be very painful and cause someone to change course if they are in the path of this wasp. In Hoodoo conjures, the effects of a wasp work in a similar way. It is not fatal in any way but it hurts exactly where it is meant to. Put this in any crossing and you give that curse a sting. This particular conjure will ensure that the target loses their job in a painful way. Of course, I can't be the one to decide what pain means for your target. That is where your intention comes in. Think of how you want this to work. Be decisive. Do you want to hurt their career or just remove whatever favor they have with the company? Use that to anchor you as you prepare this simple but potent spell.

You Will Need

- A dead wasp
- Black thread
- Vinegar

The Work

1. Cut black thread about a foot long.
2. Soak the thread thoroughly in vinegar and leave it in there for about three minutes.
3. Pick up your dead wasp. Avoid the stinger as much as possible.
4. Tie the thread around the wasp three times. Keep it loose enough to prevent splitting the wasp but tight enough to keep it secure.

5. Tie the free end of the thread to the back of the door in your boss's office and your work is done.

If you are feeling extra petty, add some pepper to the vinegar when you soaked the thread. The sting, when the conjure is done, will be twice as painful. Here is a quick tip; hang your conjure somewhere where it's not too obvious. A dead wasp is one thing but seeing a dead wasp hanging on a thread is enough to spook even the staunchest non-believer. You don't want your target to know that someone is out to get them. It wouldn't change the outcome significantly, but they might suspect that their misfortune was the result of some spiritual assistance.

LOVE SPELL BREAKER

This is another common conjure that clients ask me to prepare for them. If you have never experienced what it is like to be cheated on by your partner with someone you know, be thankful. The pain from such an experience is unbearable. Can you imagine being betrayed by the one you love and then being forced to fight them?

I usually recommend communicating with your partner and then attempting to erase whatever hold the other person has on your partner. Beware, the third party in your relationship might resort to spells and other love-binding potions to keep your partner's attention, but if that's the case, this conjure will terminate that spell and give you a chance to reclaim your relationship.

For this conjure we'll work with two powerful roots; the High John root and the Jezebel root. Both play a strong role in spells that require dominance. Throwing your urine into the mix ensures that you are the one who has dominance. This way, not only are you removing the spell that has been cast over your loved one, but you are not leaving an empty space for someone else to occupy. You are asserting yourself as the dominant romantic figure in your partner's life. This can help prevent cheating in the future and if you perform other conjures along with this one, you can solidify your relationship and get the kind of justice you will not find in a courtroom.

You Will Need

- High John Root
- Jezebel root
- Lavender
- Cinnamon
- Your urine
- Transparent jar
- Picture of the target
- A tray

The Work

1. Pour your urine into a transparent jar.
2. Add the roots, lavender, and cinnamon into the urine.
3. Seal, shake vigorously, and set aside for eight days.
4. On the ninth day, place on a tray the photograph of the target who you suspect may be under a love spell. Pour the contents of the jar onto it.
5. Remove the picture and allow it to air dry before placing it on your altar.
6. Dispose of the spell by burying it.

Recite Psalm 37 as you perform this conjure. If you are preparing this for someone who is not your spouse/partner, swap out the urine with ammonia. And instead of putting the picture on your altar, bury it along with the contents of the spell. Don't forget to hold the jar away from your face when you open it on the ninth day. The smell can be quite overpowering!

ENEMY DUST

Enemy dust, or goofer dust, as it is more popularly known, is a conjure designed to bring harm to your enemies. The gravity of this rootwork tells you that this is not something you should do lightly. However, since this chapter is about getting justice, we can assume there is someone in your life who has declared themselves your mortal enemy. And in that case, you have every right to defend yourself, including by employing all the spiritual resources at your disposal. When my ancestors came to this land, they were subjected to impossible conditions and had no one to stand up for them. It felt like everyone was against them, but this conjure gave them a fighting chance.

Graveyard dirt is a powerful tool to use in a conjure. You don't touch that stuff unless you mean business. It is possible to buy it from a Hoodoo store but the best way to obtain it is to go to the cemetery yourself and collect it. You must be very careful not to collect dirt from the grave of a person who was malicious in life, though, or you will have a malevolent spirit on your hands. It's best to collect dirt from the grave of someone related to you and whose life you have some basic knowledge of. But don't just collect the dirt; be sure to leave some kind of offering on the grave, like snacks, rum, or even flowers, as these are a few of the offerings favored by spirits.

You Will Need

- Graveyard dirt
- Charcoal
- Hot pepper (dried)
- Sulfur
- Iron filings
- Poppy seeds

- Storage jar

The Work

1. Blend the charcoal, pepper, sulfur, and poppy seeds separately until they turn to powder.
2. Put the blended ingredients together in a bowl and add graveyard dirt and iron filings.
3. Stir the mixture slowly counterclockwise 99 times.
4. Pour the contents into the storage jar and keep in the jar until you are ready to use.
5. To make your enemy sick, sprinkle some enemy dust in their shoes. Their legs will become swollen and develop sores.

Psalm 37 and Numbers 5:23 are scriptures you can recite as you stir the mix. There are many ways to use enemy dust, depending on the outcome you want. If you want your target to leave town and never return, sprinkle it on their path. If you want to destroy their marriage, put their names and that of their partner in a black bag filled with broken glass and enemy dust and then bury it at a crossroads. If you intend to bring long-term suffering, then refer to spell eleven.

LUCIFER'S DUST

In Christian mythology, Lucifer was one of the most beautiful angels. Because he was beloved and favored, he began to believe his beauty, talent, and angelic status entitled him to god-like devotion. This pride led to him being cast out of heaven. There are many like this among us, who possess an overinflated sense of self-importance. Their pride and narcissism cause them to treat people they consider beneath them in a deplorable way. Lucifer's dust will humble them and cause them to fall like Lucifer did.

You might think that with a name like this, you'd need the eye of a double-headed newt or something to make it happen. But the tools for this spell are simple kitchen ingredients that you have easy access to, like onions. This spell has the power to dissolve things that have an inherently dark nature. Things like debt, pride, and even curses can be melted down by onions. If your target is a prideful, narcissistic nightmare, the onions, along with the rest of the tools in this conjure will purge them of that spirit by serving them a healthy dose of humble pie. Think of this conjure as the needle that will deflate their ballooned egos. The outcome is always very satisfying.

You Will Need

- Onion powder
- Garlic powder
- Chili powder
- Granulated sugar (white)
- Doll

The Work

1. Make a slit in the doll representation of the target and set it aside.
2. Pour one tablespoon of sugar and onion powder into a clean mixing bowl.
3. Stir nine times clockwise.
4. Add one tablespoon of garlic powder to the mix and stir counterclockwise nine times.
5. Add one tablespoon of chili powder and seal the bowl.
6. Shake vigorously before setting down.
7. Empty contents of the bowl into the doll through the slit and sew it closed with nine stitches. Speak your intention clearly with each stitch.
8. Store the doll in a dark place until the conjure is no longer required.

Hoodoo dolls should be made for you by experts as per your requirements. The dolls are named and consecrated for your intended target. However, if you are making them yourself, the easiest way to do so is to use the personal effects of the target on the doll. The doll's hair should be made from the hair of your target. The fabric should be from clothes they have worn. Other personal effects like blood, nail clippings, and so on should be put in the belly of the doll. And finally, name the doll after the person it represents.

TORMENT YOUR ENEMY

There comes a time in your life when playing nice will only sink you deeper into a hole of despair. When that time comes, you have to be ready to take off your gloves, bare your fangs and let your enemy know that you are not someone to be trifled with. A conjure like this one is used to prolong the suffering of your enemy. If they are not backing down in their plot to ruin your life, there is no reason you should either. This is another conjure into which you can pour your malice and hatred. Naturally, I don't like the idea of hurting another person. But I also don't believe in being someone's doormat. If someone is stepping on you and you have talked to them and tried every reasonable means to stop them and they continue to be the source of your pain, it is perfectly acceptable to return the favor.

Candles are a very strong spiritual element in almost every faith. The use of candles during prayers and meditations is common. The light of a candle flame serves as a beacon in Hoodoo. It signals your ancestors and any spirits around, letting them know that their help is needed. Candles are also used as representational magic, which is what we will be doing in this conjure. There are figurine candles that you could use to represent the target, but for this spell, a regular candle will work fine. The color of the candle also plays a role in the conjure. A red candle is used in rootwork for passion or love workings. A yellow candle is used to enable you to focus and concentrate and it also creates an enhanced atmosphere of happiness. Black is used commonly for curses and that is exactly the kind of candle we will use here.

You Will Need

- Black candle
- Enemy dust
- Vinegar
- Cursing oil
- Name paper
- Jar
- Mixing bowl

The Work

1. Pour one cup of vinegar into a mixing bowl.
2. Dip the black candle into the vinegar, avoiding the wick completely.
3. Gently massage the cursing oil onto the candle as you hold it over the bowl of vinegar.
4. Set the candle down and light it. Perform the rest of this conjure under the light of this candle.
5. Write down the name of your target on the name paper three times.
6. Put the name paper into the jar and pour the vinegar over it.
7. Add the enemy dust and cursing oil into the jar and mix well.

8. Make your petition known as the candle burns. Be very clear and specific and repeat it as many times as needed until the candle burns out.

9. Seal the jar and take the candle scraps along with the cursed jar to bury at a very busy crossroads.

It doesn't matter how far away this enemy is from you. You will achieve the results you desire. And rest assured that this is a long-term thing. Your enemy will be trapped in a cycle of bad luck, misery, and suffering. The cursing oil used here is easy to prepare and I share the recipe in spell seventeen.

THE WITCH'S HAND

In the old days, people used to accuse female Hoodoo practitioners of being witches. That was their ignorance talking but we never bothered to correct them because, as much as they hated witches back then, they also feared them. The curse of a witch prevented many people from doing terrible things. This particular curse has nothing to do with a witch but we call it a witch's curse because a woman places it on a man. If you have a husband or partner who is abusive and just plain evil, and you feel that divorce is not an option, then you are in luck. A witch's curse is exactly what the doctor recommends in this instance.

The crow gets a bad rap in this world. Perhaps the color of its feathers and its piercing gaze make people uncomfortable, but they are wrong to associate it with evil just because of its appearance. In Hoodoo, crows bring good luck. When you see a crow on your path, you know good luck is coming to you. If you use the feathers of a crow in your conjure, you are simply summoning the magic of your ancestors. Crows are messengers from ancestral spirits and unless specifically stated otherwise, your ancestors often come bearing good-will messages. When you use crow feathers in a conjure like this one, you are amplifying the reach of your ancestors to make this curse more potent.

You Will Need

- Crow feathers
- Damiana
- Honey
- Almond oil
- Red clay soil
- White candle
- Mixing bowl
- Heat-resistant tray

The Work

1. Place a handful of crow feathers on a heat-resistant tray outside (for safety reasons).
2. Burn the feathers and wait until they turn to ash. Collect the ashes and move to your ancestral altar for the rest of the spell.
3. Light the white candle at your altar table.

4. In a bowl, mix the ashes, damiana, honey, almond oil, and red clay to form a thick paste.

5. Rub the paste on the palm of your hand. Let every inch be covered in it.

6. Kneel with your hands lifted and palms facing up and petition the spirits of your ancestors for help. Let them know the anguish you have suffered at the hands of this man.

7. Carry on until the clay is dry and then wash the conjure off without soap. It's best to do the wash outside so the spell goes straight to the soil. After this, your work is done.

At the end of the conjure, you will be imbued with the powers you need to dominate this evil man. The air of authority he has over you will diminish. You just need to be ready to rise to the occasion by asserting yourself. To maintain the power that this conjure gives you, renew it every six months. Some men are extremely stubborn in mind and spirit. To completely overpower them, you might need to renew it sooner or as soon as you notice the effects waning. Another option is to use the domination oil in place of the almond oil.

THE EVIL EYE BANISHER

There is a saying: Keep your friends close and your enemies closer. While it makes a lot of sense, you must understand that keeping your enemies close does not mean giving them access to you. The eye of the enemy is a curse, and it is constantly looking for what it can devour. Their access to you is one of the things that gives them power over you. But if they are unaware of what you are doing or of progress you are making in your life, they will not know where or how to attack you. A conjure like this blinds the eyes of wicked people and diminishes the power of their curse. Without access to you, their powers are useless. Use this spell to banish or diminish whatever means they have been using to monitor your movements.

This conjure is more like a daily cleanse than an actual spell. You may not know who your enemies are, as they like to operate from the shadows. They use the evil eye to send curses that fester and grow without your knowledge. A cleanse like this will reactivate every time you take a bath, making sure you do not fall victim to them. The main ingredient is salt. Salt is a powerful cleanse. It is more commonly used in protection spells than in spells for justice because it nullifies or renders spells useless. But for this purpose, we are using it to not only keep the evil eye out but to ensure that it does not affect you. If you are going to be casting spells of revenge and justice, a spell like this one ensures that you have the strength and invisibility required to stay powerful.

You Will Need

- Sea salt
- Bath soap
- Water

The Work

1. Sprinkle a tablespoon of sea salt into the water you wish to use to bathe.
2. Bless the soap you use on your skin.
3. Proceed to bathe as usual.
4. Perform the bathing ritual morning and night.
5. Drain the water from the tub as usual and allow your body to air dry.

If you have just performed a conjure seeking revenge or justice, wait until midnight of that same day to take this bath. If your spell is active (in the incubation time for the spell), you should carry out the salt cleanse every midnight until the conjure is set and then you can resume your normal routine. This is because spells can be physically and spiritually draining and you need to stay powered up. Understand that salt not only protects, it also rejuvenates. That is what we are using it for in this conjure.

END YOUR RELATIONSHIP

We've covered spells for ending relationships with outsiders. This one is for terminating your current relationship.

Sometimes, bringing a relationship to an end can be the most difficult decision you can ever make. You never know how your partner is going to take it. A spell like this will ensure that your relationship ends on a sweet note.

When creating conjures in Hoodoo, you focus on certain elements to create a desired result. You use a sweet tool for sweetening or a sour tool for souring. For this conjure, we are going to combine both elements so that we can ignite a breakup but still infuse some sweetness into it so that your partner, and yourself as well, don't suffer negative repercussions from that decision. While it is possible for exes to remain sweet towards each other, in most cases you need help from the other side to maintain the desired level of sweetness.

You Will Need

- Lemon peel
- Sugar (1 tbsp)
- Salt (1 tsp)
- 9 Brand new pins
- 3Licorice roots
- Name paper
- Jar

354 | ANGELIE BELARD

The Work

1. Write down your name and full birthday as well as that of your partner on the name paper three times.
2. On the other side of the paper, write down your intention, which in this case would be "gentle break up" nine times.
3. Fold the paper away from you and then speak your intentions over the paper before placing it in the jar.
4. Hold the licorice in your hands and summon every strength that you can. This is a command tool and by connecting it to your will, you dominate the spell. Put the licorice in the jar.
5. Next take a single pin and speak your intentions to it before adding it to the tools in the jar. Repeat the same process for the other eight pins.
6. For the salt, sugar, and lemon peel, put them individually in the jar but also ensure that you speak your intentions over them before you do so.
7. When you have put everything in, seal the jar tight and shake vigorously. Call out your name and that of your partner and demand the break-up.

Your tone as you call out your name and that of your partner should be commanding. This is not you making an request. Rather you are compelling the results you desire to manifest. Shake this jar as many times as possible throughout the day and store it in a dark but warm place. For extra potency, you can put a few drops of the domination oil you made earlier. The call-out and the shaking of the jar will continue until your relationship has come to a conclusive end. The moment it does, take the jar to your backyard and bury it there.

SILENCE YOUR ACCUSERS

Any rootwork you perform that involves the use of animal parts is going to be creepy by nature, and this is one of those. We don't delve into the creepy stuff because we want to, even though there are people who take pleasure in such things. This spell is used in cases where you have someone willing to testify or say something against you that could destroy your reputation, typically a witness in a court case. A conjure like this can silence that person and perhaps give you a fighting chance. Please note that this spell is not long-lasting. You are dealing with flesh, so as long as the meat remains, the spell will be active. Still, we know meat rots over time and so will the effect of the spell. So timing is important. Make sure you use it precisely when you need it.

Cow tongue is used in Hoodoo, Voodoo, and surprisingly, in ancient mystical arts as well. The tongue of a cow symbolizes the tongue of the target. When you nail that tongue down, the target is immobilized in their speech and will remain so until you either destroy the spell or nature takes its course. Here is a note of warning: the truth will always find its way out. So if what the other person is saying is the truth, this conjure will only give you temporary control over when it comes out. But if it is a lie, you have greater chances of subduing that person completely. There are forces you cannot mess with in life and the truth is one of them.

You Will Need

- Cow tongue
- Black thread and needle
- Domination oil
- Rusty nails
- Name paper
- Flat wood
- Preserving fluid and jar (optional)

The Work

1. Write the name of the target on the name paper nine times and set it aside.
2. Place the cow tongue on the wood and make a small incision in the center.
3. Fold the name paper away from you and insert it into the slit.
4. Soak the black thread in the domination oil for nine minutes and sew the incision shut with nine stitches.
5. Place the rusty nails nine points around the tongue to form a circle and nail the tongue down.
6. Command the tongue to be silent in matters against you and bury it far away from you as is.

7. If you need more time, put the tongue as it is into a jar big enough to hold it and pour the preserving fluid into the jar before sealing and burying it, as in step six.

You must bury this spell as soon as it is done. The tongue must not see the light of day. Also, remember that this is a temporary fix. There is some disagreement on exactly how long this conjure lasts, but I would say you have from as little as nine days to as much as three months, so time it carefully and make the most of the time it buys you. But never forget that if you are trying to silence the truth, you are fighting a losing battle, because it will come out eventually.

ASHES TO ASHES CURSE

Ashes to ashes is a secret family recipe designed to bring your enemies to their knees. I use this curse on people who have made themselves a nuisance in my life. Perhaps due to familial relationships, I cannot completely sever ties with them. However, it doesn't mean that I have to put up with their annoying behavior. A curse like this puts such people in their place and makes them unable to negatively affect you in any way, as they are too busy cleaning up the mess their lives have become after this curse.

When you burn something, you generally reduce its significance to you, making it less likely to have any power over you. You often turn the table of power in your favor and gain dominance over something. In Hoodoo, we believe that the essence or spirit of a person/spirit can be found in the ashes of items attached to them. Say, for instance, your target's name is John. Burning a picture, cloth or name paper belonging to John will leave ashes in its wake. Those ashes carry the essence of John and because you are the one who burned the items, you gain dominance over John. So if John happens to be an enemy, you will have the power to crush him.

You Will Need

- Item linked to your target
- Mustard
- Sulfur
- Dry pepper
- Jar

The Work

1. The first step is to work on the item linked to your target. You have several options. You can burn their clothes, pictures, hair, or nail clippings. If you have none of these, you can carve their full names on a log of wood and burn it down to ashes.
2. Gather the ashes and put them in a jar.
3. Add mustard, pepper, and a pinch of sulfur to the ashes and mix thoroughly.

4. Seal the final product in the jar and store it in a dark place until you are ready to use it.

5. To use, just sprinkle a little bit of this powder across their path. I like to sneak a few drops of it onto their doormats.

Ashes to ashes puts a busybody in their place. It forces them to take their nose out of your business and put it back where it belongs; in their own business. The beauty of this curse (if there is such a thing) is that it wears off in a month or so. If they learn their lesson after the chaos you bring about, they can get their lives back. However, if they continue to be pesky and annoying, you can reach into that jar of reserves and toss a few drops their way again.

JOB LOSS CREATOR

Why would you want to cause anyone to lose their job? I had a client who, after nearly a decade in the industry, finally landed his dream job. The industry he was in is very competitive but that did not worry my client. It was the only place where he felt he could thrive in his natural element. His immediate supervisor, however, was a stumbling block to his success. For nearly three years, he tried to manage that relationship but things only seemed to get worse. His mental health deteriorated to the point where he was having nightmares. Leaving his job would mean giving up decades of work and his dreams as well, so the simplest solution was to cut off the thorn. And that is where this conjure came in handy.

The work is easy. We will be working with the enemy/goofer dust that we created earlier, as well as salt. We are also going to work with ashes, which we used in the previous conjure. Basically, we're making three different conjures for this circumstance. The caustic nature of this spell means you don't want this in your face, so the salt helps to cancel out that blowback, making it safe to use malice in this conjure without compromising your safety. We will talk about this more in the next chapter when we talk about protection spells.

You Will Need

- Enemy dust (Spell Nine)
- Salt
- Ashes (Spell Sixteen)
- Address of the target's place of work
- Jar

The Work

1. Prepare the enemy dust according to the previous instructions if you don't have any on hand.
2. Prepare the ashes for your target according to the previous instructions.

3. Mix enemy dust, ashes, and salt and store in a jar until you are ready to use it.

4. Scatter the mix at the target's place of work. Places where they are likely to step would be perfect.

5. If there is any left over, dispose of it at a crossroads and rinse out the jar with salt and water so that it can be used in the future.

My client's story is a very compelling reason to perform this conjure. You don't need to fabricate a story to justify your need for this conjure. You might be worried about what other people think but I am certain you have a good reason and the only person who needs to be okay with your decision is you. Doubts have a way of tampering with the effectiveness of a good conjure. So if you have doubts, maybe you should let this one go. But if you are certain that this is the right path to take, then by all means, get out there and take your pound of flesh.

THE CURSE OF AHITHOPHEL

David was one of my grandmother's favorite people in the Bible. She saw him as a man who was after God's heart and as a result, he enjoyed a lot of favors from God. One story she told me frequently was that of Ahithophel. You see, David's son, Absalom, was planning to destroy his father and take over the kingdom, so he surrounded himself with powerful and wise people. One of the wisest was Ahitophel.

David knew that with the counsel of this wise man, Absalom would succeed. So what did he do? He prayed for the wisdom of Ahithophel to become foolishness to anyone who heard him, and that was exactly what happened.

This conjure will make those who plot against you develop Ahithophel's curse. They don't become stupid or have decreased function of their brain but it will feel as though their counsel is not trustworthy enough to be applied. When they share their ideas with their bosses, potential clients, and investors, those people will not listen to them because what they hear sounds foolish. It is a perfect way to punish someone who has underestimated you. There are many ingredients in this spell but I am going to talk about the mustard seed. Mustard generally is used for planting seeds of doubt through gossip, and because we want to afflict the target with the curse of Ahithophel, that is exactly how this is going to play out. Their credibility, in terms of knowledge, will be called into question because of gossip.

You Will Need

- Brown paper
- Domination oil (Spell One)
- Poppy seeds
- Mustard seeds
- Black pepper
- Black thread
- Water

The Work

1. Cut a square shape from the brown paper and write your target's name on it nine times.
2. Dress the name paper by putting several drops of domination oil on it.
3. Add half a teaspoon of poppy seeds, mustard seeds, and black peppers to a mortar and grind them together.
4. Cut about 30cm of thread and another thread twice as long. Dip it in domination oil.
5. Place the name paper with the name of your target facing up and pour the ground seeds on the center of the paper.
6. Fold the edges of the paper around the center and use the thread to tie the base so that it forms a head.
7. Twist the rest of the paper to form arms and a body so it looks like a weird paper doll.
8. Use the second piece of thread to tie the arms and the body.
9. Dunk the paper doll in water three times and say the target's name every time you bring it out of the water.
10. Put the doll in your freezer and leave it there until you are done.

The spell concentrates on the head of your target and because it is now in a freezer, their wisdom will be frozen. The poppy seed in the mixture will guarantee confusion and fog up their mind so they are not able to think clearly. When you feel your target has paid the price for whatever it is they did to you, you can remove the doll from the freezer and dispose of it with fire.

MAKE YOUR ENEMY FAT

Sometimes attacking your enemy where you are sure it hurts them most is the key to stopping them. Some people are very vain about the way they look. If something were to alter their appearance for the worse, their pride and ego would take a hit. This conjure is designed to make the target gain weight no matter what they do. I am not a malicious person by nature but I can tell you that there are one or two people in my life whose dramatic weight gain would give me joy. I think I already mentioned one of them. If this is something you desire, this conjure is perfect for you.

One of the tools for this conjure is cinnamon. You use cinnamon to draw things to yourself. If you want to attract money into your life, for example, you use the tools that are associated with money, and then you include cinnamon to ensure that you attract the spirit of money. If you want to bring love into your life, you use the necessary tools for love, and then you include a dash of cinnamon to ensure that you attract love into your life. For this conjure, we are trying to attract a gluttonous spirit that pushes the target to eat more than they normally would, exercise less, and slowly eat themselves into their new weight. It is sneaky and may be petty but the outcome is always satisfying.

You Will Need

- Cinnamon
- Hot pepper lollipop
- Vinegar
- Name paper or picture of the target
- Jar
- Black candle
- Domination oil

The Work

1. Put the picture of the target in a jar. If you don't have a picture, you can write the person's name three times on a paper and put that in the jar.
2. Add a cup of vinegar, one tablespoon of cinnamon, and a few hot lollipops into the jar.
3. Stir clockwise and seal.
4. Dress the candle in domination oil and place it on top of the jar.
5. Call the target name three times and make your petition known. Command them to lose control over their eating habits.
6. Let the candle burn out completely and then wrap the spells in a black bag and toss it away in the trash

or bury it if you prefer to keep them this way for a long time.

If you use cursing oil instead of the domination oil, your target will develop stomach troubles that will lead to their weight gain. The domination oil ensures total loss of control over their eating and exercise habits. To end this, you can perform a reversing spell with their consent or let the spell out of the bag.

SEND SOMEONE AWAY SPELL

The presence of some people in our lives is overrated. The fact that they were at one point near and dear does not mean that they remain that way forever. It is possible that you have both served your purpose in each other's lives. Prolonging such relationships can create a negative atmosphere that will slowly eat away at you. However, simply leaving them might not be convenient. In a situation like this, you can perform this conjure and they will receive a letter or offer that will take them far away from you. It will not harm them in any way but it will save you the stress of having them remain in your life.

This conjure calls for the use of a red, seven-day candle. Seven-day candles are meant to be used for seven days, as the name implies. It does not mean that you must use them this way, but if you have a conjure that is supposed to follow a seven-day ritual, then a candle like this is more useful instead of buying one candle for each day. The use of these candles depends on the color. Red is for love work or cursing, black is definitely for cursing and white is for clarity. For this work, you will not be keeping a seven-day vigil but the energy signature bound to this particular candle is essential for this spell.

You Will Need

- Seven-day candle (red)
- A pinch of ground hot chili
- A pinch of garlic powder
- A few tiny drops of camphor essential oil
- Carving tool

The Work

1. Use the carving tool (could be a small knife, pin, toothpick, etc.) to carve the name of your target on the candle.
2. Poke three holes at the top of the candle.
3. Put all three ingredients in each of the holes in this order: pepper, garlic powder, and essential oil.
4. Set the candle down and light it.
5. Make a clear petition. An example would be, "Leave me [insert target's name] and never return."
6. Repeat these words over and over until the candle completely burns out.

7. Wrap the burned-out candles in foil paper and toss them in your trash can.

A spell like this has no malicious intent. Perhaps you even have a soft spot in your heart for your target. But their continued presence is driving you crazy. Perform this conjure once and within seven days, they will have no choice but to leave you for good. The life they will be called to is neither good nor bad. But in any case, you won't have to deal with them anymore.

MAKE A CHEATER IMPOTENT

A cheating partner is a torture for anyone. Beyond the emotional damage, there is the risk and exposure to all sorts of STDs. If your partner can't seem to control his sexual appetite, this conjure will help guarantee that he is unable to perform. If you still intend to have sex with or make babies with this person, this is not the right conjure for you. But if you want to punish a cheater, you are in for a treat.

Hoodoo often uses representational magic, meaning the items you work with are meant to represent your target. In this conjure, you will be working with an item that is meant to represent a specific part of the target's anatomy. Some people like to work with eggplant. Some use potatoes. My grandmother once used a banana. I prefer to work with something that best resembles the person's offending tool. So before you do anything, picture the organ that has now become public property and go to the market to find a food item that looks like it. It could be a zucchini, a carrot, cucumber, etc. Once you've found it, assemble the other tools.

You Will Need

- A food item that represents target's anatomy (must be solid)
- Pepper (the hotter, the better)
- Vinegar
- Name paper
- Black thread
- Nine pins
- Domination oil

The Work

1. Write the target's name and their date of birth on the paper three times.
2. Make an incision on the food product you are working with and put the name paper inside.
3. Bruise the pepper a little to release its oil, fragrance, and heat, and squeeze it into the cut next to the name paper.
4. Make smaller cuts on the food item/tool and insert bits of bruised pepper into it.
5. Dip the thread in the domination oil and then use it to tie around the food item nine times. Say these

words as you do, "[Insert full name of the target] listen to me. Your penis is now a dead tool. As you have brought me pain with it, through it, you will now know pain."

6. Use one pin to hold down one end of the thread to the food and use another pin to do the same to the other end.

7. Stick the remaining seven pins into the food item and imagine the actual organ receiving searing pain as you do so.

8. Put the food in a jar in which it can be completely submerged and pour vinegar over it.

9. Bury the jar in the middle of a crossroads. Perform a cleanse when you get home and relax. Your work is done.

For extra malicious work, bury the jar in a graveyard or toss some rusty nails into the jar of vinegar before you bury it. Your target will feel a burning heat from within his penis as it withers away on the outside. The long-term effect of a conjure like this is that even when the curse is reversed, it may never again properly rise to the occasion… if you know what I mean.

SUBDUE A CONTROLLING PERSON

Some people need a taste of their own medicine before they can learn their lesson in life. I made this conjure recently for one half of a gay couple. His partner was controlling, abusive and manipulative. When the couple first met, my client was a happy real estate agent who, even though he wasn't wealthy, was more than able to take care of his needs and even contribute to the upkeep of a home. But his partner was insecure and self-obsessed. He demanded that my client quit his job, drop his "crazy" friends and devote all his time to their relationship. Being young and in love, my client did just that, but this did not stop the demands.

In the end, his partner dumped him for someone younger, so to get back at him, I made this conjure to take away his independence and make him weak in mind so he would become subject to the control of others. The not-so-secret ingredient for the success of this conjure is rum. Traditionally, rum is a favored offering of spirits. A conjure like this causes the target to let their guard down and loosen their inhibitions. With the help of the other tools in this spell, you will expose the scared little child within the target and exploit all their vulnerabilities. Their willpower will be compromised, and they will have no choice but to submit to the will of other people.

You Will Need

- Licorice root
- Black pepper
- Cloves
- Rum

- Corn silk
- Name paper
- Black thread
- Jar

The Work

1. Write the name of the target on a paper three times.
2. Place the corn silk in the paper and wrap it up.
3. Use the black thread to bind the name paper and make sure it is completely covered by the thread.
4. Put the bound name paper in the jar with black pepper, licorice, and cloves.
5. Pour rum over it and then cover the jar.
6. Shake it vigorously and store it in a dark place.
7. Repeat this every day until you are sure they have learned their lesson.

Please note that their newfound submission will not be to just one person but to everyone who gives them a command. They will be aware of their responses and despair at how helpless they feel to disobey or go against anyone. They will have the same ugly spirit they had before but will be powerless to stop themselves from being obedient.

BAD NEIGHBOR BANISHER

A good neighbor can make a world of difference in how you experience your home. Having good neighbors can help you feel safe, and when you are distressed, they can be an additional source of comfort to you. However, if you are unfortunate to have bad neighbors, your home can become the last place you want to be. A nosy neighbor can be very annoying, but they are rarely mean-spirited. A bad neighbor, on the other hand, is something that has to be dealt with decisively. This conjure will bring about their eviction or swift relocation.

Hot pepper can be a terrible nuisance in our waking life. A little smudge on the skin can create great discomfort and this is precisely why we use it in curses and crossings. It offers enough torment and discomfort to make the target run for their lives. While this particular conjure targets your neighbor, it can be used on anyone who you have access to that you want removed from your environment. People who torment you in any way deserve an equal measure of what they do to you. However, you need physical access to them.

You Will Need

- Hot peppers (the spicier the better)
- Cooking oil
- Three rusty nails

- Nose mask (the fumes from the preparation can cause you to choke)
- Fire-resistant container

The Work

1. Set half a cup of cooking oil on a fire for about one minute, letting it heat up nicely.
2. Bruise the peppers so their oils and fragrance are released.
3. Put the pepper and the nails into the oil.
4. Stir clockwise and recite Matthew 11:28. Visualize your target as the yoke that will be taken out of your life.
5. The fumes from the oil will be strong. Be sure not to expose yourself to them.
6. Set the oil down and allow it to cool.
7. Extract the nails and place them under the doormat of your neighbor.
8. Toss the oil and pepper mix at a busy crossroads.

For those who still don't know, a crossroad is formed when two roads intersect to form an X. It is a spiritual point where the worlds between the living and the dead collide. The disposal of the leftovers from most conjures can be done here, so the spirits can consume the part of the conjure that is potent, leaving behind the harmless bits. If you want to use this banishing spell on someone other than your neighbor, you have to get it to a place where you are certain their feet will step.

SPEED UP DIVORCE

Divorce is never easy. It is a deliberate decision to separate yourself from someone whom you once loved and believed you would spend the rest of your life with. But sometimes things just don't work out. As painful as this process is, some spouses make it even harder by being extra difficult in court. They make unreasonable demands and see the court process as a means to punish their ex's. If you are saddled with such a person, this conjure is for you.

The foundation for almost every marriage is love. Whether it was real or imagined, love once existed between the two people involved and there is always evidence of it. A love note, the ticket from a play or movie watched together, the invitation to the wedding ceremony… whatever it is, this item can be used as the basis to petition the spirits for a swift divorce proceeding. This conjure is much easier if you had a church wedding or if a minister of the church officiated the wedding. If not, you will have to retrieve dirt from a place that represents your faith to include in the work.

You Will Need

- A love letter or some other item that symbolizes the love you shared

- Dirt from a courthouse
- Dirt from a church (or any religious building that represents your faith)
- Jar

The Work

1. Burn the item representing your token of affection until it is nothing but ash.
2. Gather the ash and pour it into a jar.
3. Add dirt from the courthouse and dirt from your place of worship.
4. Shake it up and spread it at the entrance of the home you share.
5. Cleanse the jar for future use and your work is done.

If you are making this for another couple, you must pour the mix at the entrance of the home of that couple. A swift divorce proceeding will ensue. If the conjure is for you, keep in mind that you will not be able to slow down the divorce process if you change your mind later on.

MAD WOMAN POWDER

Out of all the conjures in my book series, this is the most malicious and the most dangerous. I always ask my readers to apply caution before performing these conjures, but for this one, I am asking you to be twice as cautious. Some of the herbs you will work with are dangerous to ingest, so make sure you don't prepare this anywhere close to where you prepare your food. Also, wear gloves before you touch them. Another note of warning: do not use this conjure lightly. As the name implies, it will drive your target mad. If they have a history of mental health issues, this might make their madness permanent.

Mandrake root is a key ingredient in this spell. It is a member of the poisonous nightshade family and is known for its potent hallucinogenic properties. If used properly, it can cause an enemy to see their worst nightmares in their waking life. My grandmother told me that a spell of this nature is designed to torment the target to the point where they can no longer distinguish their nightmares from their real life. The madness that ensues is not chemically induced. And even when it is reversed, the target might never fully recover.

You Will Need

- Gloves and mask
- Mandrake roots (dried)
- Nightshade seeds (dried)
- Henbane flowers (dried)
- Four tablespoons of coconut flour
- Enemy dust (Spell Nine)
- A recent picture of the target

The Work

1. Put on your gloves and wear a face mask. Avoid hovering directly over the herbs as you prep them so you don't accidentally inhale.
2. Put the dried herbs together in a mortar and pound until they become powdery.
3. Pour in the coconut powder and set aside.
4. Prepare enemy dust according to spell nine. If you already have it, skip to the next step.
5. Burn the picture of the target and collect the ashes.
6. Add the ashes and enemy dust to the mandrake mixture.
7. Put contents in a jar and store in a dark place until you are ready to use it.

To use the madwoman powder, spread it on the path of the target or put it directly in their shoes. Perform a cleanse before and after you perform this conjure. The herbs used here are not commonly found, and for good reason. But if you know a good Hoodoo store, you should be able to place an order. Remember, just because you know how to do something doesn't mean you should do it. These spells are about getting justice. If you choose to ruin someone's life out of spite, it will come back to you in spades, so be careful.

5

Peace is something we take for granted until we no longer have it. We are either not aware of the gift of peace or we assume that it will always be there so we focus on our other needs. We want to be loved. We want wealth. We want health and we want the good things in life. But we don't realize that without peace, those things will be like a feast of ashes. Everything on our plate will look beautiful but will taste like ash.

When you dabble in spirit work, you cannot be too careful. A protection spell will ensure that whatever conjure you perform does not leave trails that lead back to you. Negative spirits can ride on those trails and use them as a means to torment you. Not because you did anything wrong but because that's their nature. Hoodoo takes us outside our physical world and into a world beyond. Not much is known about this other world. The only thing you can do is to ensure that you and your loved ones are well protected.

Another element you need to protect yourself from is people who are looking for opportunities to hurt you spiritually. You are not the only one who is practicing Hoodoo. And apart from Hoodoo, there are other spiritual practices that are similar but quite malicious. You or your loved ones could be put under a curse at any given time. The things you love and hold dear to your heart might be a source of envy for someone else who might take measures to destroy your happiness. Learning the basic art of protection spells can help to protect your peace, your life, and secure your happiness.

25 Spells for Peace and Protection

The spells in this chapter are designed to protect your health, mind, body, home, and love. Some spells can be made from common kitchen ingredients. A few of them will have to be bought from professional Hoodoo practitioners. All the spells here are easy to perform. Most importantly, you need to maintain a calm state of mind when you prepare a protective spell. Set your emotions aside, and focus on your breathing. Meditate if that's your thing, or maybe focus on scriptures, which we are going to use a lot here. The state of your mind can influence the outcome of the conjure so it's crucial to have it under control.

PROTECTION FOR THE MIND

When the enemy wants to attack, the first place they focus their resources on is your mind. Before they do anything physically, they destabilize you mentally. And so, when you enter the world of Hoodoo, you need to prioritize the protection of your mind. If your mind is an impenetrable fortress, there is very little someone can do on the outside that would negatively impact your peace. Apart from that, you need a calm and stable mind to be able to effectively perform conjures.

A simple, common but very effective ingredient in a protection spell is basil. Basil can be used in its herb form, or you could use the essential oil. One of the reasons we turn to essential oils is for the preservation of the integrity of that spell. When you use herbs in their plant form, the conjures expire sooner. So if you want something you can rely on to last longer, use the oils. However, if you have no problem making your protection spells weekly, you can use the herbs in their natural form.

You Will Need

- Almond oil (5 tbsp)
- Angelica oil (1/2 tbsp)
- Bay leaf
- Basil oil (1/2 tbsp)
- Sage oil (1/2 tbsp)

- Storage bottle

The Work

1. Warm-up your base oil (almond oil) a little. Putting it over hot water works perfectly. You don't want it hot, just warm enough to help it bond.
2. Crush the bay leaf and put it in the base, as it is warm.
3. Add the basil oil and twirl a bit.
4. Next, add the angelica oil and the sage oil.
5. Allow to sit for 10 minutes on your ancestral altar before transferring it to the bottle you will store it in.
6. Set the bottle under the light of a waning moon to fire up the energy in the oils.
7. Let the mixture sit for a week before you use it.

This oil is meant to be applied topically and in small doses. Apply it on your temporal lobes when you feel like you are being attacked mentally or dab a little on the palms of your hands and rub together before you perform a conjure. To get the most out of it, make this conjure at the start of a waning moon. If you are having nightmares, this oil is perfect, especially if they are of the spiritual variety. Recite Psalm 3 over the oil.

ALTAR OIL

Every rootwork in Hoodoo requires the blessings of your ancestors. This altar oil is a variation of what people commonly call Abramelin oil. You use this to summon the spirits that help you empower the conjure. This particular variety is also made to be a protection spell so you don't accidentally summon the wrong kind of spirit that might mess up your conjure or decide to be mischievous. So after protecting your mind, the next place you want to protect is the altar from where the power will be seeping in.

We are making a type of barrier oil. The stars of this conjure are frankincense and myrrh. They have long historical roots in almost every religion and are known to have healing properties, not just physically but the type of healing that restores spiritually, which is what we need for the mind. We are going to be using essential oils in this conjure because it saves time from preparing our own oil. Plus, if you want to start from scratch, you may not have easy access to the base ingredients.

You Will Need

- Olive oil (10 tbsp)
- Cedar oil (1 tbsp)
- Frankincense (4 tbsp)
- Myrrh (2 tbsp)
- Dark storage bottle

The Work

1. Start with the base oil first. Then add frankincense, myrrh, and cedar oil, in that order.
2. Optionally, you can add cedar wood chips to bring an earthiness to the mix.
3. Pour the oil mixture into the dark bottle and seal tightly.

Use this oil on your altar every morning. Recite Psalm 23 and call on the spirits of your ancestors to walk you through your day. Thank them for the help they offered you previously. Make your petitions for the day known to them and lean into the sense of safety they provide you. This is a relationship of trust, so you have to reach out, not just with your petitions but with your emotions.

PROTECTION CLEANSE

In the previous chapter, I shared a protection cleanse mainly for conjures that have to do with heavy emotions, like getting revenge or ensuring that justice is served. That's because some of the herbs you will tamper with and the feelings you have to confront in that process will elicit some malicious emotions. A protective cleanse like the one I shared will protect you from that. This one, on the other hand, is meant to set up barriers so you are always in a safe space.

The key ingredient in this conjure is hyssop. It's great for its medicinal uses and healing properties, but in Hoodoo, the use of hyssop is inspired by its role in the Bible. From the Old Testament when it was used for purification and cleansing to the New Testament when it was used on Jesus when he was bruised and battered, you can see the importance of it. If you have had a traumatic day or performed a rather hectic conjure, using this cleanse will heal you spiritually and at the same time create a protective barrier to ensure that the after-effects don't come into play in your day-to-day life.

You Will Need

- Hyssop
- Apple cider vinegar (2 tbsp)
- Salt
- Cedarwood essential oil
- Coconut milk (1 cup)

The Work

1. Bundle the hyssop in small bundles and set in a pot of water to boil.
2. Add salt to your bathwater while the hyssop heats up.
3. Add in the coconut milk, the apple cider vinegar, and a few drops of cedarwood essential oil.

4. When the water with the hyssop boils, add it to what you already have in the tub.

5. Step into the tub when the temperature is right for you and completely immerse yourself.

6. Sit up and use the hyssop bunches to wipe down your body. Visualize the negativity leaving your body as you do so.

7. Step out of the tub and air dry. Strain the herbs from the tub and drain the rest. Dispose of the leftovers at a crossroads.

Recite Psalm 51:7 as you rub your body down with the hyssop. Visualization is key here to imagine whatever you feel is plaguing you leaving your body. If you are into crystals, putting amethyst crystals in the tub water can enhance the healing and protective ambiance for your conjure.

SELF-PROTECTION

The world can be a scary place and while your home might be the place you feel safest, it still doesn't guarantee your safety. There are measures you can put in place to keep you protected at home, but what happens when you're out? What do you do when you encounter someone who curses you with an evil eye? My grandmother always advised me to be proactive. Don't wait until something happens before protecting yourself from it. Building a barrier of protection around yourself makes it difficult for such things to affect you.

As I've discussed throughout, Christianity played a significant role in the formation of Hoodoo. As a result, it often includes the use of saints and biblical scriptures for protection. In Hoodoo, it is believed that the church or dirt from the church is a protective haven for everyone. The church is considered sacred ground that evil spirits and malicious intentions cannot penetrate. In this particular conjure, we will be using church dirt to manifest a wall of protection around you.

You Will Need

- Your picture
- Salt
- Silver coin
- Three clear nails
- Six smooth river stones
- Dirt from a church ground
- Black pouch

The Work

1. Fill the black pouch with salt.
2. Put your picture into the pouch and add the dirt from the church.

3. Add the nails to keep you anchored, silver coin for spiritual protection, and river stones to push back any tide of affliction, then seal the pouch.
4. Bury it in your backyard, or on church, mosque, or temple grounds.

If you are burying the pouch on church grounds, you can skip the church dirt. If you are not a Christian, you need dirt affiliated with your place of worship, whatever that may be. This is because prayers are performed there and this attracts protective beings and entities. Psalm 59 is perfect for this conjure.

PATH PROTECTION

You can see how easy it is to step on a curse. Anyone can prepare spells that can be tossed on your path to create chaos in your life and all you have to do is to step on it for their intentions to be activated. If you suspect you have stepped on a curse, this simple conjure is a way to get rid of it before it sets in. It is most effective when you carry it out before the spell begins to manifest in your life. Of course, it's not always easy to know if you've stepped on something. You have to be spiritually intuitive and extra vigilant. Perhaps you saw something suspicious that looked like the remnants of a spell? In any case, acting swiftly will prevent further damage.

Onion has a way of drawing something out. My grand-mother used to hate it when I left half an onion out for later use because she believed that a half onion, when exposed, draws into itself whatever is in its environment. That is what we will rely on for this conjure. Once it is positioned in the right place, it will draw out any negative energy or residue a spell has left behind. You can do this as a protective measure every time you come home, since you can't be sure what you stepped on while you were out.

You Will Need

- Onion
- Hyssop cleanse (Spell Three)

The Work

1. Cut a nice medium-sized onion vertically in two.
2. Rub your right foot with one half and your left foot with the other half.
3. Put on a clean pair of socks when you are done and proceed to execute the steps in Spell Three.
4. Toss out the onion and the leftovers of the hyssop cleanse.

The common Bible verse for protection is Psalm 91. Recite this as you soak in the bathtub. Use the power of visualization to picture whatever negative energy or spell you might have stepped on leaving your body. You need to see it to enhance the potency of the conjure.

BLOCK BLACK MAGIC

Before we are attacked, we often receive signs, especially if we are spiritually intuitive. We all have guards who watch over us. Have you ever met someone new and barely talked to them but all your alarms went off anyway? Something was warning you about them. That is your intuitive process kicking in. When you are spiritually attuned, something similar happens. You experience a sense of urgency that demands you to take action. My grandmother told me that most of the time this is your spirit guide alerting you to the danger ahead, and this conjure can be the first of many steps to keep yourself protected.

In rootwork, a juniper is considered to be a power plant that offers strength and protection. Because of its strong spiritual energy, we often use it in rootwork that gives us courage, strengthens our willpower and in this case, blocks out black magic. We are going to enhance the power levels of this plant by inserting it into a mojo bag that we will carry with us everywhere we go. Think of it as your spiritual bodyguard.

You Will Need

- Nine juniper berries
- Salt
- Camphor essential oil
- Red felt bag
- Bowl

The Work

1. In a bowl, mix two tablespoons of salt with three drops of camphor essential oil.
2. Pour the mix into the red bag and add the nine juniper berries.
3. Seal the bag and leave it overnight on your ancestral altar.
4. By morning, it is set. Carry it on your person at all times. Feed it with a protection oil every nine days.

I recommend this conjure if you are traveling through some place where dark magic is practiced a lot. You may not be the direct target of those dark spells but you could easily be caught in the crossfire. This mojo bag protects you from black magic, be it deliberate or accidental. If your stay in this place is longer, you might need to work on a protection spell that lasts longer.

HOME CLEANSE

When you arrive at a new place, be it for business or work, you need to do what you can to make it your own. The first step is to clean it up. You can hire a cleaning crew to help out but you would still need to perform a spiritual cleanse to remove any negative energy and drive off spirits that might want to do you harm. A cleanse of this nature is simple. You just need Florida water.

Florida water is rumored to be made from the legendary and mythical fountain of youth. Of course, this tale was fabricated for marketing purposes. The part that is real, though, is the spiritual properties of this water. It heals, cleanses, and helps to amplify protection spells. Initially, rootworkers used just one recipe. But over time, we discovered that it can be adapted to suit each individual. This is thanks in large part to the increase in the production of a variety of essential oils. I will give you the base formula here and you can create a blend that matches your identity based on gender, personality, element, and so on.

You Will Need

- White Rum [or vodka if you prefer]
- Orange peel (from one orange)
- Lemon peel (from one lemon)
- Cinnamon stick
- Bergamot essential oil [10 drops]
- Clove essential oil [10 drops]
- Rosemary essential oil (or the sprigs if you prefer) [10 drops]
- Orris root [one teaspoon]
- Rose petals [one cup]
- Basil [a few leaves, either fresh or dry]
- Three of any of the following oils: lavender, vanilla, jasmine, ylang-ylang, sage, neroli) [five drops of each]
- Bowl

For home cleanse:

- A broom that has never been used before
- Water

The Work

1. For your work to be very effective, begin preparations on the night of a full moon. This means that you need to gather your tools the day before.
2. In a bowl, mix one cup of white rum/vodka, essential oils, rose petals, orris root, basil, cinnamon stick, lemon, and orange peels.
3. Stir clockwise nine times and allow to sit for nine minutes on your altar.
4. Transfer the mix into a jar and then seal tight.
5. Place the jar in your window at midnight. Choose somewhere that the moonlight touches and leave it there until the moment just before the sun rises.
6. Set it aside somewhere cool and dark. Leave it to sit for the next 29 days.
7. Strain the herbs from the jar if you want and toss them in a pool of running water or use them as is.
8. To use in a home cleanse, mix one part Florida water and three parts water.
9. Sprinkle the mixture on your windows, door frames, corners of the house, and the floor.

10. Use the new broom to sweep the entire house towards the entrance. Continue sweeping down to the path. Let the whole house/room air dry and you are done.

Florida water has multiple uses. You can feed your mojo bag with it, wear it as a cologne, or spray it on your doorway as a shield. I like to put some drops in a bowl of water and put them beside my bed when I am having trouble remembering my dreams. Buying Florida water from professionals can save you time and effort too.

CALL ON THE SAINTS

Every traditional Hoodoo worker believes in the power of the saints. Each saint has a designated role. Some help to bring love into your life, some help you to get justice when you have been unfairly treated. Because we are dealing with protection, we are going to focus on the patron saint of divine protection and deliverance, Saint Michael. In the Christian faith, Saint Michael is believed to be an archangel, a warrior who can be depended on in the fight for good.

My grandmother taught me that no matter how much we think we know about Hoodoo and the world that lies beyond our own, we are not invincible. There are spiritual battles that will bring us to our knees and make us fear for our life. In such times, your powers, knowledge, and herbs might feel worthless, but this is not the time to give in to despair. It is instead when you must call on the divine to come to your aid. And this protection prayer/conjure is one of many you can perform during such periods.

You Will Need

- Image of Saint Michael
- Red candle
- Coffee powder
- Petition paper

The Work

1. Set down the image of Saint Michael at the center of your altar.
2. Light a red candle in front of it.
3. Write down your petition and your name three times.
4. Sprinkle coffee powder on the paper and fold towards you.
5. Burn the paper in the candle flame and pray to the archangel as you do so.
6. Pray for guidance, protection, and spiritual aid as you watch the candle burn out.
7. Gather the ash and candle residue to bury in your backyard. Leave the image of the saint on your altar until that feeling of dread is completely gone.

When you have finished, donate to either the police, veterans, or firefighters. People who have officially served in this capacity are close to the heart of Saint Michael, since he is the patron saint of protection. Donating to them will put you in his good graces. You can also leave offerings at your altar daily.

TRAVEL PROTECTION

When you or someone you love are going on a long journey, whether by road, air, or sea, it is natural to worry about your own or their well-being. Accidents happen and sometimes cannot be avoided. However, some accidents are instigated by malicious spirits who simply wish to harm and there are things you can do to ensure that you or the person you love can reach their destination safely without any negative incidents. And even beyond malicious spirits, if many people are aware of the trip, there could be someone who wants to see the traveler reach a tragic end. This tool can prevent that from happening.

Mugwort, which is the main ingredient in this conjure, is often used for astral travel. When you are on the astral plane, there are spirits that want to keep you trapped there. Mugwort repels such spirits and keeps you safe. Even though accidents happen, there are elements of spiritual attacks in certain accidents, and using this conjure will help to keep the target protected from those spiritual elements so that their journey is smooth and safe. For an added layer of protection, it will invite friendly spirits associated with travel to ensure safety to the destination and even a safe return.

You Will Need

- Mugwort
- Personal effect or name paper
- Green thread

The Work

1. Place the mugwort on a table. Spread the leaves out like a fan.
2. Place your personal effects at the center of this fan. If you are performing this conjure for someone else and you don't have their personal effect, you can write their name down three times on a piece of paper.
3. Roll the plants around the personal effect or name paper in a way that it completely covers it. Tuck in any rough edges.
4. Use the green thread to secure the mugwort so it stays in place. Fasten the thread to the wrapping so that one end of the thread is left dangling.
5. Use the dangling end to tie to the belt you are wearing or the handbag you will be carrying. Another way to use this is to hang it somewhere close to your seat. Just make sure it is close to you throughout your trip.

Before you use the thread to wrap the plant, you could allow it to soak in protection oil for a while. This is optional. But if you have protection oil on hand, it will help by adding extra power to the spell. When you are back from your trip, you must dispose of it properly, either by burying it at a cross-roads far from your home or wrapping it in tin foil and discarding it in your trash can.

BONE POWDER

Despite what the name implies, bone powder is not made from any bone, whether human or animal. It is made from crushed rocks. We will be using three varieties here. The objective is to protect every conjure you make from eyes that might reveal your secret. My ancestors believed that the best fruit on a tree can attain its ripeness and beauty when it is hidden from everyone else. In the same way, your spell is potent and strongest when no one is aware of it. This is one of the reasons we bury our conjures when we've finished making them or hide them in a place no one can see.

Dirt and rock in Hoodoo hold strong spiritual properties. The things you find under the rock are also valuable but for this conjure, we are going to focus on the rock itself. In biblical times, certain grounds were considered hallowed because of the properties of the rock. Moses himself was asked to take off his shoes because the ground he stood on was holy. The rocks we work with here are not divine but they do possess the ability to erect spiritual barriers that will keep prying eyes out. The nature of the second requires a little bit of courage, as earth spells are not as malleable as those made from plants. Be strong.

You Will Need

- Mortar, dry and crushed
- Red brick dust
- Clay, dry and crushed
- Ashes obtained from burned cedar or pine tree wood
- Offerings for spirits
- Mixing bowl

The Work

1. Put all the crushed rocks into a mixing bowl.
2. Stir counterclockwise nine times. As you do so, make your petition known in clear and concise language. What you want to communicate is that the powder you make from this conjure will form an impenetrable ring of protection whenever you cast a circle and no one can enter that circle without your permission. Be very clear and deliberate about saying no one.
3. When you are done with your petition, put the contents of the mixing bowl into a jar and seal it shut.
4. Go to a graveyard or cemetery with the jar and offerings for the spirits.

5. Place the jar in front of the cemetery and speak to the spirits guarding it. Let them know that you have come with a petition and that you would like those who guard the place to answer your petition. Leave the jar and the offerings there for three nights.

6. The morning after the third night, pick up your jar and take it home. Whenever you want to prepare a conjure, use the dust from the jar to form a circle and perform the conjure within that circle. Nothing will be able to see or sense what you are doing within that circle.

Be very cautious about the type of cemetery you go to. Avoid abandoned and unkempt cemeteries, as angry spirits tend to roam such places. They might answer your petition but it will come at a cost that you might not even be aware of or be ready to pay. If you have ancestors at a particular cemetery, that would work best. But you have to make it a habit to visit the cemetery with offerings from time to time. Don't go there only when you need their help.

CLEAR EYES POWDER

There sometimes comes a point in our lives when we are confused. We look for answers but aren't able to find them because our mind is clouded with doubt, regrets, and other emotions that act as shackles. To break free, we perform conjures that will open our minds to the truth around us and keep us internally balanced. This is probably why when enemies attack, they flood our minds with doubts. The second you start questioning yourself, that will be the moment your defenses will become shaky and eventually fall apart ... unless you fix it. That is what this conjure is for.

Sage is a cleanse that is used in Hoodoo, Voodoo, and even witchcraft. Its spiritual properties are highly revered, but people have overused it to the point where it has become a cliché. But don't doubt its strength. In this conjure, we are going to use sage along with other herbs to open up your mind and set you free from the lies that keep you bound and unable to fulfill your potential. Use it to rid yourself of fear so you can stand strong and defend yourself. No matter what the enemy throws at you, a clear mind can intuitively intercept attacks and keep your heart, hearth, and body protected.

You Will Need

- Eucalyptus leaves [dry]
- Sage [dry]
- Lemon leaves [dry]
- Mint [dry]
- Cornflower petals [dry]
- Five drops of protection oil
- Blue candle
- Jar

The Work

1. Put one cup each of all the dry herbs in a blender and grind them to powder.
2. Empty the herbs into a jar and then bless it.
3. Mix two tablespoons of the herbs and five drops of the protection oil you made in Spell One. It should form a loose paste.
4. Rub the blue candle with the paste you have made.
5. Light it for one hour until it completely burns out. Concentrate on the flame of the candle and picture the fire burning away any sense of doubt that has been imprinted in your mind.
6. On the day the candle burns out, gather the remnants and dispose of them at the crossroads. Your mind will be free and clear.

The clear mind powder can be used in multiple ways. If you have an enemy who is masquerading as a friend, putting a pinch of this powder in your shoes before stepping out will reveal that person to you. They will be the one who notices your shoes or steps on them. If you are feeling confused and torn between multiple decisions, grab a handful of this powder with some cloves and toss it into an open fire. A clear path will be revealed to you. The jar of powder should be stored in a cool dark place for future use.

PROTECTION FROM INJUSTICE

The world might sometimes seem like a place where life is fair to all but the reality is far different. At some point, most of us experience injustice that has the potential to derail us from fulfilling our destiny. Fate plays a role in the hand that life deals us, but the beauty is that it creates a balance where you can reclaim control and decide your own fate. One way to do that is to protect yourself from injustice in the world. This is especially important if you live in an environment where discrimination is rampant and the concept of fairness is foreign.

Oregano is one of the key ingredients in this conjure. It is a common herb used for cooking, but its spiritual properties are highly coveted. In Ancient Greece, oregano was believed to have been favored by the goddess of love, Aphrodite. This is probably why they used it in rituals for young married couples. And when you think about it, what greater protective force is there in life than love. Oregano conjures attract spirits that will feel protective towards you. The rum and salt in this spell will create a likable energy around you that makes it difficult for people to treat you unfairly. When you are favored, negative biases go out the window and when that happens injustice toward you becomes a rarity.

You Will Need

- Name paper
- Oregano
- Rum
- Black feather
- Salt
- Cotton wool or linen and twine
- Jar

The Work

1. Write your name or the name of your target on the paper three times.
2. Fold it towards you and put it in a jar.
3. Add the oregano, half cup of rum, six black feathers, and a teaspoon of salt.
4. Stuff the top of the jar with a fist full of cotton wool. If you don't have that, spread a piece of linen over the jar and tie it around the top with the twine.
5. Leave the spell outside among shrubs or under a tree. Every time you or the target of the spell is accused of something, shake the jar. The spell will be activated.

You can also use this spell whenever you feel threatened. The effect is pretty much the same. Think of the jar shaking process as ringing the bell that summons your protectors. Feed the jar with good quality rum at every full moon. This is not a moon working but it charges the spell and gives it a power boost. When it runs completely dry, it is time to prepare a new one.

SEXUAL PROTECTION

Cheating, whether physical or emotional, has destroyed countless relationships. But it is not always the actual act of cheating that brings a relationship down. What often does it is when sex is used to manipulate the person already in a committed relationship into continuing with what was supposed to be a one-night stand. Some women use this to hold a man down, either by getting pregnant or by sexually manipulating him into a submissive position in which he does whatever she wants. This can also happen when a man tries to claim a woman as his and then manipulate her into leaving her committed relationship. A conjure like this protects the target from being in such a position.

To inspire passion, with you having total control, we will use licorice root. This root is popular in candy but in spiritual work ranging from Hoodoo to European mysticism, it plays a significant role in spells and conjures that have to do with lust. It is used to compel the targets and also to strengthen romantic relationships, both of which are perfect for what we hope to achieve with this spell. Licorice root has a very strong essence and because we are going to be using it with domination oil, we need something to balance it out, like hickory nuts, which embody strength but flexibility at the same time. This is a balanced conjure that will not overwhelm the willpower of your partner. However, it will make them open to suggestions that will protect them from becoming sexually manipulated by anyone else, even if that person is using magic.

You Will Need

- Licorice root
- Hawthorn thorns
- Hickory nuts
- Domination oil
- Purple mojo bag
- Mixing bowl

The Work

1. Put one tablespoon of all the herbs into a mixing bowl.
2. Add three drops of domination oil and stir the mix clockwise.
3. Put everything into the mojo bag and hang it somewhere over the bed where you and your partner sleep.
4. Tonight, to prepare the conjure, ensure that you and your partner make love under that bag.
5. When you've finished, store the bag in a dark place. Your work is done.

Making love under a mojo bag enhances fidelity. When you put the mojo bag under the bed you make love on, it enhances passion in a relationship that is lacking it. Fair warning, after this conjure, your partner is going to experience a significant boost to their libido. So, prepare yourself for raunchy activities around the house.

BLACK SALT

Building a protection spell around your home is as basic as it gets. You want to keep negative energy out while ensuring that your home is open to spirits that come with goodwill and good tidings. Witches in olden days used to simply cast circles with salt or special crystals to achieve that result. But in Hoodoo, we prefer to add depth to that salt. Before you start making conjures, one of the first things you should learn how to do is to make the space safe where those conjures are performed, not just for you but for the spirits that show up, as well as the inhabitants of the home. This protection spell enhances the ambiance of your home, making it conducive for performing conjures.

To make a good protection spell, you need look no further than salt. Salt is a powerful protection agent in any spell or conjure. It has neutralizing powers, especially when you combine it with ashes. If you pour salt and ash over a conjure, it's a bit like pouring water over the flames of a roaring fire. You might not be able to put it out completely but you tamper with the energy of that spell, significantly reducing its potency. To make this combination fully protective, you need to be intentional about the type of salt used and how you integrate the ingredients.

You Will Need

- Sea salt
- Black pepper
- Charcoal
- Wood ash
- Jar

The Work

1. Blend the black pepper with the charcoal until it has a powdery consistency.
2. Add salt and wood ash to the mix. Stir clockwise 13 times.
3. When it is thoroughly mixed, put it into a jar and set it aside for when you need it.

Using black salt is simple. You can put it on a building, on a person, or on an object. Whenever you want to use this black salt, add a little bit of protection oil and rub it on whoever you want to be protected. If you are Catholic and have participated in Ash Wednesday, then you understand how this works. The mark doesn't have to be on their forehead or in any visible place. Just having black salt on their body is enough to identify them to the spirits you summon as beings who need to be protected. The same thing can be done to property that you want to keep out of evil hands. If you are protecting a building, use the black salt to cast a circle around it. For this conjure, it is best to work with wood ash extracted from pinewood. If you don't have access to that, you can work with regular wood. Reciting Psalm 91 as you prepare this conjure gives it a boost.

PROTECTION AND POWER HAND

Whether we like it or not, the art of Hoodoo is not an exclusive club. There are millions of people practicing it and they do it for a variety of reasons. Some people prefer to focus on darker workings; the type that involve dangerous spirits. These types of workings create curses that can permanently destabilize a person's life. In the previous chapter, we touched on one or two areas that might feel dark. But those are very mild compared to what people can do with Hoodoo. You can't control the actions of other people and so in this case, the best mode of attack is a strong defense. And that is what this conjure is for; to protect you from dark magic.

The working for this conjure is very messy, as you will be using your urine or the urine of the target you want to work with. You need to use your hands to prepare the work and this might require touching that urine. If you are squeamish about that, you can substitute urine for the person's cologne or if the conjure is for you, your own cologne. I strongly recommend using urine though, as it adds a personal element that binds the conjure to the target. This is about protection against dark magic. Cologne can be infused with some other ingredient that might not interact well with the tools you use for this conjure and might have an undesirable effect on the spell. Urine brings a personal signature that makes it binding and therefore stronger.

You Will Need

- Name paper
- High John root
- Red cotton thread
- Urine
- Salt

The Work

1. Use your hand to cut out a square shape from brown craft paper the size of your palm.
2. Write down your name or the target name on the paper three times using a pencil or permanent marker.
3. Drench the name paper in about two tablespoons of urine (or cologne, if that's what you've chosen).
4. Measure half a teaspoon of salt and sprinkle it on the name paper.
5. Place the High John root at the center of the name paper and then wrap the paper around it until the root is completely covered.

6. Bind the paper wrapping with red thread to make sure the paper is secure and stays in place. Be careful not to pull too tight, as the paper is completely drenched in urine!

7. Place it under the sun to dry for three days. When it is dry, you or the target must carry it with you at all times.

As always, I like to dip the thread that I work with in a conjure oil that is suitable for my intention. For example, since this is a protection conjure, I will use the protection oil on the thread. Mind you, this is not mandatory but simply a personal preference. Using it gives me an extra layer of comfort in the knowledge that I am getting full protection. To keep the power of this conjure strong and effective around the clock, you need to feed this charm with Florida water every seven days or every Monday. The recipe I shared in Spell Seven would be perfect for this.

EGG CLEANSE

If you have been hit with a curse or you suspect that you have been hit with a curse, a quick way to fix that is with an egg cleanse. This practice is very common in Hoodoo. Voodoo practitioners also use this method. When you use an egg in a conjure like this one, two things happen. You can divine if you have been cursed and then you can cleanse yourself from the curse. The egg will remove any doubts you

412 | ANGELIE BELARD

may have and also draw out whatever it is that has been placed in your body. You don't have to wait until you are manifesting the physical symptoms of the curse. The second you suspect it or have received signs that you might be cursed, you should take this action.

For this ritual, we are going to combine holy water with the egg cleanse. You can obtain holy water from a church or make your own. As a Christian, I prefer to use holy water from my church but I know that not all of us share the same faith, so you can make your own according to your belief. The primary ingredient in making holy water is salt. The water should be obtained from a natural source, while the salt should be sea salt. Bless the salt and the water using the scriptures and then combine them. People who practice Buddhism, Hinduism, and others have their own versions of holy water. Research that and create a version of their recipe that you are comfortable with.

You Will Need

- Egg
- Frankincense (incense)
- Holy water
- White candle
- Jar

The Work

1. First, light your candle and place it on your altar.
2. Concentrate on the candle flames and draw strength from them. Know that you are safe, regardless of what the enemy might have done to you.
3. Place an uncooked medium-sized egg at the center of the altar.
4. In a small bowl, pour out the holy water and then dip the egg into it three times.
5. Starting from the crown of your head, rub the egg in a downwards and outwards direction without actually touching your skin or any part of your body. If you can have someone else do this for you, that would be ideal. You can be standing or lying down for this. Just ensure that the egg sweeps every part of your body.
6. When you are done, place the egg gently inside a jar and seal it. Take this jar to a crossroads where you will smash the egg at midnight. Declare that whatever curse was placed on your body is now done and gone.

Check the color of the egg after you have smashed it. If it is clear, it means that there was nothing on you. But if it is spotty or colored, it means that your suspicions were right; there was indeed a curse but it has now been lifted. Go back home and perform the hyssop cleanse to ensure that you are thoroughly purified and protected inside and out. If the curse has started physically manifesting in your body as some kind of sickness when you are rubbing down your body with the egg, you can touch the egg to the affected part of your body. One more tip: if you are using the Bible as you prepare your conjures, recite Psalm 23 and Psalm 91 when you light the candle before doing anything else.

MIRROR HONEY

When you work in a company or at an established organization, your biggest asset is not the number of degrees you have or the references that vouch for you, it is the quality of your ideas. If you can consistently bring in great ideas that drive up sales and push the company closer to its goals, you become a valuable asset. Especially if you know how to stand up for yourself and play office politics. This probably explains why some people are willing to steal ideas so they can secure their place in their organization. If you have an idea and are worried that someone might claim it as their own, a conjure like this one will protect your idea and keep it yours until you are ready to share it.

One of the tools we are going to use in this conjure is honey. People think of honey as a sweet ingredient and therefore think it can only be used in sweetening spells or in things that have to do with romance. While this is true, there is an aggressive side to honey if you know how to combine it with the right ingredients. Many protection spells can be made using honey. The idea is to sweeten the spirit that you summon so they favor you more. And when you are favored by spirits, you automatically fall under their protection. In this case, we are not trying to protect you, but your idea.

You Will Need

- Honey
- Silver mica powder
- Clove essential oil
- Wood ash
- Mixing bowl
- Jar

The Work

1. For this conjure, it is very important to be clear about what you want. So before you even start, write down two important petitions. The first one should clearly state what you want, which is to protect your intention or idea from a specific person or group of people. The second one is to appeal to the spirits you summon to keep your secret for you.
2. In a mixing bowl, add one tbsp of silver mica powder, five tablespoons of honey, and 10 drops of clove essential oil.
3. Stir the mixture clockwise and recite your first petition. Do this 12 times.

4. Now, stir the mixture counter-clockwise and recite your second petition. Do this 12 times.

5. Repeat the last two steps until the mixture has achieved an even consistency.

6. Pour into a jar and store in a dark place until you are done with what you are protecting.

When you are ready to execute your idea, take out the jar and bury it in your backyard. Alternatively, you can go to a crossroads and empty the contents of the jar there. Pour water over it when you are done and cleanse the jar. Wash your hands thoroughly when you finish handling the spell. Silver mica is relatively safe but it doesn't hurt to be cautious. This conjure can also be used to protect a person. You just need to modify your petition so it includes the name of the person you want to protect.

ASH PROTECTION JAR

When someone you love is in grave danger and you have no one to rely on for their protection, this ash protection jar comes in very handy. I have already talked about how useful ash is in protection spells. This one is a variation of one of the many conjures for protection made from ashes. When you need to protect someone other than yourself and you have zero to little experience performing conjures, this is the one I recommend. It is difficult to mess up, easy to make, and very, very effective, no matter how great a threat is posed.

One of my clients was a young wife of a soldier who was on active duty in a place where his life was constantly in danger. This protection jar was one of the many things we did to ensure that he carried out his missions successfully and came home with very little damage to his mind and body. For this conjure, we are going to be focusing on ashes made from burnt oak wood. Oak is synonymous with strength. Its roots go deep and it has a strong spiritual essence that is recognized in various faiths. Oak is considered the protector of the forest, so taking ashes from wood cut out of this tree extends that protection to whomever you prepare it for.

You Will Need

- Pinewood
- Oakwood
- Elmwood
- Name paper
- Jar

The Work

1. Gather the woods needed for this conjure together.
2. Look for somewhere safe and light the wood. Try not to use any chemical accelerant to get the fire started.
3. Recite Psalm 91 repeatedly over the flames as you wait for it to burn out.

4. When the flames are out, separate the coal and gather the ashes.

5. Write the target's name three times on the name paper.

6. Sprinkle a little bit of protection oil on it before putting it in the jar.

7. Cover the name paper with the ashes you have collected and seal it.

8. If you own your property, bury the jar next to your house. If not, take it to a church and bury it there.

This is one of the few conjures you cannot prepare without reciting a Bible verse. This Bible verse in particular is a very important part of the preparation process. So if you are not a person of faith, you might have to try some of the other simple protection spells I have shared with you throughout this book. You could throw some herbs into the flames to enhance it. A little bit of cinnamon will speed up your conjure. Some bay leaves or nutmeg will add some luck. Just be creative with it. As I said, it is difficult to go wrong with this one.

GATEKEEPER POWDER

The Bible mentions building a hedge of protection around a person's habitation, or home. This hedge of protection is meant to keep out evil spirits or people with evil intentions. When you lay this conjure around your home or place of business, you automatically put up a wall that keeps all within safe from evil. After using Florida water to cleanse the interior, I use a conjure like this to secure the perimeter. Your building becomes a fortress and no evil can reach you within its walls. The best part is that you can source the tools for the conjure from around the house and it is super easy to perform.

Red brick dust, which is one of the tools in this conjure, has its roots in early Hoodoo practice in New Orleans. My grandmother told me the homes back then were made from red brick, which represented security, so when protection conjures were made, they used red brick from existing buildings. It has something to do with anchoring the spiritual barrier to the land. To get the most out of your conjure, use old red bricks. The older they are, the richer the history, and the richer the history, the stronger the barrier spell. Nothing unnatural that is evil will be able to pass through the barrier without your permission.

You Will Need

- Cedarwood
- Red brick dust
- Churchyard dirt
- Mixing bowl
- Storage jar

The Work

1. Burn the cedar wood in a safe place and collect the ash.
2. Put the ashes, churchyard dirt, and red brick dust in a mixing bowl. Stir clockwise nine times and counter-clockwise nine times. Repeat this 11 times.
3. When you are done, put the mixture into a jar.
4. To use, hold the jar upright as you pour a line around what you want to protect. Whether a space or an entire building, the line you draw must connect end to end, so either draw a circle or a square.

To increase the potency of the conjure, you can add iron filings to it. I didn't include this in the main recipe because these are not easily found around the home. But the recipe is fine without it. You just get something stronger when you include iron filings. Some people use this gatekeeper powder at their windows to keep bad spirits from entering the home. For practical reasons, I don't do this because a strong wind could blow that line in and cause a mess. A much more convenient way to use it is to sprinkle it around the space you want to protect and then sweep it out with a broom that has never been used before.

BLACK SWEEP

Old age is something we don't have a cure for. We can use the services of a beautician and a surgeon to slow down the aging process but the reality is we still get old. One of the things I hate the most about aging is memory. As we get older, our memory starts to embarrass us. I remember once when I was looking for my reading glasses only to find them perched on my nose. People who don't practice Hoodoo remind me of myself in that situation. The solution to their problem is right under their noses but because they don't know about it, they scramble around helplessly in search of it.

For example, did you know that a feather can be used to cleanse and provide protection in a home? With a handful of feathers, you can curse someone who is troubling you, cast out an evil presence or negative energy from your home, create a protection spell that is impenetrable or even cure a disease that is the manifestation of a spiritual attack. It is that simple and because we are focusing on protection spells, this conjure is going to teach you how to use black feathers to set up a protection perimeter around yourself or your home. Black feathers have always gotten a bad rap but in Hoodoo they have strong, positive spiritual properties.

You Will Need

- A fistful of black feathers
- Florida water

The Work

1. Mist the person, space, or object you want to protect with Florida water. When you are using it on a person, you don't need to dilute it. When you're using it in a space, the water needs to be one part Florida water to four parts regular water.
2. Assemble the feathers in an orderly way with the pointy end facing upwards.
3. Band the pointy ends of the feathers you have assembled so the result looks like a bouquet and then tie it with twine. Hold the shaft and use it to make a downward sweep if you are protecting a person. For the space or object you want to cleanse and protect, make an outward sweep towards the main entrance.

As simple as this spell is, you need to understand that your intentions matter. When you sweep, don't just do it without thinking. Focus on what you hope to achieve and concentrate on the outcome. One thing that helps me is to visualize myself living in the results of what I have done. This anchors your intention to this particular moment and stays with you until what you intend to happen has manifested.

DEVIL TRAP

When you have pests like snails invading your garden, using pesticides can damage or destroy the plants growing there. The most effective way to get rid of them could instead be a beer trap. This trap has beer in it, which attracts snails, but when they come to drink it, they drown. This conjure works in the same way. It is a barrier type of protection that attracts any evil spirits patrolling the borders of your territory with what they like and then traps them like the snails. Mind you, it doesn't call evil spirits to your domain but simply ensures that those that are circling too close to your protected zone do not have the chance to break the barrier.

Iron sand is actually less sand and more a variety of metals. It has a magnetic component that makes it appealing in spiritual work. It is believed to attract wealth and luck. Its main purpose in this conjure is to amplify the power of the spell. Trapping evil spirits requires a lot of spiritual power. Adding iron sand to the mix will give you the power boost you need. It will also aid in keeping luck on your side so your protection spell, in addition to this devil's trap, holds up against the attack of the enemy. Perform this conjure alongside the Gatekeeper spell we learned earlier.

You Will Need

- Iron sand
- Honey

- Holy water
- Urine
- Long-neck bottle
- A bowl

The Work

1. In a bowl, pour half a cup of holy water, half a cup of urine, and half a cup of iron sand.
2. Mix the ingredients by lifting the bowl and slowly but steadily moving it around. Be careful not to move too vigorously so the ingredients do not spill on you. This doesn't affect the conjure. It is just a precaution for those who might be squeamish about working with urine.
3. Slowly and gently empty the contents of the bowl into the long-neck bottle. If there are remnants of iron sand at the bottom of the bowl, pour back some of the liquid from the bottle into the bowl and then back into the bottle until it's all in the bottle.
4. When you have completed the last step, take a little honey and smear it around the mouth of the bottle.
5. Take the bottle to the back entrance of your house or building. Bury it up to the neck and leave it there.

You can leave the bottle buried there for up to one week. On the seventh day, seal the bottle and carry it to the crossroads. Face east and throw the bottle over your left shoulder towards the west, say the words "evil be gone," and walk away. Do not look back.

DREAM PROTECTION

One of the clear indications a person has been cursed are recurring nightmares. The kind that come every single night and leave the victim emotionally drained and broken down. These dreams are often echoes of what the enemy has done to you. But they also could be your subconscious warning you that you are in imminent danger. In some cases, they are a tool that the enemy uses to invade your mind with fear and make you more susceptible to their attacks.

A conjure like this one is not as labor-intensive as some of the other ones we've learned. It is very easy to put together and works perfectly in emergencies. All you need is a bunch of hyssops. I have talked about the protective properties of hyssop and we are going to use that to our advantage here. What you need to do is grab a bundle of hyssop and sprinkle it with holy water or Florida water, if you have either on hand. Do not use both. Place the hyssop under your mattress where you lay your head. You should be able to sleep that night without having a nightmare.

A conjure like this protects you from dream attacks and can be effective for up to a month before you need to replace it. While this conjure works powerfully in keeping your nightmares at bay, you have to remember that this does not fix the problem. It only protects your mind to give you a fighting chance. You will still need to perform other conjures to counteract the effect of the curse.

MIRROR WORK

Sometimes, the things we wrestle with are very physical and ordinary. But the damage they cause can take years to fix, if fixing it is even possible. One such battle is when your reputation or name is being tarnished by vicious gossip. Other forms of possible problems could be the reckless behavior of others. At one point in our lives, many of us have had that friend who seems to have a disregard for the law, but we like them because they seem courageous and make us feel like we're invincible. The problem with these kinds of friends is that their actions can have negative consequences for you in the long term. A conjure like this protects you from physical problems like these and even spiritual ones too.

The main tool we will work with in this conjure is a mirror. The reflective nature of mirrors show you your true self, and in rootwork, they are used to bounce back arrows that have been thrown at you. It is not exactly a 'return-to-sender' type of spell, but just as the surface of a mirror has depth that cannot be penetrated, in Hoodoo it provides you with a barrier that keeps you safe from attacks brought on by gossip or the actions of other people. It is another simple spell that can be modified as you grow in the practice of Hoodoo.

You Will Need

- Two pieces of a mirror
- A name paper
- Black thread
- Protection oil
- Piece of red clothing

The Work

1. Write your name or the name of the target on both sides of the paper three times.
2. Apply three drops of protection oil to the names on each side.
3. Place the name paper on the back of one of the mirrors. If any edges of the name paper show from the sides of the mirror, fold them inwards.
4. Place the backside of the second mirror on top of the name paper.
5. Use the black thread to bind the mirrors together. Ensure it is securely in place.
6. Wrap the conjure in a piece of red clothing and store it in a dark place. It will continue to work for a long time.

The protection oil adds a spiritual layer to the protection spell so you are not just protecting yourself from physical attacks but spiritual ones as well. Hiding the conjure in a dark place ensures that it is secret and no one knows where it is coming from. And wrapping it in a cloth guarantees that the conjure continues to work even though it is hidden. Every other week or so, apply three drops of protection oil to the thread and continue doing this until you feel you are out of danger.

FOUR THIEVES' VINEGAR

This is one of the few conjures I prepare for myself and for clients that does not have its roots in the Bible or in old Hoodoo practice. According to the stories my grandmother told me, the four thieves' vinegar became popular around the time of the bubonic plague. Four thieves were caught stealing things off the bodies of victims who had died of the plague. People noticed that the thieves didn't become sick, even though touching the bodies and interacting with the deceased's clothes should have infected them. When the thieves were caught, they bargained for their lives with the recipe for the four thieves' vinegar in exchange for their freedom, and that was how the rest of the world became blessed with this knowledge.

Vinegar, despite its sour acidic taste, is very useful in any home. It has its domestic uses, which can be for cleaning, stain removal, and emergency first aid treatment. When ingested, it can help to cure a range of illnesses, from tummy troubles to skin diseases. It is not meant to be a treatment plan but it can help you stay away from the hospital for a long time. In Hoodoo, the traditional type of vinegar used is white vinegar. But for this conjure, we are going to go with apple cider vinegar. It is more stable and less excitable but twice as strong for protection spells.

You Will Need

- Apple cider vinegar (1 cup)
- Garlic
- Sage (2 tbsp)
- Lavender (2 tbsp)
- Rue (2 tbsp)
- Mint (2 tbsp)
- Thyme (2 tbsp)
- Rosemary (2 tbsp)
- Wormwood (2 tbsp)
- Jar with a plastic cover
- Mixing bowl
- Sieve

The Work

1. In a mixing bowl, add the apple cider vinegar, dry sage, rosemary, mint, lavender, thyme, rue, and wormwood.
2. Stir clockwise nine times and then pour the ingredients into the jar. Close tight and leave in a dark place for three weeks.
3. On the last day of the third week, bring out the jar.

4. Strain the contents through a sieve.
5. Set the herbs aside for disposal at a crossroads.
6. Return the liquid to the jar.
7. Slice two garlic cloves and add to the liquid in the jar.
8. Seal and leave the garlic in the liquid for three additional days.
9. On the third day, strain one last time and return the liquid to the jar. Your four thieves' vinegar is ready.

To use the four thieves' vinegar, you can add a few teaspoons of it to your bathwater. Alternatively, if you are carrying out a cleanse, adding two tablespoons in whatever type of cleanse you are performing should suffice. This is believed to ward off diseases and provide spiritual protection. In this particular conjure, every herb, apart from the garlic, is dry. But if you are going to work with fresh herbs, you need to let them sit in the vinegar for six weeks as opposed to three weeks. You cannot mix dry and fresh together. If you want fresh herbs in the conjure, then everything must be fresh.

HEALTH PROTECTION

Health is wealth, they say. To protect your health is to protect your wealth. Hoodoo conjures are not designed to take the place of medicine in your life. If you are sick, it is important to go to a doctor and get the right medical treatment. However, we make conjures to ensure that our overall health is protected. It is like protecting a house. We don't need a Hoodoo practitioner to build the house for us. We go to the experts for that. But to provide protection that ensures nothing evil affects our house, we use conjures. So think of your health as a home that houses everything about who you are and this recipe I am about to share with you is the thing that ensures it stays safe from evil.

Hospital dirt is very tricky to use in conjures. Some people believe that a hospital is a place of sickness and that using the dirt from the hospital will only invite more sickness into your home. I disagree. A hospital is not where people go to die; it is where they go to find healing. Hospitals were built for this purpose. In any hospital, you find people who have actually dedicated a large portion of their lives to understanding the art of healing. This creates an essence in the building, and taking dirt from such a place will invite spirits that are inclined to help with healing. You only use hospital dirt in extreme cases, like if you are very sick and undergoing treatment. A conjure like this one will speed up the healing process.

You Will Need

- Protection oil
- Hospital dirt (one cup)
- Name paper

The Work

1. Write your name or the name of the target for whom you want to perform this healing conjure.
2. Apply seven drops of protection oil on the name paper.
3. Place their hair in the center of the paper and then fold it away from you.
4. Take this folded paper to a crossroads.
5. Make a hole in the middle of this crossroads about the length of your hand.
6. Sprinkle some hospital dirt at the base of the hole and then place the folded paper in it.
7. Pour the rest of the hospital dirt on top of the paper and then cover up the hole with the dirt you dug out of the crossroads.
8. When you are done, walk backward three paces and then turn in the direction you are supposed to go. Do not look back.

If I sense that the sickness has been spiritually manipulated, when I turn my back on the hole, I toss salt over my left shoulder before leaving. When you or the target gets home, you (or they) should take a healing bath. The cleanse I recommended earlier would be perfect for this. Please remember, this does not mean you should abandon any medical recommendations or treatment you are undergoing.

This spell merely helps to create an added layer of fortification that can help speed up your healing and prevent recurrences.

CONCLUSION

The practice of Hoodoo is 70 percent knowledge and 30 percent curiosity. What I've shared with you in this book has laid a solid foundation, but you still need to be curious about how the process works. Be excited about exploring the interactions between the different tools you use. Keep an open mind as you practice because you will receive messages from the spirits telling you what to do and what not to do. These instructions may serve you personally or might be helpful for those around you. It is only through an open mind that you can figure these things out.

I feel very fulfilled in sharing what I know about Hoodoo. This is knowledge that has been passed down to me and some of what I shared with you is from discoveries I've made throughout my life. However, there are some things you will have to learn on your own, like patience, for example. While some conjures deliver satisfying results overnight, some will take their sweet time. There are conjures that will deliver the desired outcome almost immediately, but the results are not visible. But as we all know, just because you can't see something doesn't mean it isn't there. Giving up because you can't see what you want will only set you back. This is why you need to remember patience.

This book is just one of three that I have written so far. I implore you to read the previous works. They contain spells for love, wealth, and general happiness. I believe you can create the life you want. Life will hand you some tough moments, but those moments do not have to be the thing that defines your entire life. You can take the resources that Hoodoo has placed at your disposal to turn your situation around and create more opportunities to succeed. My ancestors did it. They came here broken, battered, and dehumanized, but they didn't allow that to be their story or the story of the generations to follow them.

They reclaimed power for themselves and built a community for their children and the children that follow. It doesn't matter what you have done, where you come from, or what people have said about you. You may not find willing help among your peers but the world beyond can help you reach your goals and build the life you want. I am truly honored to have played a part in showing you the way. Honor yourself by honoring the gifts left for us by those early Hoodoo practitioners.

Made in United States
Troutdale, OR
02/01/2024

17376676R00244